Self-Analysis in Literary Study

Literature and Psychoanalysis
General Editor: Jeffrey Berman

1. *The Beginning of Terror: A Psychological Study of Rainer Maria Rilke's Life and Work*
   by David Kleinbard

2. *Loathsome Jews and Engulfing Women: Metaphors of Projection in the Works of Wyndham Lewis, Charles Williams, and Graham Greene*
   by Andrea Freud Loewenstein

3. *Literature and the Relational Self*
   by Barbara Ann Schapiro

4. *Narcissism and the Literary Libido: Rhetoric, Text, and Subjectivity*
   by Marshall W. Alcorn, Jr.

5. *Reading Freud's Reading*
   edited by Sander Gilman, Jutta Birmele, Jay Geller, and Valerie D. Greenberg

6. *Self-Analysis in Literary Study: Exploring Hidden Agendas*
   edited by Daniel Rancour-Laferriere

7. *The Transformation of Rage: Mourning and Creativity in George Eliot's Fiction*
   by Peggy Fitzhugh Johnstone

Self-Analysis in Literary Study

Exploring Hidden Agendas

Edited by
Daniel Rancour-Laferriere

NEW YORK UNIVERSITY PRESS
New York and London

NEW YORK UNIVERSITY PRESS
New York and London

© 1994 Chapter 3 by Norman N. Holland; chapters 1, 2, 4–8 by New York University
All rights reserved

Library of Congress Cataloging-in-Publication Data
Self-analysis in literary study : exploring hidden agendas / edited by
Daniel Rancour-Laferriere.
p.   cm.—(Literature and psychoanalysis ; 6)
Includes bibliographical references and index.
Contents: Introduction : self-analysis enhances other-analysis /
Daniel Rancour-Laferriere—"The grief that does not speak" :
suicide, mourning, and psychoanalytic teaching / Jeffrey Berman—
How I got my language / David Bleich—A cyberreader defends /
Norman N. Holland—Pulkheria Alexandrovna and Raskolnikov, my
mother and me / Bernard J. Paris—Why Natasha bumps her head : the
value of self-analysis in the application of psychoanalysis to
literature / Daniel Rancour Laferriere—Wimp or faggot? :
subjective considerations in understanding the alienation of
Dostoevsky's Underground Man / Steven Rosen—Attunement and
interpretation : reading Virginia Woolf / Barbara Ann Schapiro—
Unearthing buried affects and associations in reading : the case of
the Justified sinner / Michael Steig.
ISBN 0-8147-7439-3
1. Psychoanalysis and literature.   2. Critics—Psychology.
3. Self-analysis (Psychoanalysis)   I. Rancour-Laferriere, Daniel.
II. Series.
PN56.P92S45   1994
801'.92—dc20   94-19746
                       CIP

New York University Press books are printed on acid-free paper, and
their binding materials are chosen for strength and durability.

Manufactured in the United States of America

10   9   8   7   6   5   4   3   2   1

Contents

Foreword   *Jeffrey Berman*   vii

Contributors   xiii

Introduction: Self-Analysis Enhances Other-Analysis
Daniel Rancour-Laferriere   1

1. "The Grief That Does Not Speak": Suicide, Mourning, and Psychoanalytic Teaching   *Jeffrey Berman*   35

2. How I Got My Language: Forms of Self-Inclusion
David Bleich   55

3. A Cyberreader Defends   *Norman N. Holland*   84

4. Pulkheria Alexandrovna and Raskolnikov, My Mother and Me   *Bernard J. Paris*   111

5. Why Natasha Bumps Her Head: The Value of Self-Analysis in the Application of Psychoanalysis to Literature
Daniel Rancour-Laferriere   130

6. Wimp or Faggot? Subjective Considerations in Understanding the Alienation of Dostoevsky's Underground Man   *Steven Rosen*   145

7. Attunement and Interpretation: Reading Virginia Woolf
Barbara Ann Schapiro   178

8. Unearthing Buried Affects and Associations in Reading: The Case of the Justified Sinner   *Michael Steig*   190

Index   209

Foreword

As New York University Press inaugurates a new series of books on literature and psychoanalysis, it seems appropriate to pause and reflect briefly upon the history of psychoanalytic literary criticism. For a century now it has struggled to define its relationship to its two contentious progenitors and come of age. After glancing at its origins, we may be in a better position to speculate on its future.

Psychoanalytic literary criticism was conceived at the precise moment in which Freud, reflecting upon his self-analysis, made a connection to two plays and thus gave us a radically new approach to reading literature. Writing to his friend Wilhelm Fliess in 1897, Freud breathlessly advanced the idea that "love of the mother and jealousy of the father" are universal phenomena of early childhood (*Origins*, 223-24). He referred immediately to the gripping power of *Oedipus Rex* and *Hamlet* for confirmation of, and perhaps inspiration for, his compelling perception of family drama, naming his theory the "Oedipus complex" after Sophocles' legendary fictional hero.

Freud acknowledged repeatedly his indebtedness to literature, mythology, and philosophy. There is no doubt that he was a great humanist, steeped in world literature, able to read several languages and range across disciplinary boundaries. He regarded creative writers as allies, investigating the same psychic terrain and intuiting similar human truths. "[P]sycho-analytic observation must concede priority of imaginative writers," he declared in 1901 in *The Psychopathology of Everyday Life* (*SE* 6213), a concession he was generally happy to make. The only exceptions were writers like Schopenhauer, Nietzsche, and Schnitzler, whom he avoided reading because of the anxiety of influence. He quoted effortlessly from Sophocles, Shakespeare, Goethe, and Dostoevsky, and was himself a master prose stylist, the recipient of the coveted Goethe Prize in 1930. When he was considered for the Nobel Prize, it was not for medicine but for literature. Upon being greeted as the discoverer of the unconscious, he disclaimed the title and instead paid generous tribute to the poets and philosophers who preceded him.

And yet Freud's forays into literary criticism have not been welcomed uniformly by creative writers, largely because of his allegiance to science rather than art. Despite his admiration for art, he viewed the artist as an introvert, not far removed from neurosis. The artist, he wrote in a well-known passage in the *Introductory Lectures on Psycho-Analysis* (1916-17), "is oppressed by excessively powerful instinctual needs. He desires to win honour, power, wealth, fame and the love of women; but he lacks the means for achieving these satisfactions" (*SE* 16376). Consequently, Freud argued, artists retreat from reality into the world of fantasy, where they attempt to make their dreams come true. While conceding that true artists manage to shape their daydreams in such a way as to find a path back to reality, thus fulfilling their wishes, Freud nevertheless theorized art as a substitute gratification. Little wonder, then, that few artists have been pleased with Freud's pronouncements.

Nor have many artists been sympathetic to Freud's preoccupation with sexuality and aggression; his deterministic vision of human life; his combative, polemical temperament; his self-fulfilling belief that psychoanalysis brings out the worst in people; and his imperialistic claim that psychoanalysis, which he regarded as his personal creation, would explore and conquer vast new territories. He chose as the epigraph for *The Interpretation of Dreams* (1900) a quotation from *The Aeneid* "Flectere si nequeo superos, Acheronta movebo" ("If I cannot bend the Higher Powers, I will move the Infernal Regions"). Although he denied that there was anything Promethean about his work, he regarded himself as one of the disturbers of the world's sleep. The man who asserted that "psycho-analysis is in a position to speak the decisive word in all questions that touch upon the imaginative life of man" (*SE* 19208) could hardly expect to win many converts among creative writers, who were no less familiar with the imaginative life of humankind and who resented his intrusion into their domain.

Freud viewed psychoanalysts as scientists, committed to the reality principle and to heroic self-renunciation. He perceived artists, by contrast—and women—as neurotic and highly narcissistic, devoted to the pleasure principle, intuiting mysterious truths which they could not rationally understand. "Kindly nature has given the artist the ability to express his most secret mental impulses, which are hidden even from himself," he stated in *Leonardo da Vinci and a Memory of His Childhood* in 1910 (*SE* 11107). The artist, in Freud's judgment, creates beauty, but the psychoanalyst analyzes its meaning and "penetrates" it, with all the phallic implications thereof. As much as he admired artists, Freud did not want to give them credit for knowing what they are doing. Moreover, although he always referred to artists as male, he assumed that art itself was essentially female; and he was drawn to the "seductive" nature of art even as he resisted its embrace, lest he lose his masculine analytical power. He wanted to be called a scientist, not an artist.

From the beginning of his career, then, the marriage Freud envisioned between the artist and the analyst was distinctly unequal and patriarchal. For their part, most creative writers have remained wary of psychoanalysis. Franz Kafka, James Joyce, and D. H. Lawrence were fascinated by psychoanalytic theory and appropriated it, in varying degrees, in their stories, but they all remained skeptical of Freud's therapeutic claims and declined to be analyzed.

Most artists do not want to be "cured," fearing that their creativity will be imperiled, and they certainly do not want psychoanalysts to probe their work; they agree with Wordsworth that to dissect is to murder. Vladimir Nabokov's sardonic reference to Freud as the "Viennese witch doctor" and his contemptuous dismissal of psychoanalysis as black magic are extreme examples of creative writers' mistrust of psychoanalytic interpretations of literature. "[A]ll my books should be stamped Freudians Keep Out," Nabokov writes in *Bend Sinister* (xii). Humbert Humbert speaks for his creator when he observes in *Lolita* that the difference between the rapist and therapist is but a matter of spacing (147).

Freud never lost faith that psychoanalysis could cast light upon a wide variety of academic subjects. In the short essay "On the Teaching of Psycho-Analysis in Universities" (1919), he maintained that his new science has a role not only in medical schools but also in the "solutions of problems" in art, philosophy, religion, literature, mythology, and history. "The fertilizing effects of psycho-analytic thought on these other disciplines," Freud wrote enthusiastically, "would certainly contribute greatly towards forging a closer link, in the sense of a *universitas literarum,* between medical science and the branches of learning which lie within the sphere of philosophy and the arts" (*SE* 17173). Regrettably, he did not envision in the same essay a cross-fertilization, a desire, that is, for other disciplines to pollinate psychoanalysis.

Elsewhere, though, Freud was willing to acknowledge a more reciprocal relationship between the analyst and the creative writer. He opened his first published essay on literary criticism, "Delusions and Dreams in Jensen's *Gradiva*" (1907), with the egalitarian statement that "creative writers are valued allies and their evidence is to be highly prized, for they are apt to know a whole host of things between heaven and earth of which our philosophy has not yet let us dream" (*SE* 98), an allusion to his beloved Hamlet's affirmation of the mystery of all things. Conceding that literary artists have been, from time immemorial, precursors to scientists, Freud concluded that the "creative writer cannot evade the psychiatrist nor the psychiatrist the creative writer, and the poetic treatment of a psychiatric theme can turn out to be correct without any sacrifice of its beauty" (*SE* 944).

It is in the spirit of this equal partnership between literature and psychoanalysis that New York University Press launches the present series. We intend to publish books that are genuinely interdisciplinary, theoretically sophisticated, and clinically informed. The literary critic's insights into psychoanalysis are no less valuable than the psychoanalyst's insights into literature. Gone are the days when psychoanalytic critics assumed that Freud had a master key to unlock the secrets of literature. Instead of reading literature to confirm psychoanalytic theory, many critics are now reading Freud to discover how his understanding of literature shaped the evolution of his theory. In short, the master-slave relationship traditionally implicit in the marriage between the literary critic and the psychoanalyst has given way to a healthier dialogic relationship, in which each learns from and contributes to the other's discipline.

Indeed, the prevailing ideas of the late twentieth century are strikingly different from those of the late nineteenth century, when literature and psychoanalysis were first allied. In contrast to Freud, who assumed he was discovering absolute truth, we now believe that knowledge, particularly in the humanities and social sciences, is relative and dependent upon cultural contexts. Freud's classical drive theory, with its mechanistic implications of cathectic energy, has given way to newer relational models such as object relations, self psychology, and interpersonal psychoanalysis, affirming the importance of human interaction. Many early psychoanalytic ideas, such as the death instinct and the phylogenetic transmission of memories, have fallen by the wayside, and Freud's theorizing on female psychology has been recognized as a reflection of his cultural bias.

Significant developments have also taken place in psychoanalytic literary theory. An extraordinary variety and synthesis of competing approaches have emerged, including post-Freudian, Jungian, Lacanian, Horneyan, feminist, deconstructive, psycholinguistic, and reader response. Interest in psychoanalytic literary criticism is at an all-time high, not just in the handful of journals devoted to psychological criticism, but in dozens of mainstream journals that have traditionally avoided psychological approaches to literature. Scholars are working on identity theory, narcissism, gender theory, mourning and loss, and creativity. Additionally, they are investigating new areas, such as composition theory and pedagogy, and exploring the roles of resistance, transference, and countertransference in the classroom.

"In the end we depend / On the creatures we made," Freud observed at the close of his life (*Letters*, 425), quoting from Goethe's *Faust;* and in the end psychoanalytic literary criticism depends on the scholars who continue to shape it. All serious scholarship is an act of love and devotion, and for many of the authors in this series, including myself, psychoanalytic literary criticism has become a consuming passion, in some cases a lifelong one. Like other passions, there is an element of idealization here. For despite our criticisms of Freud, we stand in awe of his achievements; and even as we recognize the limitations of any single approach to literature, we find that psychoanalysis has profoundly illuminated the human condition and inspired countless artists. In the words of the fictional "Freud" in D. M. Thomas's extraordinary novel *The White Hotel* (1981), "Long may poetry and psychoanalysis continue to highlight, from their different perspectives, the human face in all its nobility and sorrow" (143 n.).

JEFFREY BERMAN
Professor of English
State University of New York at Albany

Contributors

JEFFREY BERMAN is Professor of English at the State University of New York at Albany.

DAVID BLEICH is Professor of English at the University of Rochester.

NORMAN N. HOLLAND is Marston-Milbauer Professor of English at the University of Florida in Gainesville.

BERNARD J. PARIS is Professor of English at the University of Florida in Gainesville.

DANIEL RANCOUR-LAFERRIERE is Professor of Russian at the University of California in Davis.

STEVEN ROSEN is Professor of English at Saint Peter's College in Jersey City, New Jersey.

BARBARA ANN SCHAPIRO is Professor of English at Rhode Island College in Providence.

MICHAEL STEIG is Professor of English at Simon Fraser University in Burnaby, British Columbia.

Self-Analysis in Literary Study

Introduction: Self-Analysis Enhances Other-Analysis

Daniel Rancour-Laferriere

Self-Analysis Private and Public

To practice psychoanalysis is, among other things, to think about oneself. It is nearly impossible to conduct other-analysis without also conducting self-analysis. At the same time, however, it is uncommon to go public with one's self-analysis. One can normally get on with the work of treating patients, or psychoanalyzing cultural objects and practices, without having to say too much about oneself in the process.

This volume of essays is meant to be an exception. Its purpose is to make public self-analytic material in order to demonstrate the relevance of such material specifically for literary study.

Much of course has already been written about the psychology of reader response to literature (e.g., Holland 1968; Bleich; Seilman and Larsen). Usually, however, the reader whose responses are analyzed is not the scholar who is doing the analysis, or at least is not admitted to be the scholar who is doing the analysis. On occasion the question of the scholar's own transference is dealt with on a theoretical level (e.g., Schwartz), but very rarely will the scholar actually describe in detail his or her own specific responses to a given literary text (as did Holland 1975, for example). Public self-analysis requires rare exhibitionistic drive, and it is always limited in its depth and detail by the obvious dangers to oneself and to loved ones.

Another reason so little public self-analysis occurs in literary interpretation is that self-analysis entails an admission that literary scholarship is derived, secondary, is in a sense *littérature manquée*. In other words, many literary scholars cannot handle the anxiety of belatedness, or what Harold Bloom would call the anxiety of influence. Geoffrey Hartman has written something like a self-analysis on this theme ("The Interpreter: A Self-Analysis").

Outside of the literary field *per se* there has been some theoretical treatment of the role that the investigator's own psyche plays in scholarly and scientific research (e.g., Schepeler; Devereux 148–61; Lawton 81–94; Rancour-Laferriere 1988, 28–35; Loewenberg 3–13; and especially the various papers gathered in *Introspection in Biography* edited by Baron and Pletsch). There also exists a number of "confessions" by scholars about the personal motives behind their work (e.g., Tucker; Edel). Finally, there is an extensive clinical literature on so-called countertransference, which I will discuss below.

Most of the publications on self-analysis are to be found in the psychoanalytic literature proper. Freud started it all with the fairly large doses of self-analysis he provided in his writings from the period 1895–1901, that is, when he was in the process of inventing psychoanalysis. Indeed, it is doubtful whether Freud would ever have come up with such absolutely fundamental psychoanalytic concepts as the dream work, family romance, free association, infantile sexuality, Oedipus complex, primal scene, regression, screen memories, the unconscious, wish-fulfillment, and a number of others, outside of the context of progress in his own self-analysis (Anzieu). Freud's self-analysis did not stop, moreover, once the invention of psychoanalysis was complete. Rather, it continued (although usually not in public form) for the rest of his life, because he felt it was an ongoing antidote to the dangers of misinterpretation due to his own transferences.

Like psychoanalytic therapy generally, self-analysis is never truly complete (Freud [hereafter cited as *SE*] XXIII, 249; Anzieu 559; Fleming 21–50; Kramer; Ticho; Calder; Beiser; Chessick). Freud termed analysis "interminable." I prefer "asymptotic." At best, analysis moves asymptotically toward a point of maximum possible insight, given the situation, and then moves on toward other points, never to actually touch any one of them.

The asymptosis can be discouraging. Freud once stated that "genuine self-analysis is impossible; otherwise there would be no [neurotic] illness" (*SE* XIV, 21). I believe this idea is wrong, however, for it is based on the questionable assertion that analytic insight necessarily cures.

Self-analysis is easier than analysis of someone else in the sense that, in self-analysis, one has to overcome only one set of defenses (one's own), while in other-analysis one has to overcome two sets of defenses (one's own and the other's). Also, one should, in principle, know oneself better than anyone else does, for all the material to be known is contained within oneself.

On the other hand, in self-analysis the potential for distortion of reality is great. As Devereux says, self-scrutiny "demands that the ego—composed in part of defenses *against* insight—appraise *its own reluctance to face reality*" (149).

Freud asserted that "in self-analysis the danger of incompleteness is particularly great. One is too soon satisfied with a part explanation, behind which resistance may easily be keeping back something that is more important perhaps" (*SE* XIV, 21). A recent paper by Henry Mallard illustrates this incompleteness all too clearly. Mallard gives two examples of self-analyses (one by a patient, one by himself) which subsequently proved incomplete when scrutinized by an outside party.

But the results of self-analysis are not necessarily false, even if they be partial or somewhat distorted. If practiced, moreover, for a long period of time, self-analysis can provide ever-expanding insight (Chessick reports carrying on a self-analysis for over 25 years after his initial training analysis). Freud himself never gave up on his own self-analysis, and he advocated that therapists analyze themselves on an ongoing basis. The benefits, he believed, outweighed the disadvantages. Most subsequent clinical writers on the subject have also come down in favor of self-analysis, even while recognizing its many pitfalls (e.g.: Horney; Kramer; Bollas; Ticho; Calder; Beiser; Chessick).

The benefits of self-analysis, I believe, are particularly great when the goal is not therapy, but *intellectual discovery in the realm of applied psychoanalysis*. Not much has been written about this topic because most psychoanalysts are preoccupied with therapy (indeed most of the clinical writers on self-analysis seem absolutely oblivious to applied psychoanalysis). But even the limited insights of self-analysis may have considerable scientific consequences. These insights, moreover, can be achieved by scholars who, like Freud, have no formal training analysis behind them.

Consider an example from the history of psychoanalysis. Freud, as is well known, saw homosexual wishes lurking behind Herr Schreber's paranoid fantasies. The judge's unjustified fears, paraphrased by Freud as "He persecutes me," really signified "I love him" at a deep, unconscious level (*SE* XII, 63). This controversial claim was evidently true, for it has largely withstood the falsifying onslaughts of experimental psychology. Paul Kline, in his meticulous overview of the empirical tests of psychoanalytic theories, says that "the Freudian theory of paranoid schizophrenia is confirmed" (340). In one study, for example, paranoids recognized tachistoscopically presented homosexual words ("fruit," "fairy," "homos," "queer," etc.) much more quickly than did non-paranoids (Daston).

What was there about Freud's self-analysis that might have contributed to his discovery of the homosexual etiology of paranoia? In a recent paper Phyllis Grosskurth has shown that Freud may have been projecting something of his homosexual self into Schreber. Indeed Freud came to recognize his own homosexual preoccupations precisely during the course of his study of Schreber's memoirs: "the case seems to have provided Freud with an opportunity to work out some of his unresolved difficulties about the homosexual component of his own intense relationship with Wilhelm Fliess, from whom he had parted bitterly a decade earlier" (38). As evidence, Grosskurth quotes from a letter Freud wrote to Sandor Ferenczi in October of 1910: "Since Fliess's case, with the overcoming of which you recently saw me occupied, that need has been extinguished. A part of homosexual cathexis has been withdrawn and made use of to enlarge my own ego. I have succeeded where the paranoiac fails." In another letter to Ferenczi Freud congratulated himself for "having overcome my homosexuality." In December of the same year, he wrote to Jung: "I am all Schreber" (as quoted by Grosskurth 38).

Clearly, the homosexuality Freud saw in Schreber, with whom he intensely identified, had something to do with his own admitted homosexuality.[1] Freud felt free to admit this in letters to close colleagues, that is to say, in a genre of writing which for him was self-analytic and was in many respects the functional equivalent of a diary. But such an admission would have been out of place in his published analysis of Schreber, for it would have lessened his credibility, especially in the prudish cultural context he was working in (compare Calder, who felt free to discuss his own "negative oedipal wishes"). It is not as if Freud deviously and maliciously hid his homosexuality from the reader of the Schreber paper. Rather, it did not belong there. Certainly Freud had the right to *choose* whether or not to discuss his own homosexuality in print.

Freud, then, brought his own problem to bear on Schreber's problems. But that does not mean that what Freud saw in Schreber was only an illusion (I have already mentioned the experimental studies of paranoia). Freud might not even have taken an interest in Schreber if there had not been some objective similarity between himself and Schreber, and, more importantly, he might not have discovered the homosexual background of paranoia generally if he had not been dealing with his own homosexuality in his self-analysis.

To judge from Freud's handling of the Schreber case, self-analysis is related to both the analyst's own mental life and to the intellectual discoveries the analyst makes while self-analysis is occurring. In principle, it seems to me, this double relationship ought to hold, no matter what the particular object of psychoanalysis is. For example, it ought to hold in the psychoanalysis of literature (as most of the essays in this volume will demonstrate). Self-analysis should be relevant to both the literary scholar and to whatever conceptual constructs the scholar formulates when psychoanalyzing such literary entities as an author, a reader, a character, personal relationships between characters, a trope, a narrative structure, and so forth.

The Diary

One way to facilitate self-analysis is to write down what one is thinking. Not everyone who keeps a (regular or sporadic) diary is necessarily doing what psychoanalysts mean by self-analysis. This is as true of the famous literary artists who kept diaries (e.g., Tolstoy, Gide) as of ordinary diarists. But a private diary or journal can nevertheless be very congenial to genuine self-analytic endeavor. The diary offers a concrete external space for internal dialogue without at the same time requiring the presence of a real second person.

Some forms of psychotherapy, such as psychoanalysis, Jungian therapy, cognitive-behavioral therapy, Gestalt therapy, Japanese Morita therapy, and a few others utilize the diary as an ancillary technique. The so-called Intensive Journal method developed by Ira Progoff goes much further. Each participant in a Journal Workshop is given a black notebook with blank pages and twenty color-coded, printed dividers on such topics as "Daily Log," "Dialogue with Society (Group Experiences)," "Dialogue with the Body," "Dream Log," "Twilight Imagery Log," and "NOW: The Open Moment." The journal work is highly organized, but the approach is relaxed. Slowly and meditatively the pages are filled, inner connections are made, an overall "Tao of growth" is perceived by the writer, an ever-evolving "inner wisdom" is achieved (Progoff 16, 269–84). Over the years there is supposedly a cumulative therapeutic effect.

Some of Progoff's colleagues choose to keep a journal by proxy for a creative historical personage. One of these has been published. It is titled *A Life-Study of Franz Kafka, 1883–1924*, by Ronald Gestwicki. Most of the chapters of this curious book contain an imaginary conversation between "Ron" and "Kafka." The result is not at all Kafkaesque. The chief value of the book resides, I think, in its therapeutic function for Professor Gestwicki.

Some of the diary literature touches on self-psychoanalysis, but most does not deal with it explicitly or extensively. This is quite understandable. A diary is a private record of experience, but not all private matters are psychoanalytic in nature. For example, the written record of a dream is not an analysis of a dream, although it might be the first step of an analysis. Progoff speaks of "working with our dreams" (228–52), not psychoanalyzing them, not even interpreting them.

Tristine Rainer, in her very readable 1978 book *The New Diary*, reaches psychoanalytic explicitness in the advice she offers. There is no "right way" to keep a diary, she says. One should only be concerned with writing spontaneously, honestly, deeply. Thoughts should be allowed to flow freely. It is a mistake to try to correct mistakes. "Wrong" opinions and slips of the pen should not be crossed out:

Many diarists have regretted crossing out what they have already written. It is more valuable to add new insights to an entry than to erase or cross out or rewrite. Spur-of-the-moment negative judgments may actually be resistance to an insight that might later prove invaluable.

It takes the perspective of time to know what has significance in a diary. Some misspellings or word accidents acquire meaning upon rereading. "Freudian slips" may give you a key to subconscious attitudes or feelings. And some are quite entertaining. I once accidentally wrote "spychiatrist" for "psychiatrist." In another entry I wrote "Was" for "Wes," the name of a man with whom I was about to end a relationship. Clearly my subconscious was ahead of me in considering it already past. The hand tells the truth, so write fast and trust your body. (39)

Freud of course advocated something very similar to this with his so-called "basic rule" *(Grundregel)* that all psychoanalytic patients must abide by, namely: "say whatever goes through your mind" (*SE* XII, 135). The diarist, in some moods at least, proceeds by this same method of "free association" which the patient follows on the couch. As Rainer points out, the various terms which have grown up around this procedure—free association, active imagination, automatic writing, stream of consciousness, free-intuitive writing—all refer to essentially the same thing (62).

For some it is difficult to relax to the point of free-associating on paper. But when one does, the results can be astonishing to ordinary consciousness. Marion Milner describes this experience in her fascinating 1934 book, *A Life of One's Own*. A diary entry about the sea suddenly flies off to thoughts of God:

SEA . . . mother—perhaps derived from 'mer'—feeling ashamed when they laughed at Miss R.'s and they said I'd painted the sea blue—why did I feel such accusations always unjust, a hot fighting to deny and escape—to bathe in the sea. What does it mean? Deep cool green water to dive into, but often no bathing-dress and people watching and I never would bathe naked and damn the people—?—?—God—is this what the sea means?—lose myself—. . . . (Milner, 61–62)

These somewhat incoherent thoughts take the diarist aback:

I was surprised at God coming into it. At that time if anyone had asked me what I thought about God I would have probably given a non-committal agnostic opinion, taking into account the latest fashion in science. I would have assumed that I had thus satisfactorily dealt with the question, taking it for granted that emotional troubles about it were things of the past, no doubt quite suitable during adolescence, but no concern of the twentieth-century adult. But since the word had cropped up in my free ideas about the sea, it now occurred to me that my automatic self might not hold the same views as my deliberate self. (62)

Quite reasonably Milner asks: "Might not these apparent beliefs of my automatic self, although I had no notion of their existence, possess the power to influence my feelings and actions?" (65).

With time Milner's "automatic self" did in fact play an ever larger role in her life, sometimes sending her into a panic, or provoking intense guilt feelings. Although the few sentiments expressed about psychoanalysis in *A Life of One's Own* are somewhat ambivalent, the ultimate destination of the book's author seems inevitable. Writing more than fifty years later, Milner states: "I was so astonished at what my diary keeping had shown about the power of the unconscious aspects of one's mind, both for good and for ill, that I eventually became a psychoanalyst" (219).

Literary scholars who wish to engage in self-analysis can profit from the literature on diaries. Tristine Rainer offers some valuable practical advice, such as her seven "special techniques" (72–114):

1. Make numbered lists of things on your mind, in any order, such as things to do, things you are afraid of, chronology of the ten most important events in your life, etc.
2. Write a detailed, descriptive portrait of someone intriguing, and consider to what extent it might really be a self-portrait (projection).
3. Doodle freely, without worrying about the artistic quality of the results.
4. Do "guided imagery," i.e., while in a meditative state conjure up carefully chosen self-nurturing images, such as a pleasant landscape, a fantasy journey assisted by animal helpers, etc. Use this process to change the negative outcomes of past events such as nightmares to positive outcomes. Record the images in a diary.
5. Alter the point of view of narrated events, e.g., use the pronoun "he" or "she" instead of "I," change the tenses of verbs.
6. Write first drafts of letters or unsent letters in the diary.
7. Write down imaginary dialogues between conflicting parts of the self, or between oneself and another person of emotional significance.

The reader will no doubt recognize in Rainer's suggestions some of the very techniques employed by poets and fiction writers in their craft. That such techniques should also be useful for self-analysis is perhaps one reason why self-analysis has not been popular among literary scholars—many of whom regard themselves as failed writers. In any case, it is obvious that Rainer's chapter on overcoming writing blocks (215–28) would be as valuable to the literary scholar as to the creative writer.

My Diary

My own early experience with self-writing took the form of "field notes" about plants and animals. In adolescence I was an avid bird-watcher and amateur botanist. The notebooks I have from that period contain entries such as the following for Sunday, October 18, 1959:

> After Mass this morning I went down to the Island, and from the Island I heard a flock of this year's first Pine Siskins. Also I saw a group of Mergansers and a lone Gull there. Then I went down to the Mink Swamp and saw the following: group of three Great Blue Herons, Hooded Mergansers (males now in winter plumage), Wood Ducks, several small flocks of American Mergansers, several Herring Gulls.

In time I began spouting the Latin names of the flora and fauna of my native northern Vermont, as in this excerpt under Friday, September 2, 1960:

> Having flushed a few grouse in the woods, and on my way home down over Harris II, I found Spiranthes cernua var. ochroleuca [an orchid] in an old road. I took notes on this one plant, which I had never seen before.

Occasionally these notebooks make references to *literature*, as on March 6, 1961:

7:30 Mass
Read from Scientific American at lib.
Work as usual
Studied Latin
Practiced Echo [harmonica]
Religion class
Read Dostoevskii.

This phrase "Read Dostoevskii" is repeated again and again over the course of a month, yet I registered no opinion whatsoever of what I was reading. The plants and animals I encountered on my "field trips," on the other hand, provoked a real response:

> At the very same spot as mentioned in the last notes I saw another flock (probably the same) of Pine Grosbeaks. From the top of a medium-sized Hemlock nearby I took notes on their feeding (A-2) [another notebook]. When they left I noticed an odd voice remaining.
> It was much like a Black-Capped Chickadee, but more drawn out with a

drawl, and less lively. As I approached very closely I found it to be a Parus hudsonicus—Brown-Capped Chickadee. It was definitely of a brownish hue, rather than the slate-gray of atricapillus. The brown cap and black bib quickly identified it.

Twice also a Sitta canadensis [nuthatch] flew in very close as I took notes.

These notes may seem dull and poorly written, but as I read them now I can remember the excitement of climbing trees and watching birds up close. I had definitely decided to become an ornithologist. Dostoevsky was far from my mind.

Despite the occasional pleasant memories, looking over these earliest of my notebooks has been a sad experience. I hadn't laid eyes on the notebooks for years. After spending some hours with them I began to feel slightly depressed. I realized I was a great nature-lover in those days in part because I was trying to escape from a bad family situation, and that there is now no way to change that situation in retrospect.

In those days the more hours I could spend in the woods (or alone in the dark cellar of our house writing in the notebooks), the less time I had to deal with a too large, too noisy, and much too violent family. Toward the end, just before I escaped to college (where I majored in biology), there was a grand total of two fighting parents and eleven fighting children, all living under one roof.

The relationship my parents had might be termed morally sadomasochistic. I am not going to go into the gruesome details, but there is a relevant theoretical point to be made. It seems to me that my father idealized my beautiful mother, even as he abused her. Most of the abuse was psychological, indeed it involved a considerable amount of psychological insight about my mother. My father's attitude seemed to be:

Here is a beautiful object. Now let's tear it apart.

In retrospect this seems rather similar to what the psychoanalytic scholar of literature typically does to literature. Certainly it is what *this* scholar does. I am never inclined to psychoanalyze a text unless first it attracts me aesthetically. Then I tear it apart.

By definition a successful literary work is supposed to be "beautiful." A mother's beauty and the aesthetic beauty of literature are akin to one another. I think I am not alone in this sentiment, although perhaps not all psychoanalytic critics identify specifically with an offensive father when approaching an aesthetic object.

My father's action, transformed by my identification with him as well as sublimation of the representations of his grosser offenses, became:

Here is a beautiful object. Now let's psycho-ana-lyze it.

I hyphenate the key word to emphasize its violent etymology: Greek *ana-luein* means 'to break down,' 'to dissolve.' The destructive impulse is unmistakable. My mother was periodically 'breaking down,' 'dissolving' into tears as a result of my father's behavior. Time after time I have attempted to deal with this horror in my later diaries (the adolescent diaries demonstrate blissful ignorance of the problem).

The psychoanalysis of literature of course also springs from an epistemophilic impulse, that is, an intense desire to know and to understand. But this impulse itself, if the Kleinians are to be believed, is originally inseparable from sadistic attitudes—not the father's, but the child's—toward the mother. The little child is curious (especially about sexuality), but its curiosity is typically frustrated, so it lashes out in fantasy at the most important person in the world. In an early work (1928) Melanie Klein states:

The early connection between the epistemophilic impulse and sadism is very important for the whole mental development. This instinct, activated by the rise of the Oedipus tendencies, at first mainly concerns itself with the mother's body, which is assumed to be the scene of all sexual processes and developments. (188)

Even pre-Oedipally, according to Klein, "the subject's dominant aim is to possess himself of the contents of the mother's body and to destroy her by means of every weapon which sadism can command" (219). Apparently, then, one's (e.g., my) psychoanalytic sado-curiosity can derive from something even earlier than identification with an abusive father. Although no diary entries or personal associations come to mind in support of this idea, I sense intuitively that Klein is right.

The element of aggression in psychoanalysis may also be directed at the addressee of the analysis, not only at the object being psychoanalyzed. Strong psychoanalytic work is said to be "striking," it "hits" the reader with its insights. It can also function sadistically within a context of political confrontation. American Slavist Hugh McLean describes how, in 1958, he publicly challenged the orthodox Soviet Marxist interpretation of Gogol's works with a psychoanalytic interpretation: "I . . . took some pleasure, *not without an admixture of malice*, in writing and delivering in Moscow an aggressively Freudian interpretation of Gogol" (McLean 118, italics added).

All of this is above and beyond whatever *inherent* offensiveness psychoanalysis possesses. As Freud realized from the start, psychoanalytic truths of all kinds can be narcissistically injurious. A particular psychoanalytic discovery, by its very nature, is not quite the same as, say, finding a new species of beetle in the Brazilian rain forest, or unearthing a new draft of *The Queen of Spades* in some musty archive. A psychoanalytic discovery is more like finding a precancerous condition in an unsuspecting patient. The new information has the potential to provoke great anxiety. A possibility therefore exists that this information might be used sadistically.

In the case of self-analysis, on the other hand, there is the possibility that the information might be used masochistically. Even if the anxiety of learning something about oneself is overcome, there is still a danger that someone else might use the information against you. As with sadism, however, an ulterior, theoretical motive might make a potentially masochistic enterprise worthwhile. That is, indeed, the premise implicit in most of the essays collected in this volume.

Psychoanalytic critics practice applied psychoanalysis. Clinical psychoanalysis is somewhat different. The analyst behind the couch deals with a dysfunctional human being, not a text or some other cultural object:

Here is a sick object. Now let's fix it.

This attitude, if some of the studies on countertransference are to be believed (see below, page 21), really means:

Here is a sick object. It fulfills my wish to see others suffer.

Some few clinical analysts apparently do abuse their patients in order to keep the mental suffering going, although most are governed by a healthy reaction formation which drives them to try to cure patients instead (see Brenner; Sussman 73–77). In addition, some patients are extremely fragile, psychically, and feel "mind-fucked" by any analyst who attempts to make even a slight intervention (e.g., Giovacchini 33–37).

Psychoanalysts of literature deal with sadistic impulses by sublimation rather than reaction formation. To "tear apart" the text, offering "penetrating" psychoanalytic insight—is to sublimate aggression. Psychoanalytic scholars sublimate their aggression as they strive to impart understanding to an audience they have no particular interest in "curing." A text cannot be abused in the same way a real human being can (although the *author* of a text, if still alive, might take offense, or certain *readers* might take offense if they are being subjected to reader-response psychoanalysis; even some among the *professional readership* may be put off).

It Takes One to Know One

The psychoanalytic scholar can deal with sadistic impulses not only by directing them against the text, but also by finding texts which themselves deal with sadistic matters. To use an old Jakobsonian dichotomy, the scholar can establish not only a certain special contiguity to the text, but seek out similarity in a text as well. One can operate at the metaphoric as well as at the metonymic pole of psychoanalysis.

For example, one can study Dostoevsky. His works are riddled with sadistic and masochistic fantasy material. Even the conventional, non-psychoanalytic Slavists agree on this.

I have been studying Dostoevsky for years. To some extent I can even link this interest to my early interest in birds. One of the pleasures of bird-watching was actually sadistic. I especially liked birds of prey. During my high school years I worked in a live museum caring for hawks and owls. According to the notebooks, I once spent an afternoon in the field intently watching a family of sparrowhawks haggle over the corpse of a freshly killed chipmunk. Nowadays of course I think more about Dostoevsky's characters than about hawks.

The general principle here might be paraphrased as: It takes one to know one. Literary scholars do their best work on writers and characters they resemble. The sadistically inclined gravitate toward a Dostoevsky, or a Heine, or a Capote.

Of course there is more than one way for any particular scholar to resemble a literary person. When I was writing a psychoanalytic study of Nikolai Gogol's famous short story "The Overcoat" I was more concerned with anality than with sadism (the subject of my 1982 book *Out from under Gogol's Overcoat* is a hero named Akaky Akakievich, who I thought of as 'Akaky the kaka'). One of the reviewers even said that "Gogol has found a kindred spirit in Rancour-Laferriere" (Charney

664). On the other hand, when later psychoanalyzing Lev Tolstoy's narcissistic Pierre Bezukhov (in *Tolstoy's Pierre Bezukhov: A Psychoanalytic Study*, 1993), I became quite preoccupied with my own narcissism, as is clear from the diary entries of that period. I felt—and I hope readers will find—that Pierre and I are kindred souls too.

The identification I have experienced with the personae I have psychoanalyzed has always come undone, eventually. At the beginning of a project there is usually an intense, almost blissful feeling of oneness with my subject, almost a Kohutian merging. I think Kohut's notion of "selfobject" would apply here. I and that beautiful maternal persona are one—even when the persona in question is male. But the delusive identity of self and object cannot last, cannot survive the gathering of objective facts, cannot withstand the passage of time which is inherent in any serious scholarly endeavor. I hack away at the selfobject, gradually separating self from object, isolating object in a text that reads with neutral precision. I think this process must be a derivative of the epistemophilic sadism directed against the mother which Melanie Klein described.

It is possible for a healthy psychoanalytic scholar, at the characterological level, to be sadistic, anal, narcissistic, and perhaps many other things as well. What is essential is to *be* what one studies, at least temporarily.

Or, it might suffice to *be* some natural complement of what one studies. For example, it takes a masochist to know a masochist, but a sadist might well do.

I think this general notion applies in other regions of human knowledge, not only psychoanalysis. In biography, for example, it is important that the biographer share core traits with the person whose life is being studied. Historians, journalists, and political analysts gravitate for good reason toward figures who are like themselves.

Let's return to sadomasochism as an example. Janet Malcolm, in her interesting recent essay on the aftermath of poet Sylvia Plath's suicide, argues that all biography is tendentious: "The writer, like the murderer, needs a motive."

Like the murderer? This sounds sufficiently sadistic. For example, the motive behind Jacqueline Rose's 1991 book *The Haunting of Sylvia Plath* is characterized by Malcolm as follows: "Rose's book is fuelled by a bracing hostility toward Ted and Olwyn Hughes" (Ted Hughes was being unfaithful to his wife Sylvia Plath at the time she committed suicide, and both he and his sister Olwyn have been instrumental in blocking public access to some of Plath's papers). Rose thinks it is impossible to take sides in writing about Plath. One must be even-handed, after all, in dealing with a family tragedy. Malcolm thinks otherwise:

[Rose's book] derives its verve and forward thrust from the cool certainty with which (in the name of "uncertainty" and "anxiety") she presents her case against the Hugheses. In the "Archive" chapter, her accusations against Hughes for his "editing, controlling, and censoring" reach an apogee of harshness. If it had truly been impossible for Rose to take a side, her book would not have been written; it would not have been worth taking the trouble to write. Writing cannot be done in a state of desirelessness. The pose of fair-mindedness, the charade of evenhandedness, the striking of an attitude of detachment can never be more than rhetorical ruses; if they were genuine, if the writer *actually* didn't care one way or the other how things came out, he would not bestir himself to represent them. (148)

With expressions like "verve," "bracing hostility," and "harshness" Malcolm is clearly suggesting that Rose is directing sadistic impulses toward the Hugheses. On the other hand, she is not implying there is anything wrong about this. There has to be a desire, even if a sadistic one, for good writing to occur.

Later in her essay Malcolm introduces imagery of garbage removal to characterize what the biographer does:

Each person who sits down to write faces not a blank page but his own vastly overfilled mind. The problem is to clear out most of what is in it, to fill huge plastic garbage bags with the confused jumble of things that have accreted there over the days, months, years of being alive and taking things in through the eyes and ears and heart. (158)

Narrating biography is thus a kind of "housecleaning" in which a considerable amount of garbage must be removed. To extend Malcolm's metaphor, the Rose book on Plath still contains some bits and pieces of garbage which betray Rose's hostile attitude toward the Hugheses. And this is good. One must not clean too thoroughly, for then there is the danger of "being left with too bare a house" (158).

Janet Malcolm herself is a psychoanalytically informed writer who is quite aware of the garbage in her own mind. Again, it takes one to know one. In psychoanalytic terms, it was easy for her to spot the sadistic tendentiousness toward the Hugheses in Rose's book, if only because she has felt the same way about Sylvia Plath. Plath's depressive moral masochism, culminating in suicide, attracts sadistically inclined biographers quite as much as it appeals to outraged feminists.

But again, this is good, at least for scholarly purposes. For how can we expose another's garbage without knowing our own? The psychoanalytic scholar cannot really move forward without a load of internal garbage, however neatly bagged in plastic. Other-analysis always presumes self-analysis, however covert, even unconscious.

Anyone who is willing to free-associate for a few minutes (aloud, subvocally, in a diary) will quickly be convinced of what a load of garbage there is in the human mind. It is the task of self-analysis to organize normally unconscious mental garbage, to categorize it by its smells. In this process it is important not only to throw out the irrelevant garbage, but also to retain the relevant garbage, that is, those unpleasant details of the mind which permit one to *be* what one studies.

For example, when psychoanalyzing Tolstoy's Pierre Bezukhov I had to discard my strong feelings about head injury, for they had nothing to do with Pierre even though there was a brief moment in the narration when a slight head injury occurred (see "Why Natasha Bumps Her Head," in this volume). As it turned out, my diary was a convenient receptacle for any garbage about this topic. On the other hand, my narcissistic problems, also abundantly documented in the diary, *were* relevant to Pierre. I do not think that anyone who does not carry around this particular load of garbage can really understand Pierre.

Perhaps I have extended Janet Malcolm's garbage bag metaphor far enough. In any case, I think that what Malcolm says about a writer's tendentiousness is as true of literary scholarship as of biography and journalism. The literary scholar—including the psychoanalytic scholar—always has a hidden personal agenda. A little self-analysis should reveal just what that agenda is. When this is done, however, the experience can be quite surprising, perhaps unpleasant. *Why* am I doing a study of father-imagery in Kafka? What am *I* getting out of an analysis of androgyny in Virginia Woolf? What is there about studying Shakespeare's breast-imagery that gratifies *me*?

The self-analyst asking such questions is momentarily very self-centered, perhaps disgustingly so from the viewpoint of an outside observer. But the results can be quite enlightening to both self and other.

Normally this sort of thing is just "not done" in a public forum. The present volume of essays is meant to be a didactic exception. Every author here is admittedly being more exhibitionistic than most autobiographers ordinarily are. Yet the exhibitionism is being put to uses which are of general theoretical interest. Such is normally the case when self-analytic material is presented in the *clinical* psychoanalytic studies. It is high time self-analytic exhibits became more widespread in *applied* psychoanalysis as well.

Self-Analysis in Clinical Psychoanalysis

Some schools of psychoanalysis are more open to self-analysis than others, and some psychoanalysts are more willing to reveal (exhibit) self-analytic materials than others. The original Freudian movement, for example, was very much self-analytic in orientation. Anyone who has read *The Interpretation of Dreams* (1900) already knows some of the dark corners of Freud's soul (e.g., the analysis of the Irma dream; see Gorkin 37–52 on the countertransferential aspects of this famous dream). As Christopher Bollas says, Freud "dared to be where we must be to experience news of the self, and his writing of the experience was an integral part of the receptive capacity he facilitated by the creation of psychoanalysis" (238).

Jung, on the other hand, was an intensely private person who did not care to exhibit the inner workings of his psyche. Even in the late, autobiographical book *Memories, Dreams, Reflections* (1961), Jung is rather reticent, often lapsing into theoretical passages about the "personal myth" of himself rather than simply telling the reader about himself. When he does tell us about himself he can be quite entertaining, but Jungian "self-knowledge" (330) is not really self-analysis, and Jung's insistent occultism effectively blocks self-analysis. Here is just one example:

> I had another experience in the evolution of the soul after death when—about a year after my wife's death—I suddenly awoke one night and knew that I had been with her in the south of France, in Provence, and had spent an entire day with her. She was engaged on studies of the Grail there. That seemed significant to me, for she had died before completing her work on this subject. Interpretation on the subjective level—that my anima had not yet finished with the work she had to do—yielded nothing of interest; I know quite well that I am not yet

finished with that. But the thought that my wife was continuing after death to work on her further spiritual development—however that may be conceived—struck me as meaningful and held a measure of reassurance for me. (309)

Jung resists interpreting this dream in several ways. He attributes to its "subjective level" an "anima" which seems to be doing the dreaming for him. Then he admits that he himself has some unfinished work to do in connection with his wife's death, but that this is "nothing of interest." Then he states the dream's obvious wish—that his wife continue her work even though she is dead—in a form that implies his wife is *not* dead. In other words, Jung literally believes his dead wife is still alive, and that he really did meet her in the south of France. He has succumbed to the dream's underlying wish rather than interpreting it, that is, rather than doing self-analysis. All this occurs, by the way, in the context of a chapter (299–326) where Jung repeatedly assents to theories of reincarnation and life after death.

To some extent Jung acknowledges his refusal to do self-analysis. In the prologue to his autobiography he admits: "I do not know what I really am like" (4). Perhaps this is because, as he says, "I cannot experience myself as a scientific problem" (3).

Self-analysis is a "scientific problem" in the sense that one at least *tries* to view oneself objectively, as an "other" who, momentarily at least, is "out there."

When the situation is psychoanalytic therapy, both the analyst and the analysand may be called upon to do self-analysis. Ideally, the analyst should be primarily engaged in other-analysis, however, while it is the patient who pursues self-analysis. The analyst, after all, has already been through a personal training analysis, and should theoretically be capable of remaining relatively neutral in the face of any emotional onslaughts from the patient. The patient, on the other hand, is the one in need of analysis. Also, the patient consciously or unconsciously knows more about himself or herself than does anyone else, and should be prodded by the analyst's other-analysis to engage in self-analysis.

Reality does *not* match this ideal picture, however. Analysands can be resistant to the most tactfully proffered other-analysis, and analysts themselves are sometimes so preoccupied with their own agenda or so provoked by their patients that they need to analyze their own feelings in order to get the therapy moving. When the patient does perceive that the analyst is doing self-analysis as well as other-analysis, things may indeed get moving, for the patient gains a strong feeling of being supported in a difficult struggle (Bollas 255).

Technically speaking, analysts have to deal with a special type of *transference,* called *countertransference.* Transference generally is a psychical state in which ideas and feelings about personally archaic relationships (e.g., with parents or siblings) are "transferred" into the present interaction. For example, a patient may sincerely believe that the analyst has a limp, even though such is not the case, simply because the patient's father had a limp. Transference, as Freud originally observed, can contribute powerfully to the patient's resistance to treatment (*SE* XII, 99–108). As Otto Fenichel put it, "the patient misunderstands the present in terms of the past" (29).

Over the years the terms transference and countertransference have been extended considerably. Clinicians are not in agreement about what gets "transferred," when the "transferred" materials arose in development, and what psychological mechanisms cause the "transfer" (Ehrenreich). Some clinicians, such as Robert and Simone Marshall, believe that the terms transference and countertransference by themselves now have "virtually no meaning" (42). In any case, the two terms now do mean much more than just a "misunderstanding" due to an anachronism. For the most part they now refer to the entire array of feelings—conscious or unconscious, appropriate or inappropriate—experienced with respect to the other party in psychoanalytic therapy. Gill and Hoffman, for example, equate transference with "the patient's experience of the relationship [with the therapist]" (4). A definition of countertransference offered by Maroda runs as follows: "the conscious and unconscious responses of the therapist to the patient" (66).

A growing interest in countertransference in particular is apparent in the recent psychoanalytic literature (see, for example: Feiner; Gorkin; Giovacchini; Sussman; Bollas 173–274; Marshall and Marshall; Waldron; Slakter; Messner et al.; Tansey and Burke; Maroda; Brandell; Schwaber; see Tansey and Burke 9–37 and Slakter 7–39 for valuable historical overviews of countertransference). Analysts now recognize that serious problems may arise not only from inadequate awareness of countertransference, but also from a failure to actually parlay the countertransference into the healing process. Sherwood Waldron, Jr., finds, for example, that slips of the tongue made by the analyst, when properly attended to, can make the analysis take off in a whole new, productive direction (Waldron 575). Christopher Bollas believes that the frustration and anger he experienced in being lied to by a pathological liar helped him understand the frustration his patient must have felt in relating to an unreliable mother in early childhood (183). Bollas argues for "expressive uses of the countertransference," that is, "the clinician should find a way to make his subjective states of mind available to the patient and to himself as objects of the analysis even when he does not yet know what these states mean" (200–201). Karen J. Maroda concludes that "failure to actively use and express the countertransference can lead to negative outcomes such as stalemates, premature or forced terminations, and even sexual acting-out" (4).

Analysts should dispense with the aloof neutrality and silence they have traditionally tried to maintain with respect to the patient, according to most of these analysts. Oftentimes the neutrality is false anyway, just a mask behind which the analyst hides when the patient is being particularly provocative. There is no such thing as a perfectly analyzed analyst. No amount of training analysis can (nor should it) preclude intense emotional reaction on the part of the analyst in certain circumstances. Maroda believes that sometimes the patient *needs* a responsive (not just empathic) analyst, one who is willing to undergo "mutual regression" with the patient, one who is willing to be "healed" along with the patient (Bollas refers to a "going mad together" with the patient, followed by a "mutual curing"). In one case a depressive patient improved when Maroda allowed herself to experience her own feelings of despair in the presence of the patient (47). In another case Maroda admitted to a chronically angry patient that she was feeling defeated by him, and this brought relief to both analyst and patient (55). A severely masochistic borderline patient, after several years of treatment with no apparent improvement, made a complete turnaround after Maroda threatened to terminate treatment ("refer out") while at the same time admitting to the patient that she was feeling extremely frustrated, helpless, and angry (75–80).

Analysts have to recognize that they have their own problems, and that patients are often quite capable of discerning them. Analysts may feel sexually attracted to some of their patients, they may hate others with great intensity. They may fall asleep on their patients (as Freud sometimes did). They are not necessarily healthier than their patients, says Maroda (69); indeed there is a massive body of statistical evidence that workers in the various mental health professions, including psychoanalysis, "typically manifest significant psychopathology of their own" (Sussman 34). Psychoanalysts may also have an interest in keeping their patients sick. For example, they may be therapists out of a wish to see others suffer (Maroda 44; cf. Brenner 46 ff.; Sussman 71–83 provides a comprehensive survey of the literature about aggressive strivings toward the patient). The therapist may also envy the recovering patient (Maroda 159). I would add that there is often a financial incentive to keep the patient in therapy for as long as possible.

In the interests of therapy it is sometimes good, sometimes bad for the therapist to openly acknowledge his or her emotions, to express countertransference feelings. It is particularly important to know when *not* to disclose countertransference feelings, and to be able to detect when such disclosure fails. Maroda provides some useful guidelines in the area, for example, it is best not to disclose early in the therapeutic relationship, one should not disclose sexual feelings except in very rare cases, one should disclose only when the patient explicitly requests disclosure, and so forth. Analysts are just as obliged to develop tact in disclosing countertransference as in deciding when to venture an interpretation of some segment of the patient's transference. In any case it is obvious that ongoing self-analysis makes it easier to deal with the countertransference feelings which invariably arise in treatment.

The Literary Analyst's Transference

How can the psychoanalytic studies of transference and countertransference in the clinical situation illuminate literature? In particular, what light can these studies shed on the *psychoanalytic* study of literature? The literary work per se is not very much like a patient in need of a cure. Yet the psychoanalytic scholar resembles a psychoanalytic therapist insofar as both are in a position to interpret utterances. In the case of therapy the speaker is present and real, lying right there on the couch, free-associating, acting out, and so on. In the case of (written) literature the speaker is virtual, is *represented* as present in the form of an author, narrator, fragments of a narrator, persona of a lyric poem, characters in a novel, and so forth.[2] It is clear that the psychoanalyst in both situations—clinical and literary—is capable of having subjective feelings about the object in question. How should these feelings be handled? Do the clinical studies have anything to teach the literary psychoanalyst?

I believe they do and do not. They do not in the sense that literary personae (or fragments of personae) are incapable of truly interacting with the analyst in the way a patient (or fragments of the patient) interacts with the analyst. There is no two-way "transference-countertransference matrix," as the clinicians say. There is only the one-directional transference of the analyst provoked by the literary material, and there is no point in even calling this transference a "countertransference," for it "counters" nothing real (cf. Schepeler 114 who makes an analogous point regarding psychoanalytic biography). For example, Emma Bovary has no discernible feelings about me personally as I read Flaubert's novel. I would be deluded (in the manner of some deconstructionists) if I thought she did. However real literary personae may seem, they do not actually interact with literary analysts (unless they happen to be real authors who are still alive and provide actual feedback to the analyst—a rare situation fraught with all kinds of dangers, including legal).

However, the clinical studies of transference generally (including certain aspects of countertransference specifically) do have relevance to the psychoanalytic study of literature. Indeed, they must for purely commonsensical reasons. All people have "transferable" thoughts and feelings, not just patients and therapists. Psychoanalysis has undergone such extensive medicalization—"pure" psychoanalysis has become so hypertrophied—that "applied" psychoanalysis has been cast into shadow. Just as one does not have to be a prostitute in order to have sex, one does not have to be a clinical psychoanalyst to do psychoanalysis. Robert and Simone Marshall quote someone who dropped out of psychiatry and became productive in a related field as saying: "Therapists are emotional prostitutes and I just can't sit there and listen to these needy people all day long" (78).

From the viewpoint of transferential phenomena generally, it should not matter whether one psychoanalyzes "needy" patients, literary works, characters in works, political figures, famous historical personalities, whole cultures, or whatever. To become seriously involved with anyone or anything is to introduce the possibility of transference. This includes the applied psychoanalyst's involvement with any object psychoanalyzed.

In the therapeutic situation the issues for the analyst are: (1) how to be open to one's own (counter-)transference feelings and how to manipulate them internally, and (2) when and to what extent such feelings should be disclosed in the presence of the patient. In literary scholarship the second of these issues is irrelevant, since there is no one being "cured," to whom disclosure might be made therapeutically. However, there is oneself (or one's diary), which is to say that the first issue *is* relevant. There are also friends, colleagues, a spouse, and the like with whom discussion is possible (more so than in clinical analysis, where confidentiality of the patient's revelations ordinarily must be maintained). There is also the reader of literary scholarship itself, for example, the reader of this very volume of self-analytic exposés (which, by virtue of their explicitness, are now automatically vulnerable to other-analysis). There is actually quite a variety of objects to which transferential material about literature might be expressed.

There are also various degrees of disclosure of the transferential material. These might be classified as follows:

1. Not consciously thinking about transference.
2. Consciously thinking about it.
3. Discussing it with
   (a) someone other than the object of the transference,
   (b) with the object of the transference.
4. Writing it down (diary).
5. Publishing (some or all) of it.

Traditional clinical psychoanalysis has always advocated getting at least as far as step 2. The more radical clinical analysts today believe the therapist should at least sometimes arrive at step 3b. Literary psychoanalysts, in my opinion, ought to arrive at step 4—at least when a dead end or blockage of some kind develops in the analytic work. Finally, this volume of essays, like much of the recent clinical literature on countertransference, in many instances arrives at the exhibitionistic ultimate, step 5.

Autobiographical Criticism

In the last decade or so there has arisen a genre of criticism (I would not call it scholarship) which mingles critical commentary and theory with assorted personal anecdotes. Writers in this mode tend to be feminists. Little of this fascinating writing could be called properly self-analytic, although much of it is psychoanalytically informed. Some of it is revealing at the level of professional gossip in academe, and all of it is personally revealing.

In her *Thinking Through the Body* Jane Gallop, for example, confesses not only that Rousseau's *Julie* made her cry, but that works by Sade moved her to masturbate (18). Eve Kosofsky Sedgwick, in the context of a delightfully detailed commentary on her own poetry, tells us of her childhood association of poetic rhythm with the experience of being spanked ("A Poem Is Being Written," 114). Somewhat more reserved is the "personal criticism" proffered by Mary Ann Caws in her *Women of Bloomsbury*, for in this unconventional book the sexual habits of the author herself are not displayed.

Most recently Duke University Press has brought out a collection of essays titled *The Intimate Critique: Autobiographical Literary Criticism*, edited by Diane P. Freedman, Olivia Frey, and Frances Murphy Zauhar. This work was immediately lampooned by the *Times Literary Supplement* (30 April 1993), and it does have to be admitted that a few of the contributions are framed in the most wretched college compositionese. But the volume also contains some insightful and moving papers on the role of the self in creative criticism.

For example, Brenda Daly demonstrates that she was able to gain a deeper understanding of the thematics of child abuse in Joyce Carol Oates by drawing on her own experience of living in a family where the father was sexually abusing some of the daughters as the mother stood by, denying what was happening ("My Friend, Joyce Carol Oates").

Also included in the volume is the now-classic feminist piece "Me and My Shadow," originally published in 1988, by Jane Tompkins. Tompkins says she is fed up with having to avoid personal matters in her professional discourse: "I think people are scared to talk about themselves, that they haven't got the guts to do it" (25). Tompkins has the guts, however. For example, she feels free to mention the birds outside my window, my grief over Janice [a friend who committed suicide], just myself as a person sitting here in stockinged feet, a little bit chilly because the windows are open, and thinking about going to the bathroom. But not going yet. (28).

This is the "other" voice, the "personal" element that Tompkins wishes could find its way more often into her professional utterances. In particular she wishes she could express her personal anger at men: "I hate men for the way they treat women, and pretending that women aren't there is one of the ways I hate most" (37). In fact she *does* express this anger at some length in the essay, gratifying herself and her readers—not only feminist readers, but any readers with sensitivity to the importance of psychological issues: "The disdain for popular psychology and for words like 'love' and 'giving' is part of the police action that academic intellectuals wage ceaselessly against feeling, against women, against what is personal" (39).

Another feminist who doesn't mind emerging from the straitjacket of formal academic discourse is Nancy K. Miller. She has published a rambling collection titled *Getting Personal: Feminist Occasions and Other Autobiographical Acts* (1991). Reading this book we learn, among other things, that Professor Miller is the granddaughter of Jewish immigrants, that she makes mistakes in her spoken French, that she did not get tenure at Columbia, that she used to shop with her mother at Loehmann's in the Bronx, that she would drink coffee with her mother at a Greek-owned restaurant after shopping, and so on. In a chapter titled "My Father's Penis" (143–47) she really "gets personal," describing, for example, how her father used to walk around the house in pajamas with a partially open fly:

The pajamas, made of a thin cotton fabric, usually a shade of washed-out blue, but sometimes also striped, were a droopy affair; they tended to bag at the knees and shift position at the waist with every movement. The string, meant to hold the pajamas up, was also meant to keep the fly—just a slit opening in the front—closed. But the fly, we might say modernly, resisted closure and defined itself instead by the meaningful hint of a gap. (143)

The object, the "it" in the gap was a mystery to the child, and was "somehow connected to the constant tension in our family, especially to my mother's bad moods." Why this should have been so is never made clear. But Miller does tell us that she eventually got to see, even to feel her father's penis many years later, after he was stricken with Parkinson's disease and developed urinary problems: "I fished his penis out from behind the fly of his shorts and stuck it in the urinal; it felt soft and a little clammy" (144).

In a theoretical context of French feminism all this leads, naturally, to the Lacanian Phallus/Penis dichotomy. The Father's phallus was constituted by his authoritarianism, in particular by his acts of violence against the daughter: he physically abused her, she reports, throwing her across a room on one occasion, knocking her down in an elevator on another. The penis, on the other hand, was merely the soft, clammy organ. Rebelling against the father meant having a "chance at the phallus," even if she could not have the literal penis (146).

Yet, although a theoretical point has been illustrated by a personal anecdote, one senses that the anecdote is overly bizarre, and that too much has been left unsaid. And besides, the theoretical dichotomy of Phallus/Penis is not all that clear to Miller (cf. Gallop 131), nor does it seem to interest her very much. What Miller really wants to tell us, it seems, is some dark secret about herself (and her mother?). But she cannot bring herself to, for such a self-analytic act would be too painful, and the secret revealed would be quite beside the theoretical point. Miller seems to be inviting some supplementary other-analysis from her reader. I venture to accept the invitation, but caution that what I am going to say is only an interpretation.

The cumulative *effect* of the essay is to belittle the father's penis. Here, I think, lies a part of the secret. The penis is soft and clammy, it turns blue, its uncontrolled action raises the stink of urine in the apartment, and so on. One is tempted to laugh at the old man's urinary problems, and it is obvious that Miller intends this. The phrase "soft and a little clammy" means: not erect, small, cold—not hot, the way the mother likes her coffee.

But behind the castratory wish there appears to be an even darker secret. The final words of the chapter—and the book—are spoken by a physician in an intensive-care unit where Miller's father is being treated: " 'What do you want me to do,' she hissed at me across the network of tubes mapping his body, 'kill your father?' " (147). The answer can only be yes. The culmination of the essay appears to express a death-wish against a manifestly abusive father. Had this feeling (along with the castratory wish) been (self-) analyzed, the essay would have been much different, the trivial Phallus/Penis distinction would have evaporated, and probably the true origins of Miller's feminism would have come to the surface.

But still, even when she does not plunge to the psychoanalytic depths Miller can be interesting. By revealing oftentimes excruciatingly painful details from her personal life, Miller succeeds in attracting the reader's sympathy. Certainly she attracted *this* reader's sympathy, and not only with regard to abusive fathers. For example, Miller's account of the anxieties she experienced about her imperfect French reminded me of my own anxieties about my imperfect spoken Russian: on more than one occasion I have felt humiliated by making a grammatical error in the presence of American fellow-Slavists (especially in front of those language robots who mimic Russian so well—and who usually turn out to be mediocre scholars). Reading Miller I also remembered how chauvinistic the French can be about their language. In Paris I was scoffed at for my French, while in Moscow I have always found the Russians *grateful* for my even attempting to speak Russian.

Another association that came to mind while reading Miller was the way Roman Jakobson, my teacher many years ago, used to speak English, that is, with a thick Russian accent. If he could get away with that, I used to think, then it was okay for *me* to go into Slavic studies and try to be as brilliant a scholar as he was. The joke used to go around among Slavists that Jakobson could speak "thirty-two languages fluently—all of them in Russian." I used to find this joke irritating. Now I realize I was identifying with Jakobson more than I knew at the time.

But here I find myself doing what Miller and some of the other autobiographical critics do, running on and on with personal observations and reminiscences, without making any relevant scholarly point. That is the potential problem with all writing which—to quote the jacket of Miller's book—"interleaves the personal and the theoretical, anecdote and text."

Posing Questions about Self-Analysis

This book began as a spin-off from the manuscript of a book on Tolstoy which I had completed in 1989 (see my *Tolstoy's Pierre Bezukhov: A Psychoanalytic Study*). The original spin-off, titled "Why Natasha Bumps Her Head" (now included among the essays in this volume) prompted Professor Jeffrey Berman of the State University of New York at Albany to write me in September of 1991, and to point out that no book had ever been published on the topic of self-analysis in literary study. Wasn't it about time, he asked, that such a book be brought out?

I agreed, and proceeded to invite some psychoanalytic scholars to contribute to a volume on self-analysis in the application of psychoanalysis to literature. In each letter of invitation I raised a series of questions which I hoped the potential contributors would address:

What is the role of the critic's (counter-)transference fantasies in literary criticism?

Have literary critics who have been "self-analyzed" become better critics? Different critics? Do they understand better the relationship between their personal and professional lives? Would they recommend self-analysis for other literary critics?

Is self-analysis an ongoing process—analysis terminable and interminable?—or does its practical value end at a certain point?

Is self-analysis equally valuable for self-understanding and self-healing? Have the literary critics who have gone into self-analysis done so primarily for intellectual or therapeutic reasons?

To what extent are the critic's identifications and counteridentifications with fictional characters based on personal experiences, values, upbringing, and so forth?

Can *students* practice self-analysis in the context of a literature course?

Is the training that literary scholars typically receive conducive to/not conducive to what psychoanalysts mean by self-analysis?

What are the difficulties (resistances?) inherent in admitting that one has been "other-psychoanalyzed," and is it possible to overcome these difficulties?

What are the difficulties (resistances?) inherent in admitting that one has *not* been "other-psychoanalyzed?"

What are the *dangers* of self-analysis? Are there contexts in which self-analysis is little more than a symptom of narcissistic disturbance? Might a scholar's public self-analysis ever be used against the scholar? How important are the exhibitionistic and masochistic components of self-analysis? How can the self-destructive aspects of self-analysis be mitigated?

Can the narcissistic, exhibitionistic, and masochistic functions of self-analysis be isolated in such a way as to prevent interference with objectivity? Can they be co-opted in such a way as to facilitate empathy either with literary creativity or literary response?

These were merely suggestions of course, and no one scholar was expected to address them all in depth. Nevertheless the response to the idea of an edited volume was positive, and, as a result, many of the questions I raised in the letter are now dealt with here.

Not all of the answers are in for this new interdisciplinary research field, by any means. Hopefully my list of questions (drawn up with the assistance of Professor Berman) will serve as a stimulus to further study.

If there is one conclusion that can be drawn from all the essays in this volume, it is this: self-analysis can be a boon to other-analysis, including psychoanalysis of literature. Literary analysis informed by self-analysis is in principle superior to literary analysis not so informed.

Because of her self-analytic activity, for example, Barbara Schapiro is better attuned to issues of boundaries, narcissism, narcissistic rage, and related problems in the works of Virginia Woolf. Bernard Paris has a better grip on Raskolnikov's inner conflicts as a result of having brought to consciousness his own highly conflicted relationship with his mother. Michael Steig's self-analytic work brought an understanding of why he had repeatedly read a novel by James Hogg in a certain way (although Steig questions the possibility of 'objective' understanding of texts, it is obvious that he improved his grasp of the psychology of justified sinning depicted by Hogg). Upon recalling certain details of his personal and ethnic background, David Bleich discovered that he understood more of Kafka than he had previously realized. Jeffrey Berman, in the aftermath of a revered literature teacher's suicide, achieved insights into literary works dealing with suicide in part by analyzing his own response to his teacher's suicide. Norman Holland's thinly disguised self-character Norwood is able to deal more productively with *Paradise Lost* after taking some self-analytic "shrink time" to overcome his anxiety about the castratory "Lacanians." Self-analysis helped Steven Rosen get beyond an interpretation of certain Dostoevskian gestures as merely homoerotic, and to achieve insight into their equally important function as enhancers of masculinity and facilitators of male-male interaction in Dostoevsky's work. And of course, my own awareness of a personal preoccupation with matters of the "head" helped me to avoid attaching any undue significance to the fact that Natasha accidentally bumped her head toward the end of Tolstoy's *War and Peace*.

Analyzing oneself has a powerful narcissistic appeal. Self-analysis may indeed be the unacknowledged main goal in life for many psychoanalysts—clinical and applied. But so narcissistic an enterprise can, paradoxically, enhance other-analysis as well. One cannot observe one's self without somehow objectifying that self, "othering" it—but this is already the structural equivalent of other-analysis. Such "othering," moreover, can be provoked specifically by something which is itself "other." For example, it can be provoked by some objectively existing element of a literary work. Indeed, to modify Aristotle, nothing exists in the "othering" mind without being perceived in the "other" first. In the case of literature, it is as if some literary persona—author, narrator, character, fragment of a character, or whatever—whispers a bribe into the ear of the reader: "If thou wouldst know thyself, know me."

Marion Milner quotes Lao Tse: "I observe myself and so I come to know others" (122). I think that even the most narcissistic of self-analysts come to know others, including literary others—in spite of themselves.[3]

Notes

1. Others who have written on Freud's homosexuality (but not in connection with Schreber) include: Jones, vol. I, 317; Anzieu 165, 259, 292, 312, 393, 543, 552. My colleague Alan Elms (letter of 7 February 1990) has pointed out to me that Freud also worked through some of his homosexual feelings while writing his book on Leonardo da Vinci in 1910. What Freud says of Schreber ("I am all Schreber") is very much like what he had said of Leonardo earlier that same year ("Otherwise I am all Leonardo").
2. It is important to recognize that literary personae *are* represented by the writer and perceived as such by the reader. Those who neglect this form of personification—from the Russian Formalists down to today's Bakhtinians and Deconstructionists—tend to mistakenly personify the text or the literary discourse itself (see my study "Why the Russian Formalists Had No Theory of the Literary Person").

3. I wish to thank Barbara Milman, Jeff Berman, Alan Elms, Brett Cooke, and Kathryn Jaeger for their constructive comments.

Works Cited

Anzieu, Didier. *Freud's Self-Analysis.* 1975. Trans. P. Graham. London: Hogarth Press and Institute of Psycho-Analysis, 1986.
Baron, Samuel H., and Carl Pletsch, eds. *Introspection in Biography: The Biographer's Quest for Self-Awareness.* Hillsdale, N.J.: Analytic Press, 1985.
Beiser, Helen R. "An Example of Self-Analysis." *Journal of the American Psycho-Analytic Association* 32 (1984): 3–12.
Bleich, David. *Subjective Criticism.* Baltimore: Johns Hopkins University Press, 1978.
Bollas, Christopher. *The Shadow of the Object: Psychoanalysis of the Unthought Known.* New York: Columbia University Press, 1987.
Brandell, Jerrold R., ed. *Countertransference in Psychotherapy with Children and Adolescents.* Northvale, N.J.: Jason Aronson, 1992.
Brenner, Charles. "Countertransference as Compromise Formation." In *Countertransference.* Ed. Edmund Slakter. Northvale, N.J.: Jason Aronson, 1987, 43–51.
Calder, Kenneth T. "An Analyst's Self-Analysis." *Journal of the American Psycho-Analytic Association* 28 (1980): 5–20.
Caws, Mary Ann. *Women of Bloomsbury: Virginia, Vanessa, and Carrington.* New York: Routledge, 1990.
Charney, Maurice. Review of *Out from under Gogol's Overcoat,* by Daniel Rancour-Laferriere. *Psychoanalytic Review* 71 (1984): 663–64.
Chessick, Richard D. "Self-Analysis: A Fool for a Patient?" *Psychoanalytic Review* 77 (1990): 311–40.
Daly, Brenda. "My Friend, Joyce Carol Oates." In *The Intimate Critique: Autobiographical Literary Criticism.* Ed. Diane P. Freedman, Olivia Frey, and Frances Murphy Zauhar. Durham, N.C.: Duke University Press, 1993, 163–73.
Daston, P. G. "Perception of Homosexual Words in Paranoid Schizophrenia." *Perceptual and Motor Skills* 6 (1956): 45–55.
Devereux, George. *From Anxiety to Method in the Behavioral Sciences.* The Hague: Mouton, 1967.
Edel, Leon. "Confessions of a Biographer." In *Psychoanalytic Studies of Biography.* Ed. G. Moraitis and G. Pollock. Madison, Conn.: International Universities Press, 1987, 3–27.
Ehrenreich, John H. "Transference: One Concept or Many?" *Psychoanalytic Review* 76 (1989): 37–65.
Feiner, Arthur H. "Countertransference and Misreading: The Influence of the Anxiety of Influence." *Contemporary Psychoanalysis* 24 (1988): 612–49.

Fenichel, Otto. *The Psychoanalytic Theory of Neurosis.* New York: W. W. Norton, 1945.
Fleming, Joan. *The Teaching and Learning of Psychoanalysis: Selected Papers of Joan Fleming, M.D.* Ed. S. Weiss. New York: Guilford Press, 1987.
Freud, Sigmund. *The Standard Edition of the Complete Psychological Works of Sigmund Freud,* ed. J. Strachey. 24 vols. London: The Hogarth Press, 1953–65.
Gallop, Jane. *Thinking through the Body.* New York: Columbia University Press, 1988.
Gestwicki, Ronald. *A Life-Study of Franz Kafka, 1883–1924, Using the Intensive Journal Method of Ira Progoff.* Lewiston, N.Y.: Edwin Mellen Press, 1992.
Gill, Merton M., and Irwin Z. Hoffman. *Analysis of Transference,* vol. 2. New York: International Universities Press, 1982.
Giovacchini, Peter L. *Countertransference Triumphs and Catastrophes.* Northvale, N.J.: Jason Aronson, 1989.
Gorkin, Michael. *The Uses of Countertransference.* Northvale, N.J.: Jason Aronson, 1987.
Grosskurth, Phyllis. "Freud's Favorite Paranoiac." *New York Review of Books* 36 (1990): 36–38.
Hartman, Geoffrey. "The Interpreter: A Self-Analysis." *New Literary History* 4 (1973): 213–27.
Holland, Norman. *The Dynamics of Literary Response.* New York: Oxford University Press, 1968.
———. "Hamlet—My Greatest Creation." *Journal of the American Academy of Psychoanalysis* 3 (1975): 419–27.
Horney, Karen. *Self-Analysis.* 1942. New York: W. W. Norton, 1970.
Jones, Ernest. *Sigmund Freud: Life and Work,* 3 vols. London: The Hogarth Press, 1953–57.
Jung, C. G. *Memories, Dreams, Reflections.* 1961. Ed. Aniela Jaffe. Trans. Richard and Clara Winston. New York: Vintage Books, 1989.
Klein, Melanie. *Love, Guilt and Reparation and Other Works, 1921–1945.* New York: Delta, 1977.
Kline, Paul. *Fact and Fantasy in Freudian Theory.* London: Methuen, 1981.
Kohut, Heinz. *The Analysis of the Self.* New York: International Universities Press, 1971.
Kramer, Maria K. "On the Continuation of the Analytic Process after Psycho-Analysis (a Self-Observation)." *International Journal of Psycho-Analysis* 40 (1959): 17–25.
Lawton, Henry. *The Psychohistorian's Handbook.* New York: Psychohistory Press, 1988.
Loewenberg, Peter. *Decoding the Past: The Psychohistorical Approach.* Berkeley: University of California Press, 1985.
Malcolm, Janet. "The Silent Woman." *New Yorker,* 23, 30 Aug. 1993, 84–159.

Mallard, Henry C. "Ambiguities of Self-Analysis." *Psychoanalytic Quarterly* 56 (1987): 523–27.
Maroda, Karen J. *The Power of Countertransference: Innovations in Analytic Technique.* New York: John Wiley, 1991.
Marshall, Robert J., and Simone V. Marshall. *The Transference-Countertransference Matrix.* New York: Columbia University Press, 1988.
McLean, Hugh. "Gogol's Retreat from Love: Toward an Interpretation of *Mirgorod.*" In *Russian Literature and Psychoanalysis,* ed. Daniel Rancour-Laferriere. Amsterdam: John Benjamins, 1989, 101–22.
Messner, Edward, James E. Groves, and Jonathan H. Schwartz, eds. *Autognosis: How Psychiatrists Analyze Themselves.* Chicago: Year Book Medical Publishers, 1989.
Miller, Nancy K. *Getting Personal: Feminist Occasions and Other Autobiographical Acts.* New York: Routledge, 1991.
Milner, Marion (Joanna Field). *A Life of One's Own.* 1934. London: Virago, 1986.
Progoff, Ira. *At a Journal Workshop: The Basic Text and Guide for Using the Intensive Journal.* New York: Dialogue House Library, 1975.
Rainer, Tristine. *The New Diary: How to Use a Journal for Self-Guidance and Creativity.* Los Angeles: Jeremy P. Tarcher, 1978.
Rancour-Laferriere, Daniel. *Out from under Gogol's Overcoat: A Psychoanalytic Study.* Ann Arbor: Ardis, 1982.
———. *The Mind of Stalin: A Psychoanalytic Study.* Ann Arbor: Ardis, 1988.
———. "Why the Russian Formalists Had No Theory of the Literary Person." *Wiener Slawistischer Almanach—Sonderband* 31 (1992): 327–37.
———. *Tolstoy's Pierre Bezukhov: A Psychoanalytic Study.* London: Bristol Classical Press, 1993.
Rose, Jacqueline. *The Haunting of Sylvia Plath.* 1991. Cambridge: Harvard University Press, 1993.
Schepeler, Eva. "The Biographer's Transference: A Chapter in Psychobiographical Epistemology." *Biography* 13 (1990): 111–29.
Schwaber, Evelyne Albrecht. "Countertransference: The Analyst's Retreat from the Patient's Vantage Point." *International Journal of Psycho-Analysis* 73 (1992): 349–61.
Schwartz, Murray M. "The Literary Use of Transference." *Psychoanalysis and Contemporary Thought* 5 (1982): 35–44.
Sedgwick, Eve Kosofsky. "A Poem Is Being Written." *Representations* 17 (1987): 110–43.
Seilman, Uffe, and Steen F. Larsen. "Personal Resonance to Literature: A Study of Remindings While Reading." *Poetics* 18 (1989): 165–77.
Slakter, Edmund, ed. *Countertransference.* Northvale, N.J.: Jason Aronson, 1987.
Sussman, Michael B. *A Curious Calling: Unconscious Motivations for Practicing Psychotherapy.* Northvale, N.J.: Jason Aronson, 1992.

Tansey, Michael J., and Walter F. Burke. *Understanding Countertransference: From Projective Identification to Empathy.* Hillsdale, N.J.: Analytic Press, 1989.
Ticho, Gertrude R. "On Self-Analysis." *International Journal of Psycho-Analysis* 48 (1967): 308–18.
Tompkins, Jane. "Me and My Shadow." In *The Intimate Critique: Autobiographical Literary Criticism,* ed. Diane P. Freedman, Olivia Frey, and Frances Murphy Zauhar. Durham, N.C.: Duke University Press, 1993, 23–40.
Tucker, Robert C. "A Stalin Biographer's Memoir." In *Psychology and Historical Interpretation,* ed. W. M. Runyan. New York: Oxford University Press, 1988, 63–81.
Waldron, Sherwood, Jr. "Slips of the Analyst." *Psychoanalytic Quarterly* 61 (1992): 564–80.

ONE

"The Grief That Does Not Speak": Suicide, Mourning, and Psychoanalytic Teaching

Jeffrey Berman

In my teaching and writing I have spent many years exploring fictional characters' suicides, but I have never acknowledged in print the personal reason for this professional preoccupation: the suicide of an admired college English professor. Len entered my life in 1963, when I was a freshman, and soon became my mentor and best friend. He was, apart from my parents, the most formative influence on my adulthood, awakening my love for literature, introducing me to Freud's writings, directing an Honor's thesis on psychoanalytic criticism, and encouraging me to become a teacher. At a time when I felt like an impersonal number at the large state university where I was studying, Len showed special interest in me and enriched my life in a multitude of ways. His subsequent death, a year after my graduation, left me bewildered and devastated, searching for a clue why someone so remarkably gifted would take his life despite having so much to live for.

Len approached teaching with unsurpassed intensity, and he had an uncanny ability to make literature come alive to his students. Imbued with the activist spirit of the 1960s, he believed that literature could transform the world and change his students' lives. When asked to elaborate on his approach to teaching, he wrote the following comment, which I subsequently framed and placed on my office bookcase:

You have accurately discerned that I am not interested in the usual things English teachers are concerned about. . . . I want, in short, to change your life. But I don't feel this is at odds with the aims of literature. You see, it's my sincere belief that the function of literature is to change lives—and to let people know a lot more about themselves and the world. I am not a religious missionary because I am not religious. But I will agree that I am a kind of missionary. Yes, I want to make the world a nice place, but I am also desperately in love with literature. And I try to combine my deepest cares by teaching literature and making sure that I indicate how that literature speaks to every person in the classroom (including me). Literature, and art in general, is nothing if it is not a criticism of life. Writers are men, not distant "authors," and they write about people, not "characters." If I didn't care about and love my students I wouldn't take the trouble to get into painful self-searching.

I had no idea how painful that self-searching would become in time. I was eighteen when I first met Len, twenty-three when he died, and though I have dwelled upon his life and death for a quarter of a century, I still do not know all the reasons for his suicide. I am now twice as old as I was when he died and realize that I know him half as well as I once thought.

"Tell Me Why I Shouldn't Kill Myself"

An early and outspoken critic of the Vietnam War, Len believed that the United States was heading toward an apocalypse. That he was heading toward a personal apocalypse, I realized only slowly. The growing social and political turbulence filled him with a premonition of doom. Depression darkened his normally ebullient spirit. Idealism gave way to skepticism, then pessimism; inside the classroom, he remained lively and engaging; outside the classroom, he seemed deflated and apathetic about his life. Hired as a lecturer, he never finished his Ph.D. dissertation on the American critic Edmund Wilson despite completing all his research. When his contract was not renewed, he lost faith in himself, concluding that his academic career was over. He was also despondent over his wife's failing health, irrationally blaming himself for the incurable degenerative disease from which she suffered. Ironically, the deterioration and eventual collapse of their marriage aggravated her illness, deepening his guilt.

I was a graduate student at Cornell University in Ithaca, New York, when Len phoned me from his parents' apartment in Brooklyn, a five hour drive away, on Labor Day, 1968, to tell me, in a voice eerily composed, that he had just taken an overdose of sleeping pills. He was not calling, he stated, because he wanted me to talk him out of his decision; rather, he asked me to say goodbye to his family and friends. He was not angry at anyone, he added, and hoped that no one would be angry at him. He felt that suicide was the right decision and that everyone would be relieved by his death. He believed that he had accomplished nothing in his life, had disappointed his family and friends, had ceased to be a good teacher, and had made a mess of things.

Panic seized me, but I knew I had to remain calm and proceed deliberately if I was to help him. He refused to disclose where his parents' apartment was located or when they would be home, nor would he reveal where his estranged wife was living. When I asked how many pills he had swallowed and what kind, he replied that he had taken 40 or 50 chloral hydrates, more than enough, he said, to do the job. I did not doubt for a moment the seriousness of his suicide attempt, for in the preceding months he had often phoned me in the middle of the night, awakening me with the stark question: "Tell me why I shouldn't kill myself?" The telephone calls were always unnerving, even when I grew to expect them; and each time I urged him to speak to a therapist, he refused, believing that his problems were insoluble.

In what turned out to be a self-fulfilling prophecy or, more accurately, an example of life commenting upon art, Len had given me a copy of Camus' *The Myth of Sisyphus*, with its bold assertion that "[t]here is but one truly serious philosophical problem, and that is suicide. Judging whether life is or is not worth living amounts to answering the fundamental question of philosophy" (Camus 3). I argued that Camus' existential heroes were on the side of life, aware of the fragile nature of existence, and determined to live every moment in full consciousness and revolt. I quoted to him Camus' passionate words—"It is essential to die unreconciled and not of one's own free will. Suicide is a repudiation" (41)—but Len was not convinced. To him, Camus' tragic death in 1960, when he was killed in a car accident at the age of forty-six, only seemed to confirm the absurdity of existence.

I could not disguise the fear in my voice as I implored Len to call an ambulance or the police, a plea he adamantly refused. I found it impossible to carry on a reasonable conversation with a person who had set into motion his own death. The longer I spoke, the more I feared his life was slipping away. I found myself choked with emotion, unsure what to say or do. After several minutes I told him that if he did not hang up and call for assistance, then I would. Later, in reflecting back upon the event, I realized that I should have kept him on the phone while my wife, who was with me throughout the crisis, rushed to another phone to call the police. One always sees clearly in hindsight. Instead, I pleaded with him to go for help and, when that failed, I hung up and dialed the operator.

Just as I succeeded in getting through to the operator, Len somehow got back on the line and, in a controlled voice, reprimanded me for making—the words are etched indelibly in my memory—the "conventional response." The second call was a repetition of the first, and when I exhorted him once again to summon help, lest I would, he responded: "Then I'll go somewhere else to die." Grief-stricken, I hung up for the second time, phoned the operator who connected me to the police, and breathlessly explained the situation. A few hours later a police officer called with the news that they had broken down the apartment door but found no one inside. The next day Len's body was spotted in his old Plymouth outside the apartment, his wrists slashed. He was thirty-one.

The Aftermath of Suicide

Suicide creates intense, long-lasting guilt, grief, and anger among family and friends, and Len's death overwhelmed me. By literally hanging up on him, cutting him off, I felt like I had betrayed his friendship. He had forced me into a Catch-22 situation; had I remained on the phone, as he urged me to do, listening without intervening, I would have respected his wishes but felt greater disloyalty, blaming myself for not having done everything in my power to save his life. Years later I discovered that my situation was by no means unique: approximately one in four suicides occurs in the presence of another person or while the suicide victim is speaking over the telephone—a phenomenon that emphasizes the interpersonal nature of suicide and the crucial importance of the role of the other. Edwin Shneidman has remarked that "the concept of the 'significant other' has its sharpest operational meaning in a case of suicide where another person seems to be both the life-sustainer and the last straw, at any rate, the focus of the victim's life and the precipitating reason for the death" ("Overview" 7).

I am convinced that, contrary to his stated wishes, Len wanted to be talked out of death. Surely he must have known that I would not only disagree with his decision in the most emphatic terms but also do everything in my power to come to his aid. This was the position I had maintained during all our conversations on suicide, and he knew how strongly I felt about this subject. A basic assumption in suicide prevention is that most people who attempt or commit suicide unconsciously wish to be rescued and thus leave clues to their anticipated deaths. Suicidal behavior is highly ambivalent: one wishes simultaneously to live and die. If Len did not want me to intervene, he could have simply written a letter explaining his actions.

Following the death, Len's family and friends mourned the tragic waste of his life, feeling that part of their own lives had also been destroyed. If, by committing suicide, Len was offering a "gift" to his loved ones, they felt less relief than horror and reacted as if his death were an act of aggression—which suicide often is. As the psychoanalyst Wilhelm Stekel noted as early as 1910, "*No one kills himself who has never wanted to kill another, or at least wished the death of another*" (qtd. in Friedman 87, emphasis in original). While there are other motives for suicide, including the desire to escape from pain, the wish to be reunited with a loved one in death, and the belief that death will magically solve one's problems, suicidal individuals tend to be profoundly aggressive.[1] Len's wife went into shock upon learning of his death and had to be hospitalized immediately. She died one month later, on his birthday—a death that may have also been self-induced, a retaliation for his abandonment of her.[2] His friends and students were also horrified by his death, wondering how someone who was once so full of life, so determined to transform and humanize the world, could perish by his own hand.

Suicide Survivors

In the weeks following Len's funeral, I remained emotionally numb and confused. Suicide always comes as a shock, even when it is not entirely unexpected, and there is probably no form of death that is more difficult for survivors to mourn. There were no self-help groups in those days for "suicide survivors," a term that now refers to relatives and friends of people who terminate their own lives. Suicide survivors share many characteristics:

> marked distortions in time, especially the inability to remember the date the relative or friend died; difficulty in responding to direct questions about the number of people in one's family; emotional estrangements from other family members; a sense of foreboding; a pessimistic outlook on life, including the suggestion of an early death; overtly suicidal ideas and less overt self-destructive behaviors. (Dunne, McIntosh, and Dunne-Maxim xiii)

Although I have never been suicidal, I have found myself in the situation of other suicide survivors whose lives have been changed irrevocably. Suicide survivors have fewer support systems available to them than survivors of other tragedies because of the stigma of suicide and the tangled emotions arising from the act. Perhaps the most painful realization is that one often does feel a degree of relief over a loved one's suicide, along with anguish and remorse. In my own case, Len's nightly telephone calls had become unbearable, and while I never took the telephone off the hook, there were times when I was tempted to do so. Suicide survivors are burdened by self-reproach, making recovery problematic.

For months afterwards I could not talk to anyone about Len's suicide, not even to my wife, who was as close to him as I was and no less devastated. We both felt a gaping void in our lives. I kept asking myself what Len was thinking and feeling during the final moments of his life; each time I visualized him alone in his car, I felt heartsick. Unable to find an outlet for my grief, I could not, to cite Malcolm's lines to Macduff in *Macbeth*, "[g]ive sorrow words. The grief that does not speak/Whispers the o'er-fraught heart, and bids it break" (4.3.208–10). I immersed myself in my graduate studies, hoping to avoid brooding over the past. Yet even as I tried to concentrate on life, I was preoccupied with death.

Serendipitously, I was at this time taking a graduate seminar on Joseph Conrad and William Faulkner, taught by Walter Slatoff. Early in the semester Professor Slatoff mentioned, almost as an aside, the discovery of new biographical evidence indicating that, in a moment of depression, Conrad as a young man had shot himself deliberately in the chest. He later mythologized the wound in the semi-autobiographical novel *The Arrow of Gold*. A telegram that Conrad wrote to his uncle, elaborating on the details of the self-shooting, helps to explain the high suicide rate among his fictional characters, including characters with whom he strongly identified, such as the eponymous hero of *Lord Jim* and Martin Decoud in *Nostromo*.

Obsessed with Len's suicide, I found myself gravitating toward Conrad's suicide attempt, hoping that an understanding of the latter would shed light on the former. One of the characteristics of suicide survivors, I later discovered, with a shock of recognition, is the constant search for an explanation of suicide. I began studying the enormous body of literature on self-destruction and plunged into psychoanalytic theory, which made sense both theoretically and experientially. The result was my 1971 Ph.D dissertation, *Joseph Conrad and the Self-Destructive Urge*, which was published in 1977 as *Joseph Conrad: Writing as Rescue*. By studying the psychodynamics of suicide, I acknowledged to myself the paralyzing emotions arising from Len's death: the guilt, anger, and anguish that are the legacy—or illegacy—of suicide. It was a relief to know that I was not alone in feeling burdened by these emotions. I also joined a suicide prevention organization in Ithaca, which trains volunteers to assess the suicidal risk of callers and then decide on an appropriate course of action, ranging from counseling to emergency rescue procedures. In 1980, after receiving tenure at the State University of New York at Albany, I began three years of psychoanalytic training in New York City, an experience which has broadened my understanding of mental illness and health.

"The Nightmare of My Choice"

In retrospect, I can see why, following Len's death, I was so drawn to Conrad's stories, particularly to *Heart of Darkness*, a novella that had curiously failed to move me when I first read it in high school. I regarded Len in the same way that Marlow views Kurtz at the beginning of the story—as a "very remarkable person" (19), an "emissary of pity, and science [in Len's case, literature], and progress" (25), a person who had "enlarged my mind" (65). Both Len and Kurtz had immense plans, vast energy, lofty humanitarian aims, and an extraordinary gift for expression. Paralleling Marlow's relationship to Kurtz, I idealized Len and, despite our closeness in age, transmuted him into an admired father figure whose approval meant the world to me. Like Kurtz, Len defined himself as a missionary, and his belief in the humanizing and transformative power of literature elevated him into a heroic figure.

And yet something terrible had happened to Len, some deficiency had been revealed which rendered him, like Kurtz, "hollow at the core" (59). I pictured Len's dying words as "The horror! The horror!" (71). Marlow's observation about depression—"Even extreme grief may ultimately vent itself in violence—but more generally takes the form of apathy" (44)—seemed to describe Len's last months. Just as Marlow defends Kurtz and is prepared to risk his own life if necessary to protect Kurtz from the forces of darkness, only to draw back at the last moment, unwilling to plunge into the abyss with his dying friend, so, too, did I retreat out of self-preservation. After his death, I could not help but judge Len in the same oxymoronic way in which Marlow judges Kurtz: as a man of "exalted and incredible degradation" (67). And Marlow's dazed reaction to Kurtz's death anticipated my own reaction to Len's: "It was not my strength that wanted nursing, it was my imagination that needed soothing" (73).

This is, of course, a literary construction, an interpretation of a real character as seen through the veil of a shadowy fictional one. It may be objected that I am being overly self-conscious and literary. To regard myself like the stalwart Marlow, capable of navigating the most treacherous waters, must seem grandiose. I can hardly read a road map without getting lost, much less undertake a heroic and perilous voyage into the deepest recesses of Africa. To compare my "psychic" journey with Marlow's is like comparing (to paraphrase Mark Twain) a lightning bug with lightning. Nevertheless, to the extent that readers identify with fictional characters, I viewed myself as Conrad's captain, permitted to retreat nervously from the brink of death and compelled to narrate the story of a man who will forever remain, as Marlow describes Kurtz, the "nightmare of my choice."

For suicide survivors, life is never the same. I still feel vague anxiety when the phone rings late at night or when I hear a student casually say that he is going to "kill himself" over a grade. It has taken me a long time to recognize that I was not responsible for Len's death and that it is the victim who must bear major responsibility. It is easier to realize this intellectually than emotionally; even as I was writing earlier drafts of this chapter, I could see that I was more self-blaming than I was consciously aware of. This is the first time I have written about Len—and the most painful writing I have undertaken. I don't know whether I have penetrated many of the veils of his life or death; as Marlow observes in *Lord*

Jim, "it is my belief no man ever understands quite his own artful dodges to escape from the grim shadow of self-knowledge" (49).

Self-Analysis and Psychoanalytic Theory

For me, the grim shadow of self-knowledge has been illuminated in part by psychoanalytic theory, particularly the repetition-compulsion principle. In *Beyond the Pleasure Principle* (1920) Freud postulates the existence of a "compulsion to repeat" which contradicts the pleasure principle. Freud's famous example of the compulsion to repeat is the "fort [gone]-da [there]" ritual enacted by his eighteen-month old grandson in response to his mother's temporary disappearance. By throwing over his bed a wooden reel with a piece of string round it, the child symbolically makes his mother disappear; by pulling the reel onto his bed again, he makes her magically reappear. The game of disappearance and return enables the child to endure his mother's absence. Although Freud interpreted the repetition-compulsion principle as confirmation of a "death instinct," contemporary psychoanalysts regard it more plausibly as a reflection of the need to relive and master traumatic experiences. Many of the shell-shock soldiers of World War I would now be classified as suffering from post-traumatic stress disorder.

The repetition-compulsion principle has been striking in my own life. By converting a passive situation (standing helplessly by as a friend committed suicide) into an active one (becoming a psychoanalytic critic and doing research on self-destructive writers), I have gained a degree of control over a frightening situation. One of the driving forces behind my teaching and scholarship, I now see, is a reparative fantasy in which, by attempting to "rescue" fictional characters, I replay my discussions with Len and strive for a more positive outcome. Although I cannot bring Len back to life nor journey into the heart of his darkness, I can play the role of significant other to my students, especially to those whose lives have been touched by suicide or other traumas and who are still burdened by their own private albatross.

Writing as Rescue

The notion of "writing as rescue" which I explored in my work on Joseph Conrad applies to other writers who write out of the need to exorcise the specter of self-destruction. Although writing was at times unbearably painful for Conrad, the only thing worse than writing was not writing—the fear of artistic silence. One of his most striking pronouncements about the therapeutic nature of writing appears in his late novel *Chance*, in which the authorial Marlow observes: "to be busy with material affairs is the best preservative against reflection, fears, doubts—all these things which stand in the way of achievement. I suppose a fellow proposing to cut his throat would experience a sort of relief while occupied in stropping his razor carefully" (340). As I wrote in *Joseph Conrad: Writing as Rescue,*

> Given the pervasiveness of the destructive element in his novels, Conrad's work involved a continual sharpening of his razor—and the use of that razor against his fictional characters. But as long as he was engaged in the sharpening of the blade, and as long as his reading public could admire the deadly beautiful bite of that blade, he gained enough relief—though at times he surely nicked himself—to keep it away from his throat. (27)

Creative writers as diverse as D. H. Lawrence, Ernest Hemingway, Sylvia Plath, and William Styron have all remarked upon the mysterious healing power of self-expression. Writing cannot be reduced to therapy but it promotes both self-mastery and self-healing. "One sheds one['s] sicknesses in books," Lawrence wrote in a letter, "repeats and presents again one[']s emotions, to be master of them" (2:90). Hemingway's Robert Jordan dwells upon a similar thought in *For Whom the Bell Tolls:* "my guess is that you will get rid of all that by writing about it. . . . Once you write it down it is all gone" (165). Sylvia Plath experienced psychological relief through writing poetry, reflecting in her *Journals* that "Fury jams the gullet and spreads poison, but, as soon as I start to write, dissipates, flows out into the figure of the letters: writing as therapy?" (256). And William Styron has commented in *Sophie's Choice* on how his fiction may be viewed, psychobiographically, as an effort to work through personal conflicts. "I realize now . . . how my writing had kept serious emotional distress safely at bay, in the sense that the novel I was working on served as a cathartic instrument through which I was able to discharge on paper many of my more vexing tensions and miseries" (438).

There are many reasons why writing is conducive to psychological health. To begin with, writing enables artists to confront and master, if only temporarily, potentially self-paralyzing conflicts and fears, purging toxic emotions. Writing allows artists to descend within themselves and impose order upon chaos, defining the indefinable. Writing encourages exploration of multiple points of view and promotes greater self-detachment. Writing is an act of creation, a validation of the effort to leave part of oneself to posterity. Writing is also a way to memorialize loss and achieve a victory of sorts over death, the "love and care lavished upon the work of art serving," as David Aberbach remarks in *Surviving Trauma*, "as a permanent testimony to the artist's attachment to the lost person" (23). Finally, writing strengthens the artist's connection to the community, thus helping to offset the solitude and struggle associated with the creative process.

Neither the "talking cure" nor the "writing cure" is a panacea for fictional or real characters. Cathartic relief, if and when it comes, may be short-lived. Despite Lawrence's belief that some writers shed their illnesses in books, we know that other writers may repeat and re-present their conflicts without mastering them. Many of the strongest testimonies of the healing power of writing have come, ironically, from novelists and poets who later perished by their own hand. Both Hemingway and Plath committed suicide, the former in large part because of the recognition that his creative powers had been exhausted, the latter notwithstanding the extraordinary burst of creativity in the months preceding her death.

Nevertheless, for every artist who has failed to be sustained by his or her own art, there are numerous others who have affirmed that writing has been crucial for their psychological well-being. As Franz Kafka observed, with characteristic gallows humor, "The existence of the writer is truly dependent upon his desk and if he wants to keep madness at bay, he must never go far from his desk, he must hold on to it with his teeth" (*Letters* 335).

Classroom Diary Writing

I have found that students can also experience the therapeutic benefits of writing. In my literature-and-psychoanalysis classes I encourage students to keep a weekly introspective diary in which they write about their personal experiences and make whatever connections they wish between their own lives and those of the fictional characters whom we are studying. By writing weekly diaries and allowing me to read a few of these entries anonymously to the class, students explore conflicts which they rarely write about or even disclose to relatives and friends. In many cases, students experience significant personal breakthroughs in their lives and share these insights with classmates.

In a recent article published in the *Chronicle of Higher Education*, Swartzlander, Pace, and Stamler have called into question the ethics of classroom diary writing, but potential problems can be averted by observing the following precautions. First, students need to be assured that their diaries will remain strictly confidential (there is only one exception to this promise of confidentiality, as I shall discuss shortly) and that no one, apart from the teacher, will have access to the diaries. Second, if a student allows the teacher to read a diary aloud, it is with the understanding that there will be no class discussion of the entry, since an unsympathetic comment from a classmate might prove harmful to the diarist. Third, since diaries are obviously personal, they should not be graded. Fourth, students who are reluctant to engage in self-analysis and self-disclosure must not be pressured into doing so. Finally, teachers must not psychoanalyze their students' writings; interpretations outside a clinical context would surely be experienced by students as threatening and intrusive. Instead, teachers should limit their responses to supportive statements—praising students' honesty, suggesting books for them to read, and raising additional questions for them to pursue if they wish.

When I first started receiving diaries from my students in 1976, I was startled by their power, candor, and openness. The diaries offered a fascinating glimpse into students' lives, including their hopes and expectations, their fears and conflicts, their feelings about themselves and others. Many students wrote about subjects with which I had little personal experience: problems of being children of divorced parents, serious eating disorders such as anorexia and bulimia, drug and alcohol addiction, and sexual abuse. Other students, however, wrote about a subject with which I was familiar—suicide—and over the years I have received diaries from numerous students who write about being personally affected by the self-inflicted death of a relative or friend. In the remainder of this essay I would like to focus on how psychoanalytic literature courses can be an effective setting for suicide education and prevention.

Coming Out of the Closet

"The suicidal person leaves his psychological skeleton in the survivor's closet," Edwin Shneidman has observed (qtd. in Zinner 67). The number of these closets is startling. The American Association of Suicidology estimates that there are at least 30,000 self-inflicted deaths each year in the United States. Many authorities believe that the true figure may be closer to 100,000 deaths. It has been estimated, moreover, that each suicide directly affects at least six other people. There are thus millions of Americans who are suicide survivors, and their numbers are increasing by at least 180,000 per year.

Not only is suicide the second leading cause of death in young adults, next to accidents, but suicidal thinking and suicide attempts have become a way of life for an astonishing number of people. According to the national school-based Youth Risk Behavior Survey, sponsored by the United States Centers for Disease Control, 27 percent of all high school students thought seriously about committing suicide in 1990; 8 percent of all students actually attempted suicide; and 2 percent of all students sustained injuries serious enough to warrant medical attention ("Attempted Suicide" 633–34). The study, which surveyed 11,631 high school students from every state in the country, estimated that over a quarter of a million high school students made at least one suicide attempt requiring hospitalization in the preceding 12 months. The CDC also noted that the suicide rates for adolescents 15–19 years of age have quadrupled in the last 40 years, from 2.7 per 100,000 in 1950 to 11.3 per 100,000 in 1988. The CDC concluded its study by recommending a variety of strategies to reduce the suicide rate, including educating youths about the warning signs of suicide and the availability of suicide prevention services.

Literature courses offer an excellent forum in which to talk about suicide because the subject appears in the earliest classical plays and the latest poems and novels. A. Alvarez and others have noted that twentieth-century literature is preoccupied with suicide; it is scarcely possible to read a modern novel without confronting a self-destructive character. To speak about a fictional character's suicide is to inquire into the motives and, hence, the psychology of suicide: thus the value of psychoanalytic theory. Over the years I have taught several literary texts that focus on suicide: *Hamlet*, Ibsen's *Hedda Gabler*, Dostoevsky's *The Brothers Karamazov*, Kafka's "The Judgment" and *The Metamorphosis*, Conrad's *Heart of Darkness*, *Lord Jim*, and *Nostromo*, Woolf's *Mrs. Dalloway*, Miller's *Death of a Salesman*, Plath's *The Bell Jar*, Anne Sexton's poetry, Joanne Greenberg's *I Never Promised You a Rose Garden*, Mishima's "Patriotism," and Salinger's *The Catcher in the Rye*. Many of these texts I have discussed in *The Talking Cure* and *Narcissism and the Novel*. Suicidal literature is not necessarily depressing or morbid; the writer, like the physician, is interested in illness in the larger context of healing and health. Literature reflects, as John Clayton has recently expressed, "*gestures of healing*—reparative acts that permit writers to feel whole and to make some link, other than alienation, with the world" (4). Even if these gestures of healing are temporary or incomplete, they point the way toward health for writers and readers alike.

Prevention and Postvention

In my classes I usually spend a few minutes talking about Len's suicide. I emphasize the warning signs of suicide, the psychological dynamics, the common misconceptions of suicide, and the various treatments available. I stress how important it is for students to realize that help is available. And I tell my students that although it is difficult to talk about suicide, it is more difficult *not* to talk about it.

Diary writing is especially helpful for students who are either suicide survivors or in a suicidal crisis. For suicide survivors, writing promotes the bereavement process, first, by allowing them to accept the reality of their loss, and second, by enabling them to confront and work through the chaotic emotions arising from a loved one's suicide. Suicidologists use the term "postvention" to describe the process of helping the bereaved come to terms with suicide. For students who may be actively suicidal, writing creates a powerful bond to a supportive community. These students feel a sense of relief when their diaries are read—they know they are being heard. They also derive the comfort of knowing that others have survived suicidal crises and that help is available. For students who have not been exposed to suicide, learning about prevention and postvention becomes a valuable part of their education.

Befriending Skills

It is particularly important for teachers who receive suicidal diaries to respond as empathically and nonjudgmentally as possible. They must display what one psychologist has called befriending skills: being compassionate and humble; sharing a person's pain; listening instead of offering advice; and providing acceptance, empathy, and caring (Poland 170). Teachers must respect a student's need to grieve, and they must remain calm and reassuring, allowing students to write openly about suicide and express their feelings. Students who write about suicide require compassionate and understanding readers; a teacher's empathic failure obviously has serious consequences. Teachers must guard against countertransference responses such as projecting their own guilt, fear, anger, or disapproval onto students. Teachers, like therapists, must recognize their own limitations when dealing with a potentially life-threatening crisis. As psychoanalysts John Maltsberger and Dan Buie observe, "The three most common narcissistic snares [for the therapist] are the aspirations to heal all, know all, and love all" (627). Finally, teachers must suggest outside help when they feel it is appropriate.

Confidentiality

Confidentiality is essential for classroom diary writing, but in certain situations the need for confidentiality is outweighed by moral, ethical, and legal considerations. If, for example, a student writes a diary revealing the possibility of an impending suicide attempt, it is incumbent upon a teacher to notify the university's counseling service. I have never been in a situation where this has been necessary, but I can conceive of the possibility. There are at least two compelling reasons to seek outside help: first, a teacher, like a psychologist or lawyer, can be held liable for failure to disclose information that a person may harm another or himself or herself; second, a student's disclosure of an impending suicide attempt is a cry for help that should not go unheeded.

Talking and Writing about Suicide

There is a common misconception that talking or writing about suicide heightens a person's vulnerability. The opposite is almost always true.

People are relieved when they have the opportunity to express suicidal feelings, and they feel less lonely, stigmatized, and withdrawn. The only time a classroom discussion might become dangerous is if a student overidentifies with an author who glorifies suicide. Following the publication of the confessional novel *The Sorrows of Young Werther* in 1774, a rash of suicides occurred, all apparently copying the death of Goethe's youthful romantic hero. (Writing the novel proved more cathartic to Goethe, who identified strongly with his self-tortured protagonist, than reading the novel did for many of Goethe's followers.) In 1978 the film *The Deer Hunter*, which graphically depicts Russian roulette, provoked a spate of real-life suicides. By refusing to romanticize either real or fictional suicides, literature teachers can avoid contributing to the Werther effect.

Suicide prevention and self-help groups are effective precisely because they enable people to express themselves, to enter into reciprocal relationships with others who may have similar problems, and to avail themselves of the treatments that have worked for others. For the same reason, I have found that students are relieved when, in a response to a vague suicidal observation in a diary, I ask them if they are indeed suicidal. The question encourages them to talk about their feelings and find solutions to their problems.

Suicide Diaries

Students who write suicide diaries generally fall into one of two groups: those who write about a relative's or friend's suicide or suicide attempt, and those who write about feeling suicidal themselves. Students in the first group generally do not understand why a person would wish to take his or her own life, while students in the second group offer explanations for their actions and describe how they felt during a suicidal crisis. Students in the first group usually write only one or two diaries per semester on suicide; those in the second group often write several diaries. Predictably, students in the second group experience much more resistance in writing about suicide than students in the first group: their diaries are more intense, and they pose greater challenge to the teacher, who must decide when to read—and not read—their diaries to the class.

Almost without exception, students who write about another person's suicide or suicide attempt express shock, confusion, grief, guilt, and anger—the same emotions I experienced after Len's death. The closer students are to the deceased, the greater their devastation. A relative's suicide is generally more traumatic than a friend's, unless the friend was a former lover. The death of a relative or friend produces sorrow, but if the death is a suicide, the sorrow is tinged with anger and guilt. The tension between sympathy and judgment is particularly striking in suicide survivor diaries.

Suicide has the uncanny ability to cast a wide net, ensnaring friends, family, and even distant acquaintances. Students are unsure not only how they actually feel about a loved one's suicide but about what they are supposed to feel. Undergraduates who write about suicide are still comparatively young and have another forty or fifty years ahead of them, but they believe that the event has irrevocably altered their lives, a conclusion supported by research on suicide survivors. Suicide calls into question so many deeply ingrained assumptions about life, defies so many social and religious taboos, and shatters so many lives that virtually no one can write about it dispassionately. Many suicide survivors have never spoken about the subject before, not even with those people who have been most directly affected by the event. Consequently, the diaries reveal their first effort to write about this experience and share it with another person.

Unlike deaths from natural causes or from illnesses that cannot be medically treated, many—probably most—suicides can be prevented through intervention or counseling. This is especially true for teenagers, for whom suicide is usually a spontaneous, impulsive act rather than premeditated, as with older age groups. Moreover, for the vast majority of adolescents, suicidal crises are usually of short duration. Once adolescents successfully cope with a suicidal crisis, they find it easier coping with future crises should they arise. Most people who attempt suicide do not attempt it again.

Apart from entering therapy, I believe that it is valuable for students at risk to study the lives of authors who have written about overcoming suicidal depression. The suicide literature is extensive, but if I had to cite a single volume—and a slender one, for that matter—it would be William Styron's autobiographical *Darkness Visible*, in which he describes his descent into mental illness, from the development of his depression in October 1985, when he turned sixty, to its near-fatal conclusion in December, when he rejected suicide, hospitalized himself, and initiated the healing process. Noting that "[t]hrough the course of literature and art the theme of depression has run like a durable thread of woe" (82), Styron chronicles the long list of twentieth-century artists who have killed themselves. An intensely private man, Styron acknowledges that his frank discussion of his own suicidal depression has caused an outpouring of responses from readers who expressed gratitude to him for writing about a subject that still remains taboo for most people. Styron's conclusion in *Darkness Visible* is that while depression remains nearly incomprehensible to those who have not experienced it, one can survive its horrors and live to write about it, as he himself does eloquently:

[I]f depression had no termination, then suicide would, indeed, be the only remedy. But one need not sound the false or inspirational note to stress the truth that depression is not the soul's annihilation; men and women who have recovered from the disease—and they are countless—bear witness to what is probably its only saving grace: it is conquerable. (84)

Notes

1. Although Freud never formulated a comprehensive theory of suicide, his remarks in "Mourning and Melancholia" (1917) on clinical depression emphasize the link between suicide and internalized aggression: "no neurotic harbours thoughts of suicide which he has not turned back upon himself from murderous impulses against others . . ." (225). In his classic study *Man Against Himself,* Karl Menninger observed that no suicide is consummated unless there is the wish to kill, the wish to be killed, and the wish to die (23).
2. It is not uncommon for a person to commit suicide on a loved one's birthday or deathday. This "anniversary reaction," as Kubie notes, is even more common if the loved one has committed suicide.

Works Cited

Aberbach, David. *Surviving Trauma.* New Haven: Yale University Press, 1989.
Alvarez, A. *The Savage God.* New York: Bantam, 1973.
"Attempted Suicide among High School Students—United States, 1990." In *Morbidity and Mortality Weekly Report.* Centers for Disease Control 40 (20 September 1991): 633–35.

Berman, Jeffrey. *Joseph Conrad: Writing as Rescue.* New York: Astra Books, 1977.
———. *Narcissism and the Novel.* New York: New York University Press, 1990.
———. *The Talking Cure.* New York: New York University Press, 1985.
Camus, Albert. *The Myth of Sisyphus.* Trans. Justin O'Brien. New York: Vintage, 1955.
Clayton, John J. *Gestures of Healing.* Amherst: University of Massachusetts Press, 1991.
Conrad, Joseph. *Chance.* London: Dent, 1913. Rpt. 1969.
———. *Heart of Darkness.* Ed. Robert Kimbrough. New York: Norton Critical Edition, 1963.
———. *Lord Jim.* Ed. Thomas Moser. New York: Norton Critical Edition, 1968.
Dunne, Edward J., John L. McIntosh, and Karen Dunne-Maxim, eds. *Suicide and Its Aftermath.* New York: W. W. Norton, 1987.
Freud, Sigmund. *Beyond the Pleasure Principle. The Standard Edition of the Complete Psychological Works of Sigmund Freud,* vol. 18. Ed. and trans. James Strachey. London: The Hogarth Press, 1955.
———. "Mourning and Melancholia." *Standard Edition,* vol. 14. 239–58.
Friedman, Paul, ed. *On Suicide. Discussions of the Vienna Psychoanalytic Society—1910.* New York: International Universities Press, 1967.
Hemingway, Ernest. *For Whom the Bell Tolls.* New York: Scribner's, 1940.
Kafka, Franz. *Letters to Friends, Family, and Editors.* Trans. Richard and Clara Winston. New York: Schocken Books, 1977.
Kubie, Lawrence. "Multiple Determinants of Suicide." In *Essays in Self-Destruction.* Ed. Edwin Shneidman. New York: Science House, 1967, 455–62.
Lawrence, D. H. *The Letters of D. H. Lawrence,* vol. 2. Ed. George J. Zytaruk and James T. Boulton. Cambridge: Cambridge University Press, 1981.
Maltsberger, John, and Dan Buie. "Countertransference Hate in the Treatment of Suicidal Patients." *Archives of General Psychiatry* 30 (1974): 625–33.
Menninger, Karl. *Man Against Himself.* New York: Harcourt, Brace & World, 1938.
Plath, Sylvia. *The Journals of Sylvia Plath.* Ed. Frances McCullough. New York: Dial Press, 1982.
Poland, Scott. *Suicide Intervention in the Schools.* New York: Guilford Press, 1989.
Shakespeare, William. *The Tragedy of Macbeth.* Ed. Sylvan Barnet. New York: Signet, 1963.
Shneidman, Edwin. "Overview: A Multidimensional Approach to Suicide." In *Suicide: Understanding and Responding.* Ed. Douglas Jacobs and Herbert Brown. Madison, Conn.: International Universities Press, 1989, 1–30.
Styron, William. *Darkness Visible.* New York: Random House, 1990.
———. *Sophie's Choice.* New York: Random House, 1979.
Swartzlander, Susan, Diana Pace, and Virginia Lee Stamler. "The Ethics of

Requiring Students to Write about Their Personal Lives." *Chronicle of Higher Education* 24 (17 February 1993): B1–B2.

Zinner, Ellen. "Survivors of Suicide: Understanding and Coping with the Legacy of Self-Inflicted Death." In *Youth Suicide*. Eds. Peter Cimbolic and David Jobes. Springfield, Ill.: Charles C. Thomas, 1990, 67–86.

TWO

How I Got My Language: Forms of Self-Inclusion

David Bleich

In this chapter, I tell a story of how I think "my" language made its way into my life. My discussion of Kafka, even in its scholarly features, presupposes readings of his work I did in high school as well as presenting views I just came to. The story is partial and circuitous, but it represents a simultaneous understanding of self, society, gender, culture, and language. This understanding is founded on critical and biographical reflection as well as the conversational reporting of events and circumstances in my life. I hope to contribute to changing some of our academic purposes through the public use of self-understanding and self-inclusion. It goes along with recent efforts of Diane Freedman and Jane Tompkins to function as members of the academy by including self-reflection in the processes of criticism and scholarship. My points of greatest interest have to do with language use in an immediate sense. My English, in its struggle to emerge, has my parents' Yiddish in it, in its struggle to survive. Reading Kafka and then thinking about his work for this occasion helped to teach me new ways in which my and our languages enact many of our other memberships.

Works by Franz Kafka have always been among my preferred readings. This has been true since high school, when I had no patience for literature. But now that I do have patience, his work still seems to have the "right word." Reading him in German doesn't feel the same: it is not my native language. I did pass an examination which said I knew German well enough for it to count for my doctoral requirements. Often the sound and meaning of Kafka in German emphasize its role in my mind as a constant caricature of its culture and subject matter. I think that in German Kafka's literature is even more bitter and ironic than it seems in English. But even in English, the literary sarcasm and linguistic caricature seem to stretch through the substance of the stories to the language itself. My degree is in *English*, and I took my comprehensive oral examinations in both English and American modern literature. The literature I studied in my dissertation was written in English. My "field" is supposed to include only English-language literature, except for classical literature or Dante. However disloyal toward academic orthodoxy my interest in Kafka may be, the fact of my experience is that the works of a writer read *in translation* speak to me more than the works of any other writer.

My older brother wrote his master's thesis in philosophy on the works of Kafka. He too had read Kafka since he was young. His "field" was philosophy, but Kafka was still his subject; Kafka's literature lent itself to philosophical reflection. He and I joked about Kafka, but I can't say why he liked Kafka; I just know that Kafka played the same role in my brother's study of philosophy that he played in my study of English-language literature: an apparently "outside" figure really occupying the emotional center stage. It could be that our mother influenced us both, since she reported that she was a friend, in Poland in her youth, of Dora Diamant, Kafka's last lover. My mother was briefly involved in the Yiddish theater as an actress in New York in the early 1920s. As I will explore, there is a circle of relation between Kafka, the European Yiddish theater, and my parents' Yiddish in America, and I was substantively touched by that circle. My brother knew spoken Yiddish quite well, while I could only get along in it if I had to. Being involved in Yiddish ways of thought has something to do with liking Kafka, for both my brother and me. And Yiddish was definitely not one of our doctoral certification languages. Here, for me, knowledge and experience from outside the academy are actually the bases for my interests in teaching, in literature, in this essay, and in the academy.

I take pleasure in repeating statements like, "A false alarm answered in the night will not ever be made good, not ever," or "To write prescriptions is easy but to come to an understanding is hard."[1] This immediate, literal, experiential sense of Kafka's work that I have held from my youth led me to try to understand and conceptualize his life as a German-speaking Czech Jew, more than as a "significant literary artist," even though it seems clear enough that this latter identity was part of his own self-understanding. But in graduate school, for the first-person narrative in which the foregoing statements appear ("A Country Doctor"), Professor Leon Edel, a man I respect and admire now as then, asked us as a class assignment to "deduce" the narrator. I did this with enthusiasm, riddling my analysis with psychological speculation, writing an essay twice as long as was assigned and getting an A−. What I suppressed in that essay, however, was something that emerged when I first read Kafka in public in 1991,[2] something I am considering here: the meanings of the oral or conversational fulfillment it affords to merely speak Kafka's words.

Something I have felt for a long time, but never spoken or written about in "criticism" or even in response essays, was that the act of "speaking" Kafka's literature—as opposed to reading it silently—makes me aware of my own community memberships—an American Jew from New York—and my professional membership—a faculty member that society generally views as "an academic." In both roles I occupy a different spot than does a Christian from Iowa who now teaches in Texas. Part of this difference may be explained by the "two language" principle.

At an early age I learned to speak two languages at once—not just my parents' language Yiddish and my community's language English, but within my English I included the vocabulary of the Yiddish culture, the East European culture in which both my parents and Kafka lived, the culture which was already accustomed to external hostility. My parents' culture had already begun to respond to the population of a host culture whose German-speaking descendants finally did try to do us all in. To read Kafka not only reestablishes these historic fears and dangers in my mind—the anticipation of disaster and the attempt to remain calm and extremely ironic, as a form of readiness—but articulates my/my parents' culture's ways of naming and dealing with them through a kind of intrapersonal wit and dramatic metaphorical initiative that we Jews from New York in my generation recognize as "our language." I am not implicated in Kafka's language just because I like this author, but because I feel his voices within me represent a way of speaking and knowing that plays a role now, in these universities, in this country, in this mix of cultural interests.

Ernst Pawel's *Nightmare of Reason* (1984) developed a point of view about Kafka that helps to characterize my response to his work:

> Had Kafka not been born and raised a Jew, he would not have been Kafka, any more than Joyce, reared among Eskimos, could have written *Ulysses*. Though the point seems blatantly obvious, its significance has all too often been missed, distorted, or willfully ignored. He has been hailed as a crypto-Christian, unveiled as a pseudo-Marxist; the absence of explicitly Jewish references in the surviving texts has made literary pedants feel justified in dismissing his "religion" as an incidental biographical detail.
>
> All these simpleminded approaches, whatever their motives or causes, suffer from the same basic failure of the imagination. To grow up as a Jew in Kafka's Prague was a matter not of choice but of destiny. What Kafka made of that destiny at different points in his life, the manner in which collective fate shaped his individual vision and conduct, is part of the larger story; moreover, his attitude toward Judaism—and far more is involved here than religion as such—underwent significant changes over the years. Yet who he was, and what he did, cannot possibly be understood without a clear realization that his being Jewish—not faith, to begin with, not observance, but the mere fact of being Jewish in turn-of-the century Prague—was at least as vital a component of his identity as his face or his voice.[3]

Pawel emphasizes the absence, in critical studies, of Kafka's cultural Jewishness, as compared, for example, to the presence of Joyce's cultural Irishness in much of the criticism of Joyce. Pawel's book about Kafka is different from most other work because he highlights Kafka's cultural identity as a Jew, and then derives, not "readings" but perhaps a "reading attitude" that is more cognizant of this identity than the attitude of the great majority of academic critics of Kafka.

In Kafka's Prague, Jewish writers flourished beyond their population numbers, Pawel explains, because of the failure of assimilation:

> What fueled this outburst of frenzied self-expression was the dilemma which at that juncture faced most Western Jews: the awareness, however dim, that assimilation was a failure. The fathers, smugly content with having overcome piety and poverty, groomed their sons for roles they could never hope to play. The sons, however, found themselves locked out of the show altogether; and trapped between promise and reality, they drifted into literature as a way out of the impasse.
>
> It was a return to tradition, in its way. But whereas, to their ancestors, words were the building blocks of faith, they themselves used words to demolish faith, to bewail their loss of it, and ended up with literature taking its place. God was dead, but the running argument with his chosen people—who chose whom, and why?—continued unabated, and with no loss of stridency. (98–99)

The international critical community, many of whom were Jews interested in Kafka, could not, would not, and did not think of Kafka's work as the expression of one who was poised to be assimilated into the majority society but was prevented at every turn. The rationality that lay beneath the metaphorical surrealism of Kafka's work was not discernible if the social psychology of assimilation was not taken into account. Kafka's writing, fiction and nonfiction, is often cited for its riddles, its passion, its frustration, and of course, its paradox. In view of the new-critical literary philosophy that developed in the postwar academy, Kafka's work was made to order for critics searching for something to solve, something important to document the humanist academic need to establish paradox as a fundamental of existence, as Heinz Politzer tried to do in his classic critical study of Kafka.

To review Pawel's point about "pedants": the logic of academic work required the suppression of the issue of assimilation and the long list of uncomfortable topics it necessarily entails. Among these topics is Jew-hating and, I include, woman-hating. For them to emerge, members of the majority culture would have to acknowledge its hegemony as well as face its own ways of self-hatred.

To the extent that we can count ourselves members of a majority culture we have no need to think about assimilation. As Pawel discusses, for more than a hundred years before Kafka was born, there was some promise or hope for Jews in central Europe to get out of the ghetto and become assimilated to the majority society. Many Jews, but particularly those who spoke German, were extremely eager to join the society, just as many Jews today, including much of the State of Israel, strive in fundamental ways to "be like everyone else." On the other hand, Eastern Jews were more conservative, more respectful of the meaning and value of their historic orthodoxies, and thus, more wary of assimilation as a social goal. For Western Jews, assimilation meant adopting the philosophy of enlightenment (haskallah): secularizing their existence—expunging the vast structure of rituals and superstitions from daily life and pursuing vocations which entail regular, consequential interactions, including sex and marriage, with the members and laws of the majority culture. As Pawel describes and documents in a variety of ways, the Jews of Prague, like the Jews of Vienna and Germany, presumed assimilation, but it was resisted by the host culture. At the same time, the many Jews of Prague felt closer to Eastern Jews, and thus also felt the impossibility of actually "becoming like everyone else." The result was the rejection of the religious superstructure among Jews and the retention of their inner identity as a people, a nation, a culture, a community with a coherent history and style. Literary activity in Prague was one of the scenes of this historic movement to redefine Jewish identity.

For Kafka in particular, writing was at once a way out of the constraints of Jewish separatism, a way to work within the customs and social structures of the existing society, a way to adopt some of its aesthetic styles and interests, and still a way to use the historic discourse of Jews, to explore the feelings Jews have as they face a continuing hostility from without, a way to express the pains and problems of their own transition to a secular, nonsuperstitious culture, and as a double perspective that can *communicate simultaneously* with both Jews and non-Jews (the two-language principle). As odd as it may seem to describe Kafka's work in this way, it actually seeks a common ground with the host cultures, while nevertheless advancing its own bitterness and frustration in coping with this culture as well as with the strains within the Jewish community caused by its move toward assimilation. Because the task of assimilation exists for me in ways quite similar to how it related to Kafka, I am able to "hear" Kafka on this frequency, so to speak, and thus not respond with perplexity or a sense of its mystery that characterizes the great majority of Kafka criticism.

As Ralph Cohen has discussed,[4] generic identification works less as an element in an internally consistent abstract taxonomy than as a product and marker of history and society. The "paradoxical parable," the genre proposed by Heinz Politzer for some of Kafka's works, while offering a *prima facie* commonsense identification of Kafka's works, given their unusual style and power, is almost an inert conclusion to the intense exercise of intellectual energy given by Politzer to merely read the works, sentence by sentence, paragraph by paragraph. It seems clear that when so much energy is spent, there ought to be an explanation of why it is spent. In Shakespeare's case, people say they love his work. But this is not what critics say about Kafka. Their passion is mainly to solve the riddle, to work the paradox, to produce answers.

Academic criticism, as I have become familiar with it, separates itself from its subject, literature, and then lives and works in *its* own community, speaking its own language, rarely examining its own usually clerical role as a social institution. The distance between Politzer's community of work and Kafka's is great, and while one may link the two communities, there is no language for Politzer to acknowledge the distance between them and to include study of it in the critical project. There is no impetus for him to reach out, culture to culture, so to speak, to Kafka's own lived community, or to its descendants in today's living communities, and to begin the conversation with Kafka's literature on this more experientially authentic ground. Northrop Frye's formulation in 1957 was that criticism, not literature, was the subject we learn in school, just as we don't learn "nature," but physics, which *studies* nature. This, in retrospect, represents a philosophy of intellectual separation, strong boundaries, territory, leading to an adversarial style of thought removed from the experience of language. A more engaged critical stance, which I will now describe, will include not only language and culture, but gender as well, a factor generally absent from traditional styles of criticism.

It is widely agreed that Kafka achieved his characteristic literary voice when he wrote "The Judgment" in 1912. Although there are signs of his familiar irony and brevity in passages of his earlier work, their effects were muted by his inability to move out, metaphorically, from a kind of "correspondence"—that is, quasi-naturalistic—theory of writing. "The Judgment" moves ordinary discourse into an irrational context: from that point on Kafka's narratives found ways to de-authorize, metaphorically and dramatically, the apparent rationality of everyday life. The irrational context is presented as malicious through its indifference and sometimes directly malicious but for no expectable reason. The missing rationality is the basis for the critical perception of the Kafkaesque riddle that has occupied critical and philosophical attention. In "The Judgment," the suicide of the hero, as well as the interaction with his father that precedes it, are two events which cut the tie to "realism." The story steadily moves away from the expectable and toward its violent end, thus implying that all the events preceding the end were teleologically organized toward this end, and thus establishing a literary voice for its author. This was a "real" *Kafka* story.

Given the torment of Kafka's relationships with women,[5] Politzer's Felice Bauer reading has some appeal at the level of individual psychology. However, it is not compelling as a comprehensive explanation of either the literary breakthrough or of the "Kafkaesque" voice. Rather, Kafka's developing infatuation with Yiddish theater and its players better explains his literary metamorphosis. This view relieves us readers and critics of the need to rely on either neurosis or paradox as critical stopping points.

The material presented by Evelyn Torton Beck in *Kafka and the Yiddish Theater* (University of Wisconsin Press, 1971) was quite surprising to me after having learned about Kafka from Leon Edel. It is a bit odd that it took so long for someone in the scholarly community to notice the intensity of attention Kafka gave to his theater involvement in his diaries of 1911 and 1912. On the other hand, this task required someone who knew both Yiddish and German well, and someone who *already* understood Kafka more or less in the terms presented by Pawel in 1984. In her remarkable book, Beck tried to show that a multitude of literary, dramatic, verbal, and thematic moves in Kafka's fiction had sources in the many Yiddish plays that Kafka saw, more than once, in those two years. She relates the substance of the Yiddish plays to the substance of Kafka's writing. Pawel also notes that the plays did provide Kafka with plot devices, but he concentrates on the human or interpersonal effect the troupe of eight Yiddish actors had on Kafka, coming mostly, according to Pawel, through Kafka's friendship with Yitzchak Levi (Lowy, in the diaries).

In the biography as a whole, Pawel portrays Kafka as someone searching for an appropriate mode of being a Jew. He documents Kafka's later interests in Zionism, and he takes some pains to show that Kafka's interest in being a Jew is at odds with his father's affirmative assimilationism. Yet, he does not explore Kafka's subjective attraction to the *emotional* character of both the plays and the actors. As Beck describes, the plays themselves were a combination of so many dramatic forms, so undisciplined, compared to German theater, so indulgent emotionally, so expressive in presentation and so exaggerated in their plot materials, that they represented something genuinely new to Kafka. However, because these were strongly Jewish plays with serious, unambiguously Jewish themes, they represented the combination of culture and feeling that Kafka would normally express in his own art. But when the troupe came to Prague, Kafka still had not understood how his art would be able to make the combination consistent with his own personality and sense of life.

So it is true that he was "affection-starved" (Pawel) when the troupe came into town and that friendship with this group was needed from a personal standpoint. But it was needed as much or more from a communal standpoint: cultural self-expression for his father was prohibited in the area of earning a living. Hermann Kafka achieved *survival* in a hostile culture. But for the well-educated, personally responsive, expressive son, his father's principle of survival was completely inadequate. Franz Kafka had to come to terms with what his father was satisfied to deny: his social survival required an awareness of and the expression of his Jewish identity. What Kafka learned from the Yiddish theater experience, *both in personal and cultural terms*, was that this identity can admit of emotional release and sexual feeling.[6] Both the themes of the plays and the personal presence of the actresses exuded sexuality and explored its role in the lives of Jews who, like Kafka, were frustrated by the problems of inhibited assimilation. Over and over, the plays depicted men, and sometimes women, who were tempted by a purely secular and material life and the license for sexual indulgence. The literary and dramatic materials that Kafka took from these plays came from that context. Kafka continued, mostly, to omit direct sexual portrayals from his major literary works and to omit altogether explicit reference to Jewish themes, but he nevertheless *presented dramatic situations whose source was predicated on both sexual and Jewish issues*. It is as if the Yiddish plays were presented "in color," and Kafka reworked the material so that it appeared only in black and white, the medium that did finally correspond to the character of his own existence. Kafka placed dramatic, gestural, dialogic tropes into the narrative genre, and stuck to portraying only the persistence of rationality in the face of arbitrary acts of authority and malice. But in the plays, whose secular consciousness never entirely rejected historic Jewish religious, sexual, and cultural conflicts—that is, such conflicts were explicit in the plays—there was a directness of emotional expression that is completely absent from Kafka's literature.

Perhaps a good way to represent what was happening to Kafka in 1911 and 1912 when he found his literary voice might be to imagine an African American person today in America growing up in an assimilated, professional family, learning to speak "white" standard English from birth, attending "white" universities, but then discovering a black culture which functioned only with the vernacular "black English," which self-consciously pursued "soul" culture including its strong emphasis on music, dance, dramatic and interactive oral performances in a variety of serious and entertainment contexts, and which, because of this cultural liberation was able to better face and understand today's stubborn legacy of underlying white hostility to African Americans as a people. The cultural freedom expressed by the Yiddish acting troupes allowed them to announce what people like Kafka, reared in a German-speaking, seemingly assimilated community, could not very well see, much less think about or write about: Jews did not feel free to express their desires to love and celebrate their own history and culture; they were denied even the path to think about, in a collective way, the problems of whether and how much to join the majority culture.

The secular Yiddish community did what the acting groups did: established a second perspective for Kafka and people like him. They spoke an appropriated form of German that was riddled with Polish, Russian, and Hebrew vocabulary and other usages; it was considered a "low" language, vulgar and uneducated, just as black English is so considered by the many users, even less educated users, of standard English today. Yiddish was considered a "ghetto" language, separatist and self-hating, by speakers of German like Hermann Kafka who, as Pawel describes, was at pains to conceal his Jewishness. It was with reference to Kafka's friend Levi that Hermann Kafka said to his son "He who lies down with dogs gets up with fleas" (*Diaries* 246, 11/2/11).

As I learned from my own parents, Yiddish was also a principal vehicle for Jews to separate themselves from the historic, arbitrary irrationalities of Orthodox Judaism, whose passive qualities were rejected by Zionists as well as by Yiddishists. Jewish enlightenment in Europe was parallel with other European rejections of superstition and autocratic authority. Kafka's father was already "enlightened" to such a degree that "realpolitik" dictated to him to pretend, practically, that he was not a Jew. That is, since religious pretexts for hating Jews were no longer the main ones, other, nonreligious reasons were found, so that to counter these reasons, some Western, German-speaking Jews imagined, one only had to adopt the majority culture in order to neutralize the Jew-hating that Jews falsely believed was rooted in religious, doctrinal teachings. The Yiddish theater experience taught Hermann's son just how unsuccessful his father's assimilationist strategy had been. On the affirmative side, it provided a vocabulary which taught just what it was that Kafka could become, a gestural and figurative vocabulary for speaking the truth in a hostile culture, a schedule of values that could be announced and ones that could not, a calculus of feelings that corresponded to his own personal condition as well as those which did not. The Yiddish theater helped Kafka to identify or situate himself as a social figure, at least as a writer, and this learning emerged in his first "Kafkaesque" story, "The Judgment," whose meaning and style, Beck suggests, are largely rooted in Yakov Gordin's important play, *Gott, Mensch, und Teufel* (God, Man, and Devil, hereafter GMD). "Metamorphosis," perhaps Kafka's best known and most characteristic work, written only three months later, Beck suggests, was rooted in Gordin's other play, *Der Vilder Mensch* (The Savage One, hereafter TSO).

Like much of Yiddish literature, these two plays deal with the effect of secularization on Jewish families and community life. As detailed by Beck, GMD portrays how Hershele Dubrovner, a professional scribe whose job had been to create new copies of the Torah, is tempted by the devil's offer of wealth and freedom to change his life. Childless, he divorces his wife of long standing and marries his niece, whom he raised as his own child. After a life of selfishness and greed resulting in considerable physical harm to innocent people, including his father and his best friend, he realizes his guilt and hangs himself. The plot is much more complicated than this suggests, and the play is filled with melodramatic scenes, including the conspicuous use of a blood-soaked prayer-shawl. The radical difference between Kafka's short story and this long and complex play may have been the cause of Pawel's impatient disbelief in Beck's seemingly obscure project. Nevertheless, Beck provides enough material to demonstrate the means and terms of Kafka's adaptation of some of the material in this play. More importantly perhaps, the radical difference in form helps to document the depth of the change in Kafka's work that his involvement in the Yiddish theater helped to produce.

In GMD there are two interesting scenes involving Hershele's old father, a "jester," which seem to be sources for scenes in "The Judgment." Early in the play, as Hershele is about to give in to the temptation offered by the devil's representative, but is still his old self, his father gets drunk and starts singing. Hershele, in order to prevent his father from embarrassing himself, picks him up and carries him to bed. In gestural terms, the earnest still-devoted son is carrying the old, less-than-competent father to bed. Similarly, in "The Judgment," the beginning of the story's break with naturalistic reality comes when old Bendemann accuses his son Georg of not having a friend in Russia, where just previously, Georg's written correspondence with the friend was seemingly taken for granted by both parties. The father's peremptory accusation seems irrational and prompts Georg to pick him up bodily and take him to bed, while the father, like Hershele's father, shouts *"No! No!"* In GMD, Hershele is still respectful of his father, and the change in Hershele has not yet taken place. In "The Judgment," as old Bendemann becomes more truculent on his way to "sentencing" Georg to death, he stands on the bed, waves his arms, and lifts his nightgown. Georg calls him a "comedian." Similarly, a second incident in GMD finds Hershele's father jumping on a chair and taking on the "traditional mock-serious tone of the wedding jester."

It seems at first as if, in both the play and the story, the fathers are on their way out. But in fact Hershele is finally brought under the "old" orthodox ethic represented by the ousted father (he was sent out of Hershele's house) while Georg actually did carry out the sentence declaimed by the seemingly demented old Bendemann and drowned himself as Hershele hanged himself. Kafka took an ironic Jewish motif of a son's failed gesture toward independence (taking up the devil's offer) through the path of secularization and assimilation and boiled it down by omitting mention of culture and religion altogether, and by consigning the sexual dimension to an epistolary presentation of Georg's engagement to Frieda. One might say that the story is a "reading" of the play, a response to it, a conversion of its inner story into contemporary terms and genres that have suppressed any *local* cultural and sexual identities. Nevertheless, the issues and themes of both the plays and the stories matched very well. Where the ridiculousness of the posturing of fathers is common to the plays and to Kafka's stories, as is the gathering self-doubt of the sons, the Yiddish plays insisted on a rational conclusion to the turmoil, thus keeping a sense of collective rationality as the framework for the personal travail.

Kafka's breakthrough was his acquisition of *the means to delete the rationality and identity of "traditional Jewish values"* and carry through the arbitrary logic of the phenomenology of daily life to the conclusion dictated—literally—by the purely *verbal* activity of the dialogue. Beck says, "Kafka's narrative presents a self-enclosed world in which the characters are totally absorbed in their roles, and in which there is no commonsense perspective by which we can interpret the action" (78). There is no actual devil associated with Georg Bendemann; he is, merely, in the eyes of his ranting father, only a "devilish human being" *(ein teuflischer Mensch)*. Notice how *"Gott"* is removed from the transposed title in German, while the father's "sentence"[7] (the "judgment" of the title) is taken literally and, in the story's climactic gesture, carried out by the "prisoner" himself. The dramatic, literal presentation of the metaphorical on an extended level is one of the principal elements of Kafka's "breakthrough." There can be little doubt that the habitual, routine, ironic confounding of the literal and the figurative was a principle of the Yiddish stage and a feature of the Yiddish language, in both of which contexts, the result was, as Georg Bendemann observes, comic.

Kafka, however, had to express and imply this comedy within a style that would function in the assimilated secular world in which he knew he had to function. Levi could and would remain a self-conscious Jew engaging with Jews on Jewish topics; but for Kafka none of this could be true regardless of how much of his "extracurricular" time would be spent in Yiddishism and Zionism. In Kafka's own Czech/German context, hostile to Jews, there in fact was no "God"—certainly no Jewish God, but no expectable social rationality either. Thus, the expressive license of the Yiddish theater group, its "folk" origins and social character, could never become an open element in Kafka's already ongoing involvement in the German-speaking Prague literary circles. This necessary censorship led to Kafka's characteristic deadpan, even solemn poses in each and every piece of literature that he wrote. In a piece that is almost obviously comic, the "Report to the Academy," there is just no indication that this is, in some way, a playful or joking piece. The pattern of animal figures in Kafka, where narrators and protagonists are themselves beasts of some sort, is one of the more decisive dramatizations of verbal histrionics—you dog, you mouse, you ape (in English; in Yiddish, one does call another person a *Wanz* [an insect]—more on this shortly). Yet it seems clear that these literal *"Verwandlungen"* (transformations) of metaphors are, in an environment of censorship, undoubtedly playful acts in bitter contexts, pieces of Yiddish-style verbal behavior commonly found in the theater experiences but now sanded and polished so that their true shapes and colors are no longer perceptible to a general public that would never countenance any honest Jewish exploration of its culture and social psychology.

If my mother's figures—"cholera," "dog-like beast," "traitor" *(me-*

shummed, in Yiddish), "go get yourself killed" (*ver geharget* in Yiddish)—were echoed and more seriously given by a hegemonic community which also thought of me in this way, but literally, actually, you will get a sense of what Kafka had to do with these figures to cope with the sense of danger their use must have alluded to. As a writer, an artist trying to make his way in a mixed public, this is what Kafka had to do and did do with extraordinary power, with his father's contemptuous dismissal of Levi and the Yiddish troupe: "If you go to bed with dogs, you wake up with bugs."[8] He wrote what is now perhaps his best known story whose premise—lying in bed with dogs—is deleted, while the conclusion is slightly changed—waking up as an insect instead of with one! This new reality supplants the father's premise with his own funnier, more dramatic one, as the story is then executed on the basis of the son's, the artist's, premise. In spite of the angry but relentless mirth of carrying through a long, dark, passionate story on this basis, there is no hint in the narrative tone of just what sort of parody is taking place, and readers of all stripes, but particularly the academic critics, feel no choice but to ponder in the usual solemn, conventionally practiced modes of proper philosophical perplexity the meaning of this metaphorical riddle.

According to Beck this story, as mentioned above, also draws a great deal from a Gordin play, *The Savage One*. In this play, about the Layblikh (I am using Beck's transliterations of the Yiddish) family, the "tragic" hero is the "idiot" son, Lemekh. He and his siblings are grown and his father marries a widow much younger than himself who bleeds off the father's money. As the hero deteriorates toward idiocy, his sexual feeling toward his stepmother increases, and he is confined to his room. At the play's climax, he murders his stepmother. Beck describes how the situation in this play parallels that in "The Metamorphosis."

Like Lemekh, Gregor is barely tolerated in the home, and like him, is looked upon with disgust (particularly by the father) as an outcast whose very existence shames his family. In different ways, Gregor and Lemekh combine the same qualities of "thing" and "person." Both are presented as essentially simple, meek, self-effacing persons who become animal-like creature because of a drastic transformation which culminates in Gregor's death and Lemekh's murder of Zelde. Although Gregor's physical transformation is already completed when "The Metamorphosis" opens, while the change in Lemekh occurs more gradually, the process of progressive decay continues throughout both works. . . .

Each of the five characters in Kafka's story has a direct counterpart in

Gordin's play. Besides Gregor and Lemekh, the two defective sons, there are the two fathers, Samsa Senior and Shmul Layblikh, who are "resurrected" (Samsa by his son's decline, Layblikh by his marriage); the two mother-figures, Mrs. Samsa and Zelde, who protect their sons and are adored by them; the two sisters, Grete and Liza, half-developed girls who eventually abandon the brothers to whom they are so closely attached, and the two housekeepers, who show no fear of the peculiar son and take charge of him. (Beck 136–37)

While "The Metamorphosis" boils a long play down just as "The Judgment" did, the material of TSO was closer to Kafka's characteristic theme: the radical generic difference between the heroic son and his family and culture. Where, for Lemekh, the unconsciousness of his own position is rationally presented as a known disease, the characteristic denial of "what has happened" for Gregor is complete and does not need explanation: the change in him is so fundamental, so fully offered as a familiarity of daily life, that one proceeds literally without any need for exploring this premise. As regards relations of fathers and sons, Kafka creates similarly reduced and abstracted "rereadings" in both of his stories for both of his sources in Yiddish plays.

One reason for the emergence of "The Metamorphosis" from the "pack" of Kafka's collection of works could be its more-than-usual exploration of sexual feelings in the family. If one looks over all of his writings, including the letters and diaries, one finds characteristic ways in which the topic of sexuality emerges. TSO announces this theme, and Beck cites the key lines which show Lemekh enjoys the touch and sexual presence he feels in his stepmother, who is not, in an actual sense, a forbidden figure, but instead is in the *role* of a forbidden figure. Thus, the attraction Lemekh has for Zelde can present the *forbidden quality* of sexual attraction for traditional, religiously observant Jewish men without actually portraying an incestuous scene. Analogously, in the climactic scene in "The Metamorphosis," some of the incestuous quality of Gregor watching his mother losing her clothes and underclothes as she clings to his father is reduced by the fact that Gregor is only an insect confined to the room: he is not eligible to be involved in the love triangle at home.

It is hard to overlook just how deeply Gregor is involved in longing for the love of both his mother and sister. After this scene, as Gregor's deterioration hastens and his sister begins to exercise leadership in getting rid of Gregor, he hears and sees her playing the violin:

> Her face leaned sideways, intently and sadly her eyes followed the notes of music. Gregor crawled a little farther forward and lowered his head to the ground so that it might be possible for his eyes to meet hers. Was he an animal, that music had such an effect upon him? He felt as if the way were opening before him to the unknown nourishment he craved. He was determined to push forward till he reached his sister to pull at her skirt and so let her know that she was to come into his room with her violin, for no one here appreciated her playing as he would appreciate it. He would never let her out of his room, at least not so long as he lived; his frightful appearance would become, for the first time, useful to him; he would watch all the doors of his room at once and spit at intruders; but his sister should need no constraint, she should stay with him of her own free will. . . . After this confession [that he was planning to send her to the Conservatorium to study music] his sister would be so touched that she would burst into tears, and Gregor would then raise himself to her shoulder and kiss her on the neck, which, now that she went to business, she kept free of any ribbon or collar. (*Complete Stories* 121)

While passionate and moving, this fantasy scene is not perverse. It portrays Gregor's longing for intimacy emerging from his sense of his ineligibility of achieving it, a theme given again and again in his letters to Felice Bauer and other prospective marriage partners. Nevertheless, the images feel and imply much more beyond their topical familiarity: the crawling up to her and pulling at her skirt; the thought that she would stay with him alone in his room while he would fend off all "intruders"; and finally his kissing her on her bare neck, now free from decoration owing to her going to work. All the while her sensuous playing of the violin would remind him of his "animal" dimensions. This scene is sensual; his observance of his mother's clothes falling off was only forbidden, and in any case, he was not a participant. Now, after his "defeat" by his father and the rest of the family, Gregor experiences a new level of erotic feeling. Gregor's condition and the resulting fantasy enacts the fate of permitted sexuality in Kafka's life: the closer he comes to the likelihood of forming a family the more decisively such a possibility must be avoided. Sexual feeling is heightened and its increase is directly proportional to its ineligibility of "legalization."

This view of the paralysis of socially legitimate sexual passion for Kafka is supported by the history of how the Yiddish theater made its way into Kafka's psychology. There is a pattern in the earlier volume of diaries that neither Beck nor Pawel discussed: Kafka's participation in public life in order to meet and come into contact with "legitimate" women but who were not necessarily to be courted. As is well known from Kafka's diaries as well as from other sources, the "double standard" was a common approach taken by young men toward women. The man found sexual release and learned, in general, about sexual behavior from prostitutes, while he and his family or both sought the proper "match" and hoped and expected to "fall in love" with the proper woman. Women had no options to educate (or indulge) themselves about sex, and so the entry into a marriage had mostly to do with guaranteeing their physical survival and well-being; needs for physical passion and bodily attachment are met by bearing, nursing, and raising children. Kafka's continuing reluctance to commit himself to the "proper" woman was related to his sense that in his own circle or community, getting married was a necessary, rather than only recommended, path of living, especially in view of his parents' pressure on him in that regard: [19 July 1910]: "For without a center, without a profession, a love, a family, an income; i.e., without holding one's own . . . one cannot protect oneself from the losses that momentarily destroy one" (*Diaries* 24). Provisionally, one might read Kafka's avoidance of marriage as resistance to the double standard and a critique of what men are expected to do. The diary entries show both the resistance and his inability to remove himself from this socially masculine trope. Kafka's first extended entry in his diary is some time before May 1910 about the dancer Eduardova from the visiting Russian Ballet. He first records a dream about her in which she asks him if she is a "wicked woman." Then there is the entry about her appearance: "The dancer Eduardova is not as pretty in the open air as on the stage" (*Diaries* 10). Kafka's discussion of the Russian dancer, first seen on a stage as a performer, but then observed in the "open air" (a phrase that Kafka uses in other, similar, contexts) outlines the motif of almost all of his observations of women, from a distance, in a variety of contexts, but mostly on stage and as compared to their appearance in person. His dream of her emphasizes her face and the glamour of the attention paid to her by the "princes of Europe." But then he describes the loss of her stage-beauty, "her faded color," "the large nose . . . with which one can take no liberties," as well as her resemblance to "an elderly lady."

The recording of the dream in this early part of the diary, whose major role in Kafka's life was to last only about four years, between 1910 and 1914, is a sign of how the apparition of the idealized woman on a stage enters his subjectivity in this decisive way. Subsequent entries in the diary, especially as he first starts to attend Yiddish plays, continue this theme, but now the women are Jews, the plays Jewish, the other people Jewish men with whom he can relate. Several diary entries describe what he saw as he sat in cafes on several different occasions.[9]

While there is now a break of about six months in the use of the diary, the end of summer of 1911 and all of the fall record, following the pattern and even sometimes the vocabulary of the foregoing entries, Kafka's falling into the combined Jewish/erotic atmosphere of the Yiddish folk theater.

24 August 1911: Sitting with acquaintances at a coffeehouse table in the open air and looking at the woman at the next table who has just arrived, breathing heavily beneath her heavy breasts, and who, with a heated, brownish, shining face, sits down. She leans back, a heavy down becomes visible, she turns her eyes up, almost in the way in which she perhaps sometimes looks at her husband, who is now reading an illustrated paper beside her. If one could only persuade her that one may read at most a newspaper but never a magazine beside one's wife in a coffeehouse. After a moment she become aware of the fullness of her body and moves back from the table a little. (62)

27 September 1911: Yesterday on the Wenzelsplatz met two girls, kept my eye too long on one while it was just the other, as it proved too late, who wore a plain, soft, brown, wrinkled, ample coat, open a little in front, had a delicate throat and delicate nose, her hair was beautiful in a way already forgotten. . . . The beautiful large button, beautifully set low on the sleeve of a girl's dress. The dress worn beautifully too, hovering over American boots. . . . The powerful half-turn of the neck of a strong girl. (68)

29 September 1911: . . . Cabaret Lucerna. Lucie Koenig showing photographs with old hair-styles. Threadbare face. Sometimes, with her turned-up nose, with an arm held aloft and a turn of all her fingers, she succeeds in something. A milksop face. . . .

30 September 1911: The girl in the adjoining room yesterday. I lay on the sofa and, on the point of dozing off, heard her voice. She seemed to me in my mind to be overdressed not only because of the clothes she wore, but also because of the entire room; only her shapely, naked, round, strong, dark shoulders which I had seen in the bath prevailed against her clothes. For a moment she seemed to me to be steaming and to be filling the whole room with her vapors. Then she stood up in her ash-gray colored bodice that stood off from her body so far at the bottom that one could sit down on it and after a fashion ride along.

Kafka describes the next three or four nights as "sleepless," and writes a long entry in the diary each day reflecting on the sleeplessness as well as on the dark room at night. On 4 October he goes to the Café Savoy, where he sees and records for the first time the "Yiddish troupe. Mrs. K, 'male impersonator.' In a caftan, short black trousers, white stockings, from the black vest a thin white woolen shirt emerges that is held in front at the throat by a knot and then flares into a wide, loose, long, spreading collar"(79).

The troupe presented Lateiner's play, *Der Meshumed* (The Apostate). While Kafka is obviously disturbed by this irreverent group and their irreverent style of behaving and acting, he nevertheless records both how the play "keeps its meaning" in spite of incompetence on stage, and how the melodies get "one's body to confide itself to them" (*Diaries* 80). In particular, the female singers attract his attention: "the melodies are best expressed by a swaying of the hips, by raising and lowering extended arms in a calm rhythm" (80).

Obviously attracted by the performances and the energy of the actors, the evil of the protagonist—a man who had murdered his wife to help conceal his Jewish origin after he had become Christian—Kafka devotes four days of entries in his diary to describing the complex, violent plot and analyzing the distinctive features of the performance, such as one actor playing all three Christian parts, and the female lead, the protagonist's daughter, who, toward the climax, is the "male impersonator." It seems likely that this play, and others like it which featured a prominent father indulging himself, "caught the conscience" of the young writer seeking both cultural and sexual identity.

In describing the players, Kafka stays with his habit of focusing on the character-identity of the male parts, and the physical, personal, extra-theatrical identity of the female parts. In considering his experience of this play after five days, he elaborates on his first mention of the "male impersonator," the very first impression he recorded of his experience with the Yiddish theater:

"Male impersonator" is really a false title. By virtue of the fact that she is stuck into a caftan, her body is entirely forgotten. She only reminds one of her body by shrugging her shoulder and twisting her back as though she were being bitten by fleas. The sleeves, though short, have to be pulled up a little every minute; this the spectator enjoys and even watches for it to happen, anticipating the great relief it will be for this woman who has so much to sing and to explain in the talmudic manner. (*Diaries* 87)

In revising his first impression of both Mrs. K and her role, Kafka brings out the female in this figure, both in her characteristic gestures, which attract his ("the spectator's") attention in this play as well as in almost all the other plays he writes about, and in her singing, which also has the effect of bringing out his own "body," so to speak. Having gone out in public and recorded his impressions of the many women he saw and self-consciously observed, he, in this same trope of his life, comes upon the Yiddish acting troupe, where both its prosecution of a "pugnacious national literature" (87) and its release of exhibitionistic, yet legitimate female sexuality combine to form a very appealing place for the man whose mind and body have been struggling to come together. The fact that in this play the female characters are not only sexy but "good," in contrast to the evil and opportunistic male figures, undoubtedly made the case to Kafka that he was in the presence of a cultural situation with which he could conduct the kind of exchange that his own sense of a creative life required.

That this first experience of the Yiddish stage reached him in a decisive way is suggested on 9 October when he records the thought that "If I reach my fortieth year, then I'll probably marry an old maid with protruding upper teeth left a little exposed by the upper lip"; and he then records having had a dream the previous night of visiting a brothel:

I occupied myself chiefly with the whore whose head was hanging down, . . . I fingered her legs and then for a long time pressed the upper parts of her thighs in regular rhythm. My pleasure *[Vergnügen]* in this was so great that I wondered that for this entertainment, which was after all really the most beautiful kind, one still had to pay nothing. I was convinced that I (and I alone) deceived the world. Then the whore, without moving her legs, raised the upper part of her body and turned her back to me, which to my horror was covered with large sealing-wax-red circles with paling edges, and red splashes scattered among them. I now noticed that her whole body was full of them, that I was pressing my thumb to her thighs in just such spots and that there were the little red particles— as though from a crumbled seal—on my fingers too. (89–90)

A conscious thought about the unlikelihood of marrying one with whom one will have sexual satisfaction leads to an erotic dream about the satisfaction (or enjoyment: *Vergnügen*) with a whore becoming, suddenly, sullied, tainting himself as well. These troubling and conflict-laden thoughts are embedded in the intense experience, cultural and sexual, of the Yiddish performance he just saw and wrote about at some length. The next day, 10 October, Kafka describes the actors greeting the actresses and parting company with them and with each other, continuing,

> But while this overtaking and greeting had separated the gentlemen, the ladies addressed, as though led by the one nearest the roadway who seems to be the weakest and tallest but also the youngest and most beautiful, continue on their way quite undisturbed. . . . The whole thing seemed to me at the moment to be strong proof that theatrical affairs here are orderly and well conducted. (90–91)

Which is a conclusion quite the reverse of his first skeptical responses to the troupe, its seeming vulgarity, and its apparent failures of competence (see diary entries of 29 and 30 September, above). Between his first response of five days before and now, as the potential of the troupe to stimulate both cultural and sexual arousal became clear, theatrical affairs suddenly seem "orderly and well-conducted"! Similarly, it could be that Kafka's inner psychology, constantly dogged by thoughts of early death and suffering, has, under the influence of this involvement, also become more orderly and well-conducted, owing to the disclosure, in the dream, of just how urgent his passions were.

Kafka carried through this new theatrical initiative in a series of frequent, almost daily trips to the café, where he saw many plays, perhaps up to twenty, according to Beck. He recorded the plots and other features of about a dozen of these plays, and his diaries provide a preliminary guide as to the principal Yiddish playwrights: Gordin, Lateiner, Feinmann, Goldfaden, Scharkansky. Of these, he singled out as the best Gordin, two of whose plays contributed to Kafka's start as a distinguished writer.

The erotic accent of this development is a necessary part of it. Kafka's mostly fantasy involvement with the married Yiddish actresses cannot be written off.[10] On 22 October 1911, Kafka alludes to "my love for Mrs. Ts." (107).[11] His sexual feelings and responses to Mrs. Tschissik are part of his involvement in the total project of the actors. He takes pains to cite their low pay and lack of public recognition, and how his sympathy is drawn into their situation. Kafka's entries are similar to the public mythologizing of Marilyn Monroe in recent times, in that she is a figure virtually no one credits with acting ability, yet who is nevertheless understood, now as when she was in films, as making a statement with her "naked" personality and her body, her inability to be, to play the role of, someone else. Culturally identified American Jewish men, such as Arthur Miller and Norman Mailer, were as taken with Monroe, and in the same serious way, as Kafka was with Mrs. Tschissik, imagining, rightly or wrongly (who can tell, anyway?) that this female presence contributed to the production of literature, to the promotion of culture. For Miller and Mailer, as for Kafka, this style of involvement was undoubtedly a feature of the pain of assimilation into the hegemonic society as well as a decisive sign of trouble in their masculine identities.

Two days after this entry about Mrs. Tschissik, there is a long entry about his mother which sets out in convincing fashion, the relationship of masculine discontent with, in particular, Jewish identity. After describing how he enjoyed his mother's love and attention while he was sick, he begins to wonder why he did not feel as if he reciprocated her love:

Yesterday it occurred to me that I did not always love my mother as she deserved and as I could only because the German language prevented it. The Jewish mother is no "Mutter," to call her "Mutter" makes her a little comic (not to herself, because we are in Germany), we give a Jewish woman the name of a German mother, but forget the contradiction that sinks into the emotions so much the more heavily, "Mutter" is peculiarly German for the Jew, it unconsciously contains, together with the Christian splendor Christian coldness also, the Jewish women who is called "Mutter" therefore becomes not only comic but strange. Mama would be a better name if only one didn't imagine "Mutter" behind it. I believe that it is only the memories of the ghetto that still preserve the Jewish family, for the word "Vater" too is far from meaning the Jewish father. (111)

The passage bears on Kafka's orientation to women and sexuality, to wit: how unfortunate—the German language prevented him from reciprocating his mother's love. This explanation is a pretext: he, like other men, doesn't reciprocate properly because he *expects* this level of maternal involvement in us as a matter of course. Like other intellectuals, Kafka found intellectualizable reasons, or better, cultural rationalizations, for an emotional failure, the reason being in this case, the false, pompous attitude toward parents fostered by German mores that are marked by the language's words for the parents. The passage, therefore, because of its likely high degree of unconscious disingenuousness, relates to the pattern of masculine longing for what some theater-women and Eastern Jews seem to be bringing to Kafka—an uninhibited, expressive emotionality that includes sexual feeling and engagement alongside the sense of cultural and communal belonging, a kind of unity of experience that was missing from Kafka's life, as well as from the lives of more ordinary men who become socialized in traditional ways of career and family.

It is not, therefore, the Germanness of the parental roles that is affecting Kafka: it is their definition by androcentric standards. While German androcentrism may have its own repellent form of authoritarianism, it is not that different from how most societies see the man as "head" of the family. This role exaggerates both the rights and the responsibilities of men, and creates for them an almost impossibly distant ideal. For minority males the distance is increased by the need to retain group dignity relative to the majority while actually behaving similarly to the source of domination in the majority.

In the West, some Jewish men may blame Christianity, along with its coercive role in the majority society, for their participation in a way of socialization that is common to all societies. Yet Kafka obviously saw both in the Yiddish plays and in his home that most Jewish men did not blame Christianity for their failure: they sometimes blamed Orthodox Judaism, and usually found fault with the women in their lives, when their own longing for a life of feeling and *Vergnügen* seemed blocked by the demand for family even when there was no obvious inhibition from the surrounding culture. Protagonists such as Hershele Dubrovner and Shmul Layblikh, as well as Seidemann in *Der Meshumed*, all turn against their families in major ways, while other parts of these plays do not suggest that it somehow was "really" Christian hegemony that was the main problem.

At this point, one wants to ask why "family" becomes a problem, especially if the man is the "head" of it. As I suggested above, the answer that most convincingly suggests itself is that the hierarchy of the family is a profoundly burdensome condition, and particularly so when the women, participating in the general enlightenment of culture—Seidemann's daughter who insists on marrying a Jewish man, for example—and exercising their independence from the father, themselves seem to oppose the traditional family authority structure.

So we return to Kafka's own "neurotic" reluctance to form a family. The materials and style of the Yiddish theater actually helped to foster this reluctance, with the intimations of a freer sexuality and its depictions of the "hell" of family life, its infestation by the "devilish" purposes of a materially good life and more than just the taste of sexual passion. I believe the theater helped to teach Kafka the truth of the sexual promise of the artistic, cultural life as well as confirming his own perceptions of the repugnance of traditional, hierarchical family life. These lessons became artistically enabling, having expressed, in a context external to his own family and his own subjectivity, the terms of his own psychological struggle.

Kafka's final love relationship with a sexual partner started twelve years after his early involvement with the Yiddish theater. It was with Dora Diamant (one of my own "ways in" to Kafka and his work) and it is noteworthy because, his galloping illness notwithstanding, he found a Jewish woman who was, more or less, in his own class: one who, exercising her independence from a coercive Orthodox Jewish father, left home to go to Berlin to become, of all things, an actress. Kafka and Diamant did together in a rebellious and (ironically) "Bohemian" way what is routinely done today by men and women engaged in departing from the traditional family imperatives: lived together without marriage, without family, and without family blessings from either side. This relationship was not marked, for Kafka, by either a tortured written correspondence or an "admiration from afar" form of involvement shown in his diary entries before and during the Yiddish theater period. Rather, Diamant was already a speaker of Yiddish and a living member of the society represented by that group of folk-artists. Biographers report that Kafka became uncharacteristically optimistic in that period, all the more surprising because of the devastation wrought on him by his illness. Such a development might well be understood as a relief of *masculine* rather than filial or Jewish discontent alone, since neither of the latter two sources of pain was any less at this time.

My parents came to America from Poland in 1921, independently of one another, and met in the Yiddish theater, where my father made his career and which my mother left at her marriage to my father in 1926. I have photographs of both my parents in the early twenties in acting groups and in costume in New York City. Although my mother first became a mother in 1929, when my brother was born, she worked all her life in the garment industry as either a dressmaker or an "examiner" (a job now known as an inspector or quality control person). My father ended the main phase of his career in 1945, when I was five. The Yiddish theater as a going concern ended about then, as its main source of new material, the huge Yiddish-speaking community in Europe was, mostly, murdered. My father, in addition to having to struggle during his most accomplished years, also was the sole support of his parents. My mother cared for my brother and me, as well as for my father and his always-active ulcer, while working all the time. To manage the home was her duty, she thought, while her way of noticing its unfairness was to inform the three masculine figures in the home that she was "not a slave." My father had smoked since he was twelve and died at age sixty of angina, an illness he had, and failed to announce to us, for sixteen years. My mother died of old age, I imagine, at ninety-two after a life whose principal feature in adulthood was loneliness.

Yiddish was my parents' first language, though they knew Hebrew, Polish, German, and some Russian. Until I was about three, I was bilingual; my brother remained bilingual throughout his life. However, there was no doubt that the Yiddish I knew was my mother's. My father did not take liberties with the language, did not use it in particularly daring ways in my presence, though he often rewrote Yiddish plays for performance. It took me to get through graduate school and "learn" English "the old fashioned way"—through the literature, that is, to understand the true power of my mother's Yiddish: it was the "stage" Yiddish that my father was always using "at work" but which my mother had to bring into the home to enjoy, the same stage Yiddish of indigent, self-educated, culturally conscious, secular "folk" that Kafka heard in Prague in 1911 and 1912. My mother spoke the *same* Yiddish as Mania Tschissik, Yitzchak Levi, and Dora Diamant. Her desire for a public life was unmistakable; she cooked and sewed at a level which unfailingly won extraordinary admiration from all, but she described these performances in theater language: Is it successful? she would always ask. What housewife would worry about the "success" of her handiwork? And if I were late for dinner, which I now see was a meticulous performance, even a "public service," it was a rudeness that was not easily forgivable.

My mother's language was a performance language, and represented a richer, more literary Yiddish, than that used by most non-theater types—the merchants, the lawyers, the doctors. While she herself was always a "worker" in the garment industry, making "costumes" for everyday life, she was a "closet" artist, and a real artist of all the domestic arts. But because she was female, she was treated as a second-class citizen by us three other occupants of our home. From today's perspective it seems certain that the lives of us three male figures were seriously troubled by the discontent of this original situation. At the same time, while my mother renounced what less perspicacious people might not have renounced—material well-being—she reserved for herself a level of personal discipline and prudence that created a stable style of self-regulation, good health, and the sheer ability to survive loneliness and adversity into a remarkable old age. We men, on the other hand, with our activity, enthusiasm, and all-too-certain style of initiative, were regularly battling with ourselves in exactly the way Kafka critics (and Kafka the suitor) continuously wrung their hands, made formulations, articulated paradoxes, became transcendental and philosophical. When asked about God, my mother said: Too far from me. When asked about the synagogue: I have to make dinner. When asked about money: Always causes trouble. We men had fancier answers, but she had the right word.

My mother's language did in our home what Kafka's does in public—gave us a good stick on a regular basis. In writing this account, I am understanding the stick of her sarcasm, her buried anger and frustration that she took out of her literary involvement in the Yiddish theater for her lifetime and brought into our home. Although Kafka remained "in German," I can hear through my mother's ways of speaking and living—and enact in my everyday life—something of the culture that went into his new version of German, his new version, perhaps his appropriation and recasting, of the majority language and culture. Because of the feel of my mother's more than casual needling, I can feel her language automatically articulating the insect, the vulture, the mouse, the dog, the hunger artist, the harrow in the penal colony. Unlike what mothers are supposed to do, my mother helped to remind us men that we were not content, that our suffering would last a while and that her own standards of conduct in this life, her own language, her own wit, her own extraordinary patience and modesty did, finally, represent an alternative to our discontent.

My mother's language, and my adaptation of it in English, form the terms of my self-inclusion in the academy and in American society. I identify myself as an "English" teacher, but the foregoing account suggests, rather, that I am a "mother-tongue" teacher. This language both includes me in and includes me out. Reading Kafka and thinking through his language, the "enemy" language, in fact, leads back to the mother-tongue, and represents, albeit in a complicated way, just how I remain part of my community and my society, and how I am a part of a different culture, one that, because of the accidents of history, continues to enjoy its difference, even when it passes for the majority.

One of the deepest scenes of my inclusion in my parents' culture, in my native culture, and in academic culture is to be described as masculine discontent. This discontent links Politzer's academic frustration in really hearing Kafka to Kafka's own frustration in his domestic and cultural lives, to the frustrations of academic, cultural, and domestic character my father, brother, and I have experienced. The relatedness of the different cultures and societies that I have discussed is clearest to me in terms of masculine participation in the historically mobilized tropes of the styles and ideologies of masculine superiority. Freud did not utter such words; while he may have "self-analyzed," he did not understand his discontent as we may now read it. Rather, it was "civilization" that had discontents. Perhaps. But civilization was then, and still is, in the hands of men.

Notes

1. "A Country Doctor" (in *Complete Stories*).
2. Lecture at the University of Wisconsin, June 1991, where I read "The Vulture" aloud.
3. Pawel 54.
4. Ralph Cohen, Patton lectures at Indiana University, November 1984.
5. Glatzer.
6. Something also learned by my father. My mother already understood this but could not express it because of the reduced "object" status of women, which either prohibited a full career on stage or limited their emotional lives at home.
7. I wonder if "The Sentence" would not be a better title for the English version of this story since it alludes, in one of its usual meanings, to the verbal presentation of the father's judgment.
8. The German is: "Wer sich mit Hunden zu Bett legt, steht mit Wanzen auf." (Tagebücher 139). While the rendition of "Wanz" as "flea" works pretty

well in English, the actual German for flea is "Floh." *Wanz* is more of a generic term for bug or insect and, obviously, is closer to *Ungeziefer* than a flea may be. One meaning of *Ungeziefer* does imply a parasitic insect, which a flea is.

9. 6 November 1910: "Lecture by a Madame Ch. on Musset. Jewish women's habit of lip-smacking. . . ." 12 January 1911: "A few days ago Leonie Frippon, cabaret girl, Stadt Wien. Hair dressed in a bound-up mass of curls. Bad girdle, very old dress, but very pretty with tragic gestures, flutterings of the eyelids, thrusts of the long legs, skillful stretching of the arms along the body, significance of the rigid throat during ambiguous passages" (*Diaries* 41–42). 20 February 1911: "Mella Mars in the Cabaret Lucerna. . . . When she makes her appearance she has a tired, indeed even flat, empty, old face, which constitutes for all famous actors a natural beginning. . . Unusual changeability of her nose through the shifting highlights and hollows of the playing muscles around it" (45–46).

10. Pawel 243: "An added element was his infatuation with Mania Tschissik, a fast-fading married member of the troupe whose onstage sex appeal in his eyes more than made up for her fatuous incompetence as an actress."

11. "Ms. Tschissik (I enjoy writing the name so much) likes to bow her head at the table even while eating roast goose, you believe you can get in under her eyelids with your glance if you first carefully look along her cheeks and then, making yourself small, slip in, in doing which you don't even first have to raise the lids, for they are raised and even let a bluish gleam through which lures you on to the attempt. Out of her truthful acting flourishes of her fist now and them emerge, turns of her arm that drape invisible trains about her body, she places her outspread fingers on her breast because the artless shriek does not suffice. Her acting is not varied: the frightened look at her antagonist, the seeking for a way out on the small stage, the soft voice that, without being raised, mounts heroically in even, short ascents aided only by a greater inner resonance, the joy that spreads through her face across her high forehead into her hair; the self-sufficiency and independence of all other means when she sings solos, the holding herself erect when she resists that compels the spectator to devote his attention to her whole body—but not much more. But there is the truth of the whole and as a result the conviction that the least of her effects cannot be taken from her, that she is independent of the play and of us" (*Diaries* 107–8).

Works Cited

Beck, Evelyn Torton. *Kafka and the Yiddish Theater: Its Impact on His Work.* Madison, Wisc.: University of Wisconsin Press, 1971.

Freedman, Diane P. *An Alchemy of Genres: Cross-Genre Writing by American Feminist Poet-Critics.* Charlottesville: University Press of Virginia, 1992.

Glatzer, Nahum N. *The Loves of Franz Kafka*. New York: Schocken Books, 1986.
Kafka, Franz. *The Complete Stories*. New York: Schocken Books, 1971.
———. *The Diaries of Franz Kafka, 1910–1913*. Trans. Joseph Kresh. New York: Schocken Books, 1965.
———. *Tagebücher, 1910–1913*. New York: 1948. In German.
Pawel, Ernest. *The Nightmare of Reason: A Life of Franz Kafka*. New York: Vintage Books, 1984.
Politzer, Heinz. *Franz Kafka: Parable and Paradox*. Ithaca: Cornell University Press, 1962.
Tompkins, Jane. "Me and My Shadow." In *The Intimate Critique: Autobiographical Literary Criticism*. Ed. Diane P. Freedman, Olivia Frey, and Frances Murphy Zauhar. Durham, N. C.: Duke University Press, 1993, 23–40.

THREE

A Cyberreader Defends

Norman N. Holland

"Darkened so, Yet shone above them all [click] th'Archangel."

Norwood? Yes. "Par-Los," I said, trying to avoid his eyes. I had set my Calv down and leaned my head way back to look up where the Buckydome's polygons arched over its tipplers. I found something relaxing in their logical march through space. The moodlight that shone from the ceiling onto my table was still showing a bright blue-green, while all the tables around me were soft, deep sunset blues and purples. The lights had sensed that my fellow topers had all arrived at postworkday tranquility except for a couple of oranges talking politics at the bar. I still hadn't got to blue or indigo when suddenly his face swam into my ken, so to speak. Between me and that gently geometrical ceiling was Norwood. I didn't need Norwood. "Satan," I said.

"Right, little Norma," he replied. "Right on the button. And isn't it lovely? It's that momentary pause in the scansion—the caesura—like a tiny click—that makes it such a fantastic line."

"Isn't it a pair of half-lines?"

"Spotting it was enough, Norma. Now you're being pedantic. It doesn't become a pretty young thing like you."

"Pretty, maybe. Young, I guess so. Thing, no. And why is a grumpy old geezer like you hitting on me?"

"Sorry, Norma, sorry. I forget. Put it down to my wrecked-up condition. Let me sit, will you? I've had a formidable day."

I looked up into his bloodshot eyes, and I had to agree. Me—just the opposite. At the U, I'd been able to shed my committees and students and give myself a long and beautiful afternoon out in the Zone doing my own research. I'd been tracking animals around Bergman Triad 61–64. You see, my project for tenure is a study of 1960s and '70s movies, and you've got to include Bergman, gloomy and obscure though he may be. *I* like him, though. I was cybered into an old Projector 16. It was pretty hit or miss—hit *and* miss, really. My own projections had been swift and sweet, though, and I'd had five happy hours of wonderful cybering—full merger almost all the time and several ek-stases. The old black-and-whites were running through my mind as that strong, dark green displayed by the moodlight in the ceiling as it sensed my emotions. I wanted to clear my head, slacken my lifeline, get down to the deep purple. Where does one do that but the Buckydome? I'd been enjoying just sitting, hoisting a few, and watching my tired fingers nudge a little Nintendo. I like Nintendo for easing out of fast cybering.

I didn't need Norwood, that's for damn sure, or one of his involved, oblique, allegorical tales of woe. I'd had enough ponderously meaningful fictions out in the Bergman Triad. But what could I say? "No, don't sit down"? To a three-step full who was likely to be on my promotion committee? So much for my quiet evening. Paradise Lost indeed.

Norwood was always losing it, out in the Zone. He was a thin man, ascetic-looking, very tall but humped over, spidery hands, classical features, shaved head, although you could see there hadn't been much more than a fringe to shave. He would fold himself into a cockpit and stare into an Octavo with total concentration. You'd scarcely know he was in the pilot's chair, unless you bent down and saw that shiny dome. Then behind his round, thickish glasses, you'd see his fierce sparkling brown eyes beaming out at the screen. He was a find-out kind of guy. At sixty-five, he was a good six steps ahead of me, me still bucking for tenure. It was no bad thing that he liked to talk to me, but wrinklies like Norwood sometimes get the wrong idea, because we smoothies at the U talk pretty gamy. I could tell he was not averse to a little flirtation, but I figured I could keep it within bounds. And besides, I sometimes wondered what it would be like to do it with a famous old guy like him.

He'd been an ace in his prime, although he was a little past it now for cybering. Even in my brief time at the U I'd seen him fly some remarkable antimetaboles. A real Ancient Mariner with the genuine hunted look. Or do I mean haunted? He intrigued me. I figured I could learn a lot from him—if I had the patience. With his damned digressions, though, it would take the rest of the night for him to tell me his woes.

I nodded. He sat. He rolled his billiard ball of a head around for a minute or two, as if he were trying to work a stiff neck out. Once he settled his butt in the chair opposite me, his moodlight ran a quick spectrum on him, and settled on chartreuse. He *was* taut. And silent. "Did you lose it again?" I finally asked him.

"It was almost cut."

"Cut! Who would do a thing like that?"

"I'd like to order," he said, speaking stiffly into the space in front of him. Over his head, there was a whirring from the network beneath the ceiling. "Yes, sir?" asked the Barthing, projecting the words, complete with question mark, on the table in front of him.

"Pwi. Yi," he said, carefully, as if he didn't trust the machine. The Barthing extended its tube from the ceiling down to table level, formed a stemmed glass at its end, and flowed some white wine into it. It moved a foot to the right and hovered for a minute. "Another?" glowed invitingly on the table in front of me.

"Go ahead," said Norwood. "What's that you're drinking?"

"Calv, but not just yet," I said—to the air. The ceiling whirred again, and the tube retracted. Always a little disconcerting, those Barthings, but a lot better than the old-fashioned humans with waitervision—an eye you never could catch.

"Who?" I said again.

"Lacanians."

"Lacanians! Why Lacanians? I thought they hadn't been around in decades."

"Some old-timers are still out there. They have the old neo-Saussurean *barre* and a real yen to use it."

"What the hell happened?"

"Shall I start at the beginning?"

"Sure." Because now I really was curious. Yes, I had come to the Buckydome for a little p and q from the rigors of critical cybering. I wanted nothing more complicated than Gameboy. But Norwood had suckered me into wanting to hear his story, another story, after an afternoon cruising around Bergman. Score one for Norwood. Score one for stories.

"I'd been surfing the big ones. 17–C. Late Willie. Just for fun, you understand, just seeing what I could see. At my stage in life, you do it for fun, not like you, not for tenure." That made me mad. I wanted to say I did it for fun, too, but he might have gotten the wrong idea. "Finally I caught a semantic wave and it took me out into the Par-Los region. Not my usual country."

"What were you driving?"

"An Octavo 12."

"One for each Bk?"

"Right. But all twelve in one hyperfield."

"Fair enough. This was all in the Gutenberg Zone, I take it?"

"Where else? Do we ever leave the Zone?"

"I do. I was out around Bergman 61–64 this afternoon."

He looked faintly disapproving. "Cinespace."

"Don't you ever try other zones?"

"Maybe I should. Sometimes I think I get a little monomaniacal, cybering myself into Quartos, Octavos, Duodecimos all the time. Maybe I need something a little more 21–C."

"I'd recommend a Projector or, if you like old machines, a Movieola."

"I like movies, but I've never come to feel they're academically respectable." So much for little Norma's tenure. "I connected to an Elephant once."

I remembered the term. "Folio wasn't big enough for you? That's what I mean about you, Norwood. It's as though no matter how much you try to change, you never get out of Gutenberg."

"Not this morning, that's for sure. My route into textspace was thinking how the interplanetary stuff in Par-Los is like what we cyberreaders do."

"That sounds reasonable enough."

"Very quickly, I got into Bk5.

> Down thither prone in flight
> He speeds, and through the vast Ethereal Sky
> Sails between worlds and worlds, with steady wing
> Now on the polar winds, then with quick Fan
> Winnows the buxom Air . . ."

" 'Buxom?' "

"Yielding, in J-M's day. Indo-European *bheug*-[3], to swell or bend, bow, elbow, bight, and so on."

"You time-traveled it!" That's what classical training could do for you. Should I go back to school? I often feel I need to know more. "I like the opening anastrophe."

"A nice glide that. I used it to surf over to Bk9.

> thence full of anguish driven,
> The space of seven continued nights he rode
> With darkness; thrice the equinoctial line
> He circled; four times crossed the car of night
> From pole to pole . . ."

"These vast spaces!"

"I love cybering J-M's immensities. You've gotta like this, too, Norma, even if you are a film person. Eisenstein said he was the most cinematic of poets."

"I do like him, Norwood, I do."

"Here we're coming to the back of Bk2.

> Before their eyes in sudden view appear
> The secrets of the hoary deep—a dark
> Illimitable Ocean, without bound,
> Without dimension; where length, breadth, and height,
> And time, and place, are lost . . ."

"That's a nice scheme there, anastrophe again, and like the other, straightening out into parallels. That must have been fine coasting, Norwood. Good old J-M."

"Yes, but what got to me was—I'd never sensed it before, but these descriptions are, just *are*, what it's like when we zoom textsectors."

" 'A dark illimitable ocean, without bound, without dimension?' I suppose it could be. Is textspace zero-dimensional?"

"Or n-dimensional—there are different theories. But it isn't dimension exactly that we lose, out in textspace. It's location. As the man says, 'And time, and place, are lost.' "

"Location? Didn't you just place us? You said you were cornering around the back of Bk2 in the Par-Los Region of the Gutenberg Zone. Isn't that location?"

"In textspace. I mean location in 3-space. *Where* is Prince Hamlet? Nowhere. Or anywhere. *When* is he? Never. Or now or anytime. Location is the grammatical marker that distinguishes real people from literary characters."

" 'Real?' " I said. "You don't mean real, do you?"

"You know what I mean. Hamlet has everything a real man would have except for location in space and time. Same with events, places, settings. Like life but without location—except in textspace. Not really real at all, but real another way. We make them real, intensely real, when we cyber out into textspace—if you can make reality a matter of degree. And it's hard work, as you well know."

"But fun. Tremendous fun."

"For you maybe. For me, today, hardly fun. Not when they try to cut the line."

Norwood and his digressions! I'd gotten so lost in textthink, I'd almost forgotten that he was going to tell me about somebody's cutting his lifeline. "What happened?"

"I was mindsurfing just the way we've been talking. It was beautiful today, just like skiing moguls. You would come up against something that felt hard, but there is snow between you and the hard place, yielding. The snow lifts you up, and the next thing you know you're riding on air, then down again, do it again, down again. The old up-down, in-out, in-out—fantastic! I was traveling at full thoughtspeed, flat out, letting my wings tip this way and that.

> Sometimes
> He scours the right hand coast, sometimes the left;
> Now shaves with level wing the deep, then soars
> Up to the fiery concave towering high."

"Parallels again?"

"I felt like the Silver Surfer—oh man, I was tubing. And half-drunk on the genuine J-M unforeseen that is characteristic in its very unforeseenness."

"What?"

"You know—Miltonic discourse. Discuss. Discus. Yes, it was like a discus, spinning, flat out, I was headed for the horizon."

"It was that way in Bergman, too."

"With these majors—maybe with everybody—no matter how deep you probe or how high you get, configurations repeat. The images are different, but somehow also the same. Like a person's style or character or identity. Over and over. Repetition. Underlying order. Something to know. You know what I mean?"

I did. "Why do you think I keep on cybering? It's that great feeling. For me, it's like hurtling forward in the old *2001*. You feel these wild, wild images and yourself going forward, forward, forward, faster, faster, faster over the psychedelic images beneath, above, around you. Sometimes slower, slower, slower. Then faster again. I love it!"

"I still get *ek-stasis*—ecstasy to you," he said from the elevation of a three-step full, "when I probe a long stretch of text. The only thing I can compare it to is fractals. Deep in or far out—the same configurations, but varying. You go deeper and deeper into curves and curlicues and cusps—no straight lines, but everything else and, come to think of it, maybe there are even straight lines when the computations hit the limit. But we don't get just pixels, we get people and love and anger and fighting and fucking and money and food and—I don't have to tell you, Norma. But all without location. In null-dimensional space. Or n-space."

"You ski theory better than I do."

"You should have done more math. Anyway, I spotted that old landmark: 'Nine days they fell.'

> Nine days they fell: Confounded Chaos roared,
> And felt tenfold confusion in their fall
> Through his wild anarchy."

"Lovely!"

"Yes, but *why* lovely? I say, because it describes that feeling you get when you're falling deeper and deeper into the text. Some texts anyway. J-M certainly. Confusion, wildness, roaring, and then,

> Hell at last
> Yawning received them whole, and on them closed.

It all begins to cohere."

I objected to *that!* "J-M's Hell is coherence? Come on! If there was ever subversion, contestation—"

"Hear me out. 'Received them whole.' 'On them closed.' An enclosure. Milton never makes his Hell very painful. It's a reaction to others' pleasure. It's enclosure, separation from bliss, a kind of negative pain."

"You're confusing me. Negative pain?"

"Listen—

> The more I see
> Pleasures about me, so much more I feel
> Torment within me, as from the hateful siege
> Of contraries: all good to me becomes
> Bane, and in Heaven much worse would be my state.

Every pleasure Satan sees, he feels more pain."

"You're really saying J-M's Hell is a mental space? Like textspace?"

"He left the language there plain as day to scan—

> The mind is its own place, and in itself
> Can make a Heaven of Hell, a Hell of Heaven.

Bk1. Then, later, I spotted 'His own invented torments,' as though Satan is responsible for his own misery, which, of course, from J-M's point of view, he is. And later, 'death invented'—I flew over that one around Bk9."

"If death can be invented—. Okay, you're saying that Satan's experience, both his real travels and the torments he creates for himself are like our cybering out into textspace. Our minds make heaven, hell—whatever we want."

"Using the images we see as we mindsurf. As Satan does."

"But there are differences outside of our perceptions of them. How about the Hell in Joycetext 09?"

"Por-Art?" he asked. I nodded. "Can you say any of it?"

I reached into my backpack. "I've got a disk right here, left over from Tuesday's class. Listen, Norwood. Cyber up now." I remembered "sting," fed it into the texter, and the passage I wanted jumped up on the screen. I read it to him.

Remember, it is an eternity of pain. Even though the pains of hell were not so terrible as they are yet they would become infinite as they are destined to last for ever. But while they are everlasting they are at the same time, as you know, intolerably intense, unbearably extensive. To bear even the sting of an insect for all eternity would be a dreadful torment. What must it be, then, to bear the manifold tortures of hell for ever? For ever! For all eternity! Not for a year or for an age but for ever.

"Ow! Goddard!" He shook his head as if to empty his ears and mind. "I remember this region. It's that damned Jesuit sermon. It always hurts when I scan this particular sector of Por-Art. Ow! that hurts!"

"Norwood, you're losing it again." He seemed dazed, and I had to shake him.

"What happened?"

"You were cybering the sermon in Por-Art."

"I hate that quadrant. But this time it hurt worse than usual."

"Why was it different this time?"

"Maybe because I'd been in Par-Los where it's not so painful. Pain as the opposite of bliss is nothing compared to the agonies that that damned Father Arnall is preaching. Preaching. Feeding the kids a line. Worse than awful. Wait. Calm down. Let me check the lifeline. I was talking about Satan's fall, and then you mentioned that goddardawful sermon. I started spiralling around *hell* and *line*."

"I noticed."

"Line. The Jesuit has a line."

"Go for it, Norwood."

"Line. Lyin'. Lyin' Lacanians. I was going to tell you about the Lacanians—they're like Jesuits—trying to cut my lifeline. Line. Mascu*line*. They were trying to cut my life*line*, mascu*line*. They were trying to demasculate, emasculate, me. They were trying to castrate . . . !"

He was getting louder and louder, again, and people at other tables were beginning to turn around. His moodlight was turning orange. "Norwood!" I raised my voice. "Norwood! Come back! Come back *now! Now!!* You're in J-M Par-Los, not J-J Por-Art. Come down, now. That's right. Back. Back. J-M's Hell, not J-J's. Remember, J-M's pain is just the opposite of bliss. Not like the physical horrors that Jesuit asks you to imagine."

"I said that, didn't I? Okay, okay." He lowered his voice. "Whew! That was a bitching ride!" He was quiet for a moment, then he softly said, "Why this is hell, nor am I out of it."

"No, Norwood. Not J-M. C-M Doc-Fau. And besides this is the Buckydome, not anybody's hell, but a very pleasant bar." The Barthing must have heard "bar" and thought I was calling it, or maybe it was the yelling, because it flashed on the table, "Is anything wrong here?"

Norwood broke into nervous laughter that he couldn't stop. "Stupid goddardamn machines! Let's get humans back! Whatever happened to the beautiful cocktail waitress in a leather mini and net stockings?"

"She went the way of 'my girl will call your girl.' "

"Sorry about that. I try not to, but I'm older than you. I can remember—"

"The bad old days? When there was sexism built into all your cybering?"

"Fair enough. But, you know—"

"That's the trouble with your stories, Norwood. You keep digressing and it takes too long to navigate them." I spoke outward for the Barthing's benefit. "Another Calv for me. Norwood?"

"Okay," he meekly said, and the Barthing filled our glasses, first me, then him. He sipped, and resumed. "At this point, I skied back to that old landmark, 'Nine days they fell.' Nine. I came upon—

> Nine times the space that measures day and night
> To mortal men, he, with his horrid crew,
> Lay vanquished, rolling in the fiery gulf,
> Confounded, though immortal."

"Nice apposition there," I said, properly pedantic.

"I didn't linger, though. I had followed Satan down to Hell, where I was thinking 'enclosure.' The Garden Close. Hell as J-M's parody of the medieval *Hortus conclusus*. That made me think of Eden, and 'nine' was ringing in my ears, so I decided to go up to Bk9 and take a look."

"And?"

"On the way, I passed this—

> Our prison strong, this huge convex of fire,
> Outrageous to devour, immures us round
> Ninefold . . .

And then 'the Muses nine'—it was as though the text were trying to tell me something about nine."

"But that can't be," I blurted. Text can't do anything on its own, I thought. That's so basic.

"Finally I got it, Norma.

> Thus early, thus alone: her Heav'nly form
> Angelick, but more soft, and Feminine,
> Her graceful Innocence . . ."

"Femi*nine?*"

"Right!"

"You homed in on *that?*"

"Cryptoparanomasia. And the rhyme with 'line' in mascu*line*. Sure. And then I swooped past another negative space, 'the sweet recess of Eve.' "

"Come on! Do you really think that means what you evidently think it means?"

"What kind of question is that? Who's to say? Except me. Think *shrinklichkeit*. I overshot to 'this fair defect of nature.' Another negative space. Woman as defect, lack."

"That's the place where J-M wants the world to have nothing but men?"

"Adam does, anyway, after Eve has eaten the apple and gotten him to do the same—

>O! why did God,
>Creator wise, that peopled highest Heaven
>With Spirits masculine, create at last
>This novelty on earth, this fair defect
>Of nature, and not fill the world at once
>With Men, as Angels, without feminine;
>Or find some other way to generate
>Mankind? This mischief had not then befallen . . .

"Weird is our J-M. Sick. Really! These dead white European men!"

"I won't argue that with you. Then I backed up to, 'In her look sums all Delight.' And I backed up again, and I saw her—

>Veil'd in a Cloud of Fragrance, where she stood,
>Half spi'd, so thick the Roses blushing round
>About her glow'd, oft stooping to support
>Each Flow'r of slender stalk, whose head though gay
>Carnation, Purple, Azure, or specked with Gold,
>Hung drooping unsustain'd; them she upstays
>Gently with Myrtle band, mindless the while
>Herself, though fairest unsupported Flow'r . . ."

"J-M may be crazy, but that's really lovely, Norwood. I see why you like it."

"And there she was. Geena Davis."

"Who?"

"Geena Davis. From the old movies. She's my Eve."

"Geena Davis?"

"You remember. The old movie star. The one who did for the grin what Marlene Dietrich did for legs. Geena Davis with banana leaves an artful screen."

"Banana leaves!"

"That's the way I imagine her. Grinning. Soft brown hair—the color of yours, by the way—dark brown eyes to match, and a face and body big-boned and cheeks dimpled to make the marvelous grin. Resplendent Eve. Mother of us all. Banana leaves so that now you see her, now you don't. 'Shee fair, divinely fair, fit Love for Gods,' and grinning."

"Not Bette Davis?"

"*Geena* Davis."

"She's not in my period, so I can't picture her. I'd prefer Bette Davis."

"*Chaqu'un.* Anyway, I had set the read controls on the old Octavo to Stationary. I was just hanging there, off a cusp of Eden, around Bk9, l-435, just taking it one line at a time, watching her tie up roses and bananas among the arborets and flowers and pineapples, the roses blushing round about her . . ."

"Pineapples! There are no pineapples in the Par-Los area. Or bananas, for that matter."

"There are now. Besides, you didn't object to banana leaves."

"They were leaves. There have to be leaves in Eden."

"If banana leaves, then bananas. Stands to reason. Anyway, I was just hanging there in the endotext watching Geena, minding my own business, watching her, hovering, moving up and down just a little, in and out."

"In and out?"

"Not what you think. Into Eden, back out to my Octavo. I'd be aware of Eve, and then I'd be aware of the cockpit of the Octavo, back and forth from Eve to Geena. Geena-Eve. Geneva. It was lovely. And that's when they got me."

"Who?"

"The Lacanians."

"In textspace? How?"

"I'm a wrinkly. My generation can still feel guilt about sex. Maybe that's how. Anyway, next thing I knew, I could feel something trying to detach me—both of me, the Eve-me and the Octavo-me—from my lifeline. It was a Lacanian *barre*."

"What's a barre? And how can it cut your lifeline?"

"The idea is that the word—"

" 'Word?' Terminology, Norwood! Don't you mean textspace?"

"I mean the surfaces in textspace. For Lacanians, all there is in language is s + ants and s + és. S + ant—that's their word for a bounded surface in textspace. S + é—that's the inside of the surface, meanings. The *barre* cuts off s + ants from s + és—their word for the things we draw up the line from our liferoots. S + ants, they claim, only connect to other s + ants. When the *barre* is in place, surfaces in textspace only connect to other surfaces in textspace. None of them can go back down the chord to liferoots."

"But, Norwood, how can they do that? Language doesn't work that way. Chomsky proved, way back in 1957, that you have to have deep structures. S + ants and s + és aren't enough."

"They don't believe in Chomsky. Just s + ants and s + és, with the s + ants cut off from the s + és. S + ants—word-sounds, I guess—floating, not anchored to anything."

"I feel queasy just hearing you talk about it."

"That's not the worst. *You're* cut in two, too. Hear that rhyme? Lacanians do that to you. Puns. Rhymes. Anagrams. They all become more real than—well, than Satan's Hell or even Eve's Eden."

"Sick!"

"Too damn right. You really begin to feel seasick. You're out there, rocketing or sailing or skiing or surfing through textspace—you're just out there. Nothing going back. No chord connecting back to roots. The *barre* cuts that, too. Talk about motion sickness!" He paused and took a breath. "You see, Norma, when you're cybering, it's like surfing. You and the wave are one. Cut the lifeline and you and the wave are two. Two separated, autonomous worlds."

"But does that make sense? Is that cybering anymore? What happens to sublimation?"

"Not possible. If you can't connect the s + ants to the s + és, if you can't lifeline your self hanging out there in space back to your liferoots inside, you can't sublimate, can you?"

"I guess not. Wouldn't you starve, cut off from liferoots that way?"

"Die of thirst first, I think. No, I don't think. I rhyme. They do that to you."

I've never liked theory. I wanted him to go back to the story. "So what did you do?"

"I headed for my Merlin."

He was sixty-five if he was a day, and I gasped. "You still use a Merlin?"

"And damned glad I do. Otherwise I'd never have gotten out of this."

"Wait a minute. What kind of Merlin?"

"A regulation WOP."

I winced. "We don't use that word."

"Sorry. A WOM. An old timer. 1964 issue."

"A WOM?"

"Wise Old Man. Haven't you learned your acronyms?"

"It's been a long time since I needed a Merlin. Mine was a WOW. I terminated psychoanalysis a good five years ago."

"*Twenty* years ago for me! But I sure as hell needed one this afternoon. I pushed the Regression button on that Octavo as fast as I could. Clickety-click-click-da-dit-da-dit-dadit. I played a bloody symphony on that button. I pulled back, back, back. And I could feel the deceleration. The mind grinding to a halt. Slow, slow, slow—I thought the deceleration would pull the fillings out of my teeth, but I slowed and then, thank goddard, I was going backwards, back down the lifeline. Like a huge mental bungee cord. Thung, thunng, thunnnng. Back, back, back. And there he was."

"Who?"

"Old Threik."

"Who?"

"My Merlin, Threik."

"Really?" I said skeptically. "Who ever heard of meeting an actual person in textspace?"

"No, of course not really, silly. Just an introject. But he saved me."

"How?"

"Shrinkery. Tie the now to the then with the lifeline. Threik took me all the way back. Brown hair—the girl who dumped me all those decades ago. Why the grin is important. Brown hair—mother. Paradise lost. Mother of us all. Brown hair—John Milton, blind from looking. Primal scene. Barth's 'Night Journey.' "

"Roland?"

"No. John Barth." The Barthing must have thought it was being called, because it flashed a "Yes?" on the table in front of us. "No!" we chorused and the ceiling subsided. There's such a thing as being too eager.

"By this time," said Norwood, "I had a line from Geena-Eva to ground zero and year dot, a good strong line at that. The Merlin had reestablished all the sinews. Mother tongue. Mother land. Threik cast off and rocketed to wherever he lives. I started to cyber back out."

"Weren't you afraid they'd try again?"

"As things turned out, I should have been. But I felt cocky after a little shrink time. I felt nothing could hurt me. The Lacanians had gotten at me because I was hovering. If I kept at maximum thoughtspeed . . . The lifeline felt strong and good, and I came up to speed so fast . . . I began to pick up distance and velocity, but I could sense my being strong and clear and continuous along the line . . . I felt I could mogul out as far as I wanted, faster and faster, deeper and deeper into textspace but never lose myself."

"You know, when you describe all this faster, deeper, stronger stuff—that isn't the way I cyberread."

"Probably not. It's not a woman's way."

"I don't imagine Geena Davis?"

"Not just that. The Flynn-Schweickart effect. Women navigate differently."

"Is this more of your sexist crap?" You could kid old Norwood along.

"No, not at all, Norma. I wouldn't pull that on you."

"You could have fooled me, Norwood."

"All I mean is, we've known for decades now that men and women have different methods of finding their ways around the world, to say nothing of the Gutenberg Zone. Men navigate by a kind of dead reckoning, how long I've been going how fast. Women navigate by finding and remembering details. That's why I'm always trying for faster. Deeper into the fractal."

"Female relatedness? Male thrust? I suppose so. A Chodorow matrix—I can buy that. Anyway, it fits J-M."

"What do you mean?"

I could see I'd piqued his curiosity. "Well, if you just confine yourself to the traditional three shrinktypes, oral, anal, phallic, he is surely phallic."

"Hey! I see what you mean, Norma." He was quick for a wrinkly. "Sure! Satan flying through space. Sharp male-female distinctions. Need to put down the feminine. Woman as defect or lack. Centrality of the father-son relationship. Peeping. Knowing. Etcetera, etcetera. Sure, that fits."

"Not so fast. How about the passage where he says spirits have no sex?"

"I think I passed that today—

>Spirits, when they please,
>Can either sex assume, or both; so soft
>And uncompounded is their essence pure,
>Not tied or manacled with joint or limb,
>Nor founded on the brittle strength of bones,
>Like cumbrous flesh.

17C Puritans thought that, that sexuality was part of flesh was part of the lower part of human beings, not of the spirit."

"Damn J-M. He's saying, if you don't have a bone or a joint, you don't have sex. How chauvinist can you get?"

"You have to take J-M as you find him."

"You say that because you're the same type, Norwood, forever cybering out into textspace, faster, farther, deeper."

"But I always feel the lifeline sinewing back. Flesh. Muscle. Tendon."

"A saving grace. Otherwise you could lose that phallic self in textspace."

"But, as things turned out, losing myself was not the problem."

"What was?"

"Crashing."

That sounded a little crazy to me. "You can't crash in text space," I pointed out.

"Oh no? I didn't go back to Geneva. I'd been pretty well shaken up in her quadrant. At the speed I was traveling, I felt for my landmark. 'Nine days they fell.' Hell. Having been through what I had been through, I was interested in hell. Negative space with J-M. At full mindspeed."

"Oh?" More phallicity.

"How else should we travel, but with the speed of thought?"

"This feminist will let that one go. What happened?"

"All of a sudden, I began seeing little signs all over Eden. They were like little rectangular FOR SALE signs on front lawns, but these said GIVEN. You know what that means—"

"No."

"Then I saw pieces of Par-Los broken off and sticking up at odd angles. The Octavo started to warm up. Then I began to get that electrical smell of chips and plastic overheating."

"Friction?"

"Right."

"But there's no friction in textspace. How did you know it wasn't just your warming to Geena Davis?"

"My ride began to get bumpy. I felt as though I was trying to slide over a rubbery surface. Lots of friction. I was slowing down and warming up. I realized that, if the surface got really hard . . ."

"My goddard, Norwood, at the speed you were traveling . . ."

"It would have been one helluva crash."

"Full thoughtspeed! Whammo!"

"You could go barmy."

"But I don't understand. Textspace can't get hard. How were they doing this? *Who* was doing this? Lacanians again?"

"Different bunch this time. First time, it was Lacanians *bar*ring the lifeline. This time it was the Biactive gang. They were changing the model."

"I've never heard of them."

"Sure you have. You know. W'Iser. The little GIVEN signs—that's how I knew W'Iser was in on it. The odd pieces broken off and sticking up—that was Derry's work. The usual suspects."

"Derry Dah and the Deconstructors. U'Echo with his semi."

"Yes, he was there. Theeree the bitch-goddess was in on it, too. And behind them all, I suspected, of course, masterminding it, as if he'd never retired, Newcrix. Unchanged. Same old curmudgeon. You could like him, if it weren't for— Well, that was part of my problem."

"I've never heard them called Biactive."

"That's my name for them. They concede that you and I make part of the experience of the text—no, meaning, they never talk about experience, only meaning. And we do only part. They'd insist that the text is also active. It does things. Makes meanings or defines experiences. Two things are active, not just one. Cyberers *and* texts. Bi-active."

More theory. "Well, we know that isn't true. Texts don't do stuff. They just sit out there in textspace waiting for us to come along and mind them."

"The Biactive Gang doesn't believe in textspace or cybering. They want to take what we know as mindsurfing or readskiing and turn it into spelunking."

"I don't get it."

"For them, reading is like exploring a cave. They don't have a textspace, like us. They have text walls and space inside the walls. When you read, you are down in a cave, your body turning this way and that as you try to fit yourself to the surfaces and passages around you. You don't soar and skim and race as we do. You inch through the space which is all under and above and behind and in front of you, surrounding you, enclosing you. Naked me, right there in my mind-body dichotomy."

"Philosophy now? I'm a text person. You're confusing me."

"I started to believe in their picture. The probing can be very beautiful, after all. At your fingertips, the mica and quartz in the rock gleam like jewels and off there, twenty feet ahead of you, beyond the light from the lamp, a darkness. Darkness visible? Treasures? Dangers? Terrors? The walls are beautiful. Or so they say."

"And what did they try to do to you?"

"They tried to change the model on me. From our model to their model."

"How on earth could they do that?"

"Easy. Textspace is n-dimensional or o-dimensional—right?"

"If you say so."

"They just get you, in your mind, to convert n- or o-dimensions to 3-dimensions, which are, after all, easier to understand."

"But that can't be. Literary things have location only in textspace which is no location at all. You just finished saying that. Remember? Hamlet the man without location?"

"This is different. If they can get you to *believe* that the text is a hard, constraining surface or even a horizon, you'll behave as if it were. You'll drop back out of n-dimensional space into ordinary 3-space."

"And at the speed you were traveling, that means you'll crash."

"Or split. Split into objective and subjective. Solid and nothing."

Oh boy. "Explain."

He spread his hands to show how patient he was being. "It's like the Lacanians. If they can get you to believe it, then it will happen. If you think that the *barre* cuts your lifeline, then it is cut. You can't connect. Same thing with the Biactives. If you believe the text is hard, that it walls some things off from you, then it will. Wall-ness becomes part of the hypotheses you bring to bear out in textspace. You look for walls, so you find walls."

"Maybe. I'm not sure I believe that."

The Barthing flashed in front of us. "Another, ms.?" said the Barthing. "You, sir?"

"A Calv and a Pwi Yi, Barthing," said Norwood, and the long tube from the ceiling complied. "I guess it's timed to do that." He mused. "Although somebody told me that it remembers the weight of the drink you had, checks it through a strain gauge in the table, and comes back when your glass is empty. That seems unlikely."

"Norwood, you're digressing again. How can just thinking about it turn a text into a wall?"

"Sorry? Was I talking walls? Yes. Text as wall. It's another way of cutting what should be fractal and cybernetic and continuous. If they were right, cyberreading would consist of two different parts, an objective part and a subjective. There would be these text-walls, absolutely solid, and then a wooshy, mushy subjective fooling around within those walls."

"But you and I know it isn't solid out there. Why do they think it is?"

"Because, they say, there are some things in textspace that *everybody* sees. Eden, say. So they must be solidly, really there, like tables and chairs."

"But we don't all see the same Eden. You see banana leaves and pineapples and I don't."

"Yet. But we all see the fact of Eden, although we may see different Edens. That's why they say Eden—maybe I should say it with quotation marks around it—J-M's 'Eden' is a wall that you can't go round. A given. A fact. Remember W'Iser's signs? Then mushy non-fact inside. I have bananas and pineapples. You have—whatever. Anything goes."

"But suppose I don't know what the word means? Suppose I only read kanji? Suppose I've had too much Calv, or I dropped some mesc before cybering out. Then there is no wall of 'Eden.' "

"Exactly right again. You know more of the theory of cybering than you give yourself credit for. You see what the issue is. If you divide it into objective and subjective, if you say the text is doing things here and I'm doing things there, and we're not always doing things together, then you've cut the feedback loop."

I thought I saw what he was getting at. "Another way. Different from the Lacanian attack."

"Same principle, though. You've got to keep that lifeline intact, no matter how far or how fast you go out into textspace. You may find your way by remembering details, I may find my way by dead reckoning. But whatever we do we've got to keep that lifeline reaching back into the U-ness."

Norwood's jargon was getting stranger and stranger with every Pwi-Yi. "U-ness?"

"U-ness. You-ness. Y-O-U-ness. Same thing. Uniqueness."

I tried to put it together. "You're saying you have to connect both to your lifeline and the textspace. Otherwise you get flipped into these other models and lose the allness of it. The lifeline gets cut or you split the cybering, so that at any point you have either hard text or mushy self."

He glowed with pedagogical satisfaction. "You've got it."

"But wait a minute, Norwood. Hard text would be text independent of human cybering. If it's independent of human cybering, we can't know it, can we?"

"Right again. But it's easy to fool yourself. If you believe that the text *does* things, even something as soft as 'invite' you in, and that's an easy thing to believe, all too easy, then they've got you. You've been bamboozled into the cave. You've started thinking your perceptions are a hard out-there, and you've given up your claim to cybering."

"You're not saying it's all in the mind?"

"No, of course not," he snorted. "That's imprecise. That's what they'd say, that we think it's all 'subjective.' The fractals lose their shape, you get all mooshed up in them. But that isn't what happens. You know what it's like, sailing. You don't just slue around in wind and wave. You can't see wind, you can't define a wave, but you work with them, you shape direction and purpose out of shapelessness. Where you go and what you get depends on what you do. You do the same thing in the Gutenberg Zone."

"Yes, it feels more like sailing to me than your faster, farther, deeper."

But he didn't take my feminist hook. "Both in realspace and textspace, the answers you get depend on the questions you ask. And you've got to know how to ask, and what to ask. But the questions you choose to ask will depend on what's at the other end of that lifeline."

"The Merlin?"

"No, no, Norma." Oops, I'd goofed. "The U-ness of you."

"Are we cybering around in circles?"

"Perhaps. All I'm saying is, it's not 'all in the mind.' It's all in the mind's interaction with the space around it, be it realspace or textspace. I'm just telling you basic cybering. I can't believe you never learned this in shore school, Norma."

"They didn't encourage women to study theory."

"But you surely know that we keep testing hypotheses on the real or verbal space we inhabit. Just like the Barthing. It moves through space, testing hypotheses on what the people at the tables say."

"You're not going to compare a Barthing to Par-Los!"

"Certainly not. A Barthing is more like us than like a book."

"What?" He really had had too much Pwi Yi. "Explain."

"The Barthing is programmed to scan what comes across its cognitive field. It looks for voices, high female voices, low male voices, so it knows who to call "sir" and who to call "ms." It looks for words, but it has a very limited vocabulary. Remember when I said John Barth, the Barthing thought I was talking about it? Probably it can't hypothesize much more than *yes, no, another, Barthing* and the names of hundreds of drinks. If I said something more complicated to it— If I said, 'Did you ever see an old movie called *My Dinner with André?*' I think it would be baffled. It would lock up."

"Try it." He keeps talking about movies, I thought. Among the wrinklies, does this count as coming on to me?

"Are you serious?" I nodded, and Norwood, with a smile, looked up toward the ceiling where a tele-microphone had been pointing towards us. "See? It must have heard us say 'Barthing' and focused in. Okay." He spoke to the space in front of him. "Did you ever see a movie from back in 1981 called *My Dinner with André?*"

There was a silence of several seconds. The machine was challenged, obviously. Then the Barthing flashed on the table in front of him, "Sorry, sir. The Buckydome does not serve dinner."

Norwood scarcely paused. He was not in the least embarrassed he'd been wrong. "Okay. The machine has more vocabulary than just the names of drinks. My hypothesis failed. But that's my whole point. That's cybering for you. Now I'd have to come up with another, more complicated hypothesis. What I said still goes, though. The Barthing may not be much of a conversationalist, but it's more like us than like a book. It has a rudimentary mind of its own. It keeps guessing about us. A book doesn't."

"Even a book as great as Par-Los?"

"Even a great book doesn't *do* anything. It just sits there. If I sat there too and waited for it to act, I would wait a damn sight longer than I wait for one of these Barthings."

I saw what he was driving at. "The Barthing is active. Par-Los isn't."

"You've got it. The Barthing tries out hypotheses on what you and I say, until it understands us or thinks it does. A book doesn't do that, but a human being does."

"Not even Par-Los. Could a Barthing cyber Par-Los?" This is called trying to change the subject on a male who is getting too serious, but there was no stopping him now. This was the Norwood I liked to escape from. And, of course, the Barthing had been hearing its name.

"Another, ms.?" flashed the Barthing. "You, sir?"

"You're back too soon," growled Norwood. "Go away." It did. "The point is, *I* act on the text. I move in and around it, working it, so that what I get back is a mix. A mix of me and it, me with my lifeline and the out-there. The out-there in textspace can't do anything by itself. It only says something to me when I try my hypotheses on it, and even then I have to interpret the way my hypotheses mix into it."

"Geena Davis and bananas."

"Exactly."

"So that J-M's phallic character may be just *your* phallic character."

"Yes, I see him that way, but so, I have to point out, do you."

"Does that say something about you and me—or about J-M?"

"Both. You supplied hypotheses about what phallic characters are like because you like to find out shrinky things like that and because those issues matter to you. Men-women, moving through space, the sizes of things. His space in the Zone said yes to your hypotheses. But remember, the text doesn't cause you to read Milton that way. You bring your U-ness and your hypotheses to the text. The text doesn't do anything on its own."

"But the Barthing does."

"Yes, as you and I do."

"What about compunovels?"

"They're like the Barthing. They change, depending on what we put into them. As the Barthing changes its answers according to what we say to it. Gutenberg novels don't do that."

"They do in a way, don't they? Your Par-Los is different from mine. You supplied yours with bananas and Geena Davis."

"Yes, the interaction changes, but the space doesn't change. My mind interacts with a real textspace out there, but all I can know is that interaction. The cybering."

"The feedback from the hypotheses you try out in realspace."

"Or textspace. You see? You *do* know. But the Biactive Gang deny that. And if they can get you to believe that texts do things, then texts really begin to do things."

"How can that be?"

"They don't really, of course. But you get the *illusion* that texts do things. After all, that's the way textspace feels, isn't it? When I was peeping at Geneva, it felt as though something had really hidden me there among the banana leaves of Eden."

"Something had. The old Octavo you were surfing with."

"But I was surfing it."

"Sure, but that was just you cybering."

"You know that, Norma, and I know that, but the Biactive Gang deny it and, believe it or not, they can get a lot of people to believe them."

"Profority."

"That's part of it."

"Shame! What these profs call 'objective' stuff in textspace is merely what they say it is."

"Too right."

"It's a shame to use your authority to wall off experiences like that. Who would swap the swoop and soar of cyberreading for a cave?"

He shrugged. "People who've never known what cyberreading's like."

"You mean that the Biactives' cave is Plato's cave?"

"That's clever! I guess I do mean that, Norma. Once you've seen the light, you don't want to live underground."

"Once you've been in soft textspace, the textwalls turn into shadows."

"A trope nicely turned, Norma. Yes, you can beat them if you just trust yourself. If you don't believe them, if you hold onto your lifeline, then the psychoanalytic model holds and there are no walls. You can navigate textspace any way you like, constructing as you go."

"Bananas and pineapples."

"Exactly! Wouldn't a paradise have bananas and pineapples?"

"If you say so."

"Exact again! I do say so, and it does, and you're free to go along with me or follow your own course."

"That's cybering. Out there this afternoon, you were able to hold onto it, and that was enough to ward off the Biactives?"

"I trusted that old Octavo. I took hold of my lifeline all the way back, and I set my mind. I believed, really believed, I could ski it anywhere I wanted to go, and I could, and it did."

"What happened?"

"I just went cybering off. They— I guess they're still down there. The last thing I heard from them was a muttering from down below—

> The terms we sent were terms of weight,
> Of hard contents, and full of force urged home.

I recognized Bk6, but by this time I got my beliefs in place—defensive shields. Their terms didn't, of course, have any force or weight—that was just metaphor—or bluff—and now they're locked in their own cave."

"That was it? Belief was enough to fend them off?"

Old Norwood nodded sagely. "Faith is enough. You have to have faith, a paradoxical kind of faith because it is a faith that there are no 'givens,' no hard rocks, no fixed targets, and no prescribed courses in textspace."

Okay, okay! I had it now. "Just cybering—as we knew all along because that's what we've been doing all along. No rocks, just words. My mind mines them. My queries probe them, like fingers, and I hear them reply in my own language, my own being."

"Right, Norma. Just us humans cybering. There is no god's eye view."

"Did I hear you right, Norwood? You're talking about God's identity?"

"You think I said, 'No gods I view'? You've made Putnam's Axiom an agnostic motto. Or atheist. I can go either way. That's why cybering Par-Los is such an interesting experience for me. I have to go into all kinds of forgotten places in my brain, places I haven't been since I was fifteen."

" 'Fifteen?' "

"That's when I became an agnostic. At least so far as the J-M deity is concerned . . ."

"But you're not doubting the existence of textspace, are you? Not after surfing it all afternoon."

"I'm no agnostic there. In textspace, it's not that I don't know. It's that I don't have any way of knowing what's out there in textspace except by some human way of knowing. There's no god's eye view, no superhuman way of establishing what's 'given' or 'what's there' in some absolute sense, as the Biactive Gang thinks. And indeed, they have thought that, going all the way back to the days when Newcrix was the gang leader."

"I hear you, Norwood. I hear an awful lot of you," I said, smiling.

He was not about to be amused. "I guess I do ramble on, but I think it's important. Old Newcrix and the Biactives and the Lacanians are trying to force a quasi-religious certainty on us. But there's only the human way with a lifeline and liferoots and feedback and hypotheses—all the imperfections that cybering implies and the limits. I have only my particular style of skiing or surfing through textspace and my particular vision of what I see. You the same."

"But this is old stuff, Norwood, even to me. We all know that, even if I can't give you math-think for it."

"Yes, but I have to say it extra hard and believe it extra hard, because I was a Newcrit for many years."

"You!"

"Yeah. You forget how old I am."

"You've been cybering as long as I've known you."

"It was a long time ago, but I think that's how the Biactive Gang were able to get inside my head. I keep hankering back to that old belief that there are certainties out there, that the entities in textspace *do* things."

"There's a part of you that longs for certainty? That's a problem I just don't have."

"You're too young to know anything but cybering."

"Or maybe it's a guy thing. Men—boys—need certainty. But does that mean I'm safe? That they can't change models on me?"

"You have to keep believing. Otherwise it's so easy—for me, anyway—to slip back into my ancient way of thinking. You have to have faith in that non-faith. Then you're on course."

"Whatever 'on course' is."

"I was speaking metaphorically."

"Did you ever speak otherwise?" I was smiling, he was so serious.

"*Can* you ever speak otherwise? I'm putting a Lakoff-Johnson algorithm into effect. The operative metaphor would be MIND IS A BODY MOVING IN SPACE."

"Which it is, isn't it? Isn't that what we cyberreaders do?"

"Sort of. Old J-M thought so, apparently. At least his Satan does. And I guess that's the moral of my narrow escape this afternoon." Possibly Norwood had had enough talk and Pwi-Yi to settle down. His moodlight had long since stopped being chartreuse and was shifting toward deep blue. Mine, however, was still green. Norwood kept me wary.

"So what does all this come to, little Norma?"

What did he mean? "Par-Los? Your yarn? Theory?"

"All of it," he said, his speech slurring.

"I guess we know things we wouldn't otherwise know. Have experiences we wouldn't otherwise have."

"Knowledge of good and evil, little Norma?"

Where was this going? "Sort of," I said. "Knowledge of the kinds of beings we are."

He smiled securely. "Knowledge that what you believe determines what you see."

"Or cyber."

"Yes indeed. We are all always cyberreaders. 'Why this is hell, nor am I out of it.' "

That was too gloomy for me. "Not hell—cyberreading."

"Oh? Sometimes I wonder if it's worth the trouble. All this gallivanting around the Gutenberg Zone, I mean," he said ruefully.

That felt all wrong to me. "I don't know what I would do if I didn't do this. This is where my lifeline takes me. I know there are other chords, science, business, making money, but they're not mine."

"Nor mine either, I suppose. So there's nothing else to do but hold on to the lifeline," he sighed.

"That's all I know." But why was *I* trying to give *him* advice? Was he just amusing himself with me? Then I flashed on something. I realized that Norwood's story had had no power over me, no power at all. All along, it had been up to me, not the story. It was my own mind that had destroyed my mind's rest, wound up my evening wind-down, lost my paradise, because it was I who was curious. That's why I was still registering green, why I couldn't get to indigo or violet. I wanted to hear how a lifeline could get cut. Curiosity killed my evening. He hadn't suckered me—I had suckered myself into spending what could have been a pleasant winddown offering him Pwi and sympathy.

"Another?" flashed the Barthing.

"Sure," said Norwood, easing himself back, settling its uncertainty. "And listen, little Norma. You've got my vote, and a lot of other people's. Quit worrying."

At last, indigo with a hint of violet.

Acknowledgments

Writing this story would have been a lot harder without the e-text of *Paradise Lost* prepared by Joseph Raben of CUNY, downloadable from Project Gutenberg. Theodore Reik was the non-M.D. analyst on whose behalf Freud wrote "The Question of Lay Analysis." Reik's *The Search Within* (1956) has many wonderful series of free associations (mindsurfing?). One can derive "the Flynn-Schweickart Effect" from *Gender and Reading*, edited by Elizabeth Flynn and Patrocinio Schweickart.

The *New York Times* reported the described differences in male and female modes of direction-finding (Science Section, 26 May 1992). Putnam's Axiom appears in *Reason, Truth, and History* by Hilary Putnam. A "Lakoff-algorithm" may be inferred from *Metaphors We Live By* by George Lakoff and Mark Johnson.

I am grateful to my colleagues, Andrew Gordon and Caryl Flinn, for reading and suggesting and, as always, to Jane for the same.

If dedication is appropriate to such an oddment as this, I would like to dedicate this story to the memory of the man who first opened the glories of Par-Los to me, Douglas Bush or, as the local wits sometimes called him, "Bush with frizzled hair implicit."

FOUR

Pulkheria Alexandrovna and Raskolnikov, My Mother and Me

Bernard J. Paris

Among the reasons Raskolnikov gives Sonya for having murdered the old moneylender was his desire to save his mother from poverty and his sister from sacrificing herself for his sake. Even if he could have completed his work at the university, "it would only have meant that in ten years' time, or twelve, I might (if all went well) hope to become a teacher or a clerk with a salary of a thousand roubles." Meanwhile his mother "would have withered away with care and grief" and "even worse things might have befallen" his sister. So he decided to get "hold of the old woman's money, to use it for my first years, so that I need not worry my mother, and to launch myself after the university . . . on a large scale."[1] He then says that he has not been telling the truth and that he murdered in order to find out if he was a man or a louse, if he was capable of violating the traditional morality without conscientious scruples like his hero, Napoleon. "I did not commit murder to help my mother—that's rubbish!" (V, iv, 398–99, 401). Later, however, after saying good-bye first to his mother and then to Dunya, he exclaims, "Oh, if only I were alone and nobody loved me, and if I had never loved anyone! *All this would never have happened!*" (VI, vii, 500). How much influence does his relationship with his family have on his criminal act? Perhaps his need to prove that he was an extraordinary man was more powerful than his need to rescue his mother and sister, but why did he need to be an extraordinary man in the first place?

A great deal of attention has been given to Raskolnikov's relationships with other characters in the novel, some of whom serve as foils or as purer embodiments of aspects of his own personality. From a psychological point of view, his most important relationship is with his mother, but relatively little has been said about it. I was alerted to its significance by a fortuitous circumstance: I spent two weeks with my mother, who was undergoing surgery, while I was working on an essay on *Crime and Punishment* in November of 1976.[2] Rereading the novel while being with my mother made me aware of many parallels between her and Pulkheria Alexandrovna and between her effect on me and Pulkheria's effect on Raskolnikov. Let me hasten to add that there are many differences as well, that my mother had more positive qualities than Pulkheria, and that I have not been driven to crime.

For as long as I can remember, my mother exhorted me to make something of myself, to be somebody, to get to the top. It did not matter what I did as long as I was a great success, though she clearly would have been happier had I become a real doctor and made a lot of money. I pursued a Ph.D. in English not because of a love of literature, but because I performed well in front of literary texts and received praise from my teachers. In graduate school at Johns Hopkins I felt myself to be among the select few and could not imagine how ordinary people could endure their meaningless lives. The fierce competitiveness of the program and the fact that most of the candidates failed exactly suited my neurosis, for it made success all the more glorious. When I stumbled on my doctoral oral and had to retake it in part, I was crushed. I had an extremely difficult time writing the dissertation that was to vindicate me. The dissertation was on George Eliot, and during the terrible four years I struggled to write it, I adopted her philosophy of living for others and despised the arrogant, ambitious person I had been in graduate school. When I completed the dissertation and was told that it was publishable, I lost interest in George Eliot's philosophy, scorned living for others, and resumed my ambitious course.

The success of my dissertation enabled me to get a better job, in which I had to publish or perish. My anxiety that my writing block would return led me into psychotherapy. I soon found, of course, that I had many other problems. I had had a lonely childhood in which I was alienated from my peers because I was Jewish and smart (my parents were grocers who disliked Jewish customers and always had their stores in gentile neighborhoods) and from my parents because of my antagonism toward their business, in which I hated to work and which was my biggest rival for their attention. My parents were proud of my grades, however, and I relied on academic success to win love and esteem. This did not work with my peers, of course. In my junior year of high school, I let my grades go, joined a Jewish fraternity, and tried to be one of the boys. Love-starved, I met my future wife at the age of fifteen and married at seventeen (we are still together). She meant everything to me during our courtship, but after marriage I became obsessed with my academic ambitions and had little attention for her. Our early years were stormy as a result, and we had marital problems when I entered psychotherapy.

One of the major issues in therapy, therefore, was why I was so driven in my work. My obsession with academic success and my anxieties about it were disrupting my relationships and putting me under so much pressure that writing was a torment. I did not attribute these difficulties entirely to my mother, but she had played and continued to play a major role, and one of my objectives in therapy was to free myself from her influence.

She was in many ways a stereotypical Jewish mother. As her only son, I was her pride and joy, who was supposed to bring her *naches* (defined by Leo Rosten as "proud pleasure, special joy—particularly from the achievements of a child," 257). My mission in life was to feed her pride, to give her something to brag about. During our Sunday telephone conversations, she always asked me, "What's new?" I translated this as, "What do you have for me to tell my friends about this week?" Since the life of even a successful academic does not feature weekly publications, promotions, job offers, grants, and fellowships, I usually felt that I was disappointing her. When my books were published, she kept looking for me on talk shows, though I had explained to her again and again that my sort of book did not attract that kind of attention. After I developed hypertension, I told her during a visit that she was putting me under too much pressure, that she seemed insatiable, that she was making me ill. She was concerned and apologetic and promised to back off, but on our way to the airport the next afternoon, she asked, "Now, how many books have you published, Bernard? Is it six?" At that time it was three, and she knew it.

I worked on my relationship with my mother in therapy, trying to find ways to fend her off and, above all, to free myself of the inner pressure I felt to try to satisfy her. It was not simply a matter of satisfying her, however, since I had incorporated her expectations into what Karen Horney calls an "idealized image" of myself, what I "should" be, what I had to be if I was not going to feel like a failure. I tried to moderate my need to be a great scholar doing work of world-historical importance. I tried to relax, to be more content with the good things in life that were available to me, not to be so obsessed with the progress of my work and its reception. As a result of therapy, I was able to write with pleasure, and I became, I think, a better husband, father, and friend. I was not freed, however, from the influence of my mother.

This became clear during my two-week visit with her in 1976, a decade after the completion of my most intensive work in therapy. As soon as I entered her hospital room, she introduced me to a nurse as her son the professor, and the nurse immediately reported that in her family there were six generations of Harvard Medical School graduates. This set the tone for my entire visit. My mother showed me off to doctors and nurses, and in her conversations with friends there was a constant exchange of boasts in which I figured prominently. I realized more vividly than ever that she lived in a world in which she was bombarded with stories about the accomplishments of children and relatives, and that I was her chief source of ammunition with which to reply. She was fighting to hold her own in a very competitive environment and to score an occasional triumph. Hence her weekly question, "What's new?"

Outside of the hospital, things were much the same. I was staying with my wife's brother and his wife, who had a large family in the area. We went for Thanksgiving dinner to the home of one of my sister-in-law's sisters whose children were exceptionally bright and whose trophies were on display. Her own children, my nephews, wilted visibly in the presence of their cousins, whose parents delighted in telling stories of their triumphs. My nephews were fairly accomplished young men, but no match for their higher achieving cousins.

I felt during this period that I had stepped into my unconscious, that it was all around me, objectified in the behavior of my mother, of her friends, of the doctors and nurses who had to let me know how important *they* were, and of my brother- and sister-in-law's family. Conditioned as I had been, how foolish I was to have thought that I could escape, that I did not *have* to try to do great things. This experience

Pulkheria Alexandrovna and Raskolnikov 115

actually helped me to come to terms with some of my compulsions, to understand and accept them, to forgive myself for having them. I could not have been otherwise.

And all the time I was carrying around *Crime and Punishment*, rereading and brooding upon it. I was struck as never before by the importance of Pulkheria Alexandrovna, by the tremendous pressure she puts on her son, and by her resemblances to my own mother. Early in the novel, Raskolnikov receives a long letter from his mother that tortures him. As he finishes reading it, his face is "pale and convulsively distorted and a bitter angry smile play[s] over his lips" (I, iii). Before receiving the letter, he had been in terrible conflict about his plan to murder Alyona Ivanovna. He had carried out the rehearsal but then had felt "infinite loathing" toward the "vile, filthy, horrible" act he had been contemplating (I, i, 7). Convinced that he could never do it, he suddenly had a social impulse that took him to the tavern where he became involved with Marmeladov. Raskolnikov vacillates both before and after receiving his mother's letter, but her letter pushes him in the direction of carrying out his plan, and it is possible that without it he would not have committed the murder. I found myself oppressed by this letter and more able than ever before to enter into Raskolnikov's state of mind.[3]

In the third sentence of the letter, Pulkheria Alexandrovna writes, "You know how much I love you; you are all we have, Dunya and I, you are everything to us, our only hope and trust." She repeats these sentiments near the end, adding, "If only you are happy, we shall be happy too" (I, iii, 28, 37). Is it Raskolnikov's happiness that his mother and sister desire? I think not, unless it takes the form of becoming a great man. When his mother writes that he is their only hope and trust, she means that, as the male in the family, he is the only one who can achieve glory in which she and Dunya can vicariously participate.

Raskolnikov's career is so important to his mother and sister that they are ready to sacrifice themselves to facilitate it. Pulkheria sends money, borrowed on her meager pension, and ruins her eyes with knitting to make a few extra roubles. In order to help her brother, Dunya takes her salary in advance from Svidrigaylov, forcing her to remain in his household after he begins to harass her. The self-sacrificial disposition of both women is well known. Raskolnikov's landlady feels that there is hope of collecting the money he owes "because there is a mama who will come to Rodenka's rescue with her pension of a hundred and twenty-five roubles, if it means going without enough to eat herself, and a sister who would sell herself into slavery for him" (II, iii, 118). Dunya is, indeed, prepared to sell herself into slavery by marrying Luzhin in order to advance her brother's career. When Luzhin complains that she is not treating his interests as more important than those of her brother, Dunya heatedly replies: "I put your interests along side of everything that has until now been precious in my life, that has until now formed the *whole* of my life, and you are offended because I set *too little* value on you?" (IV, ii, 289). Rodya has been everything precious, the whole of her life. What a terrible burden for him!

Raskolnikov is supposed to feel gratitude for the sacrifices of mother and sister and to repay them by making them proud. In her letter, Pulkheria at once assures him that she and Dunya are fine, that their sacrifices are nothing, and lets him know how much she has suffered, how Dunya has been humiliated at the Svidrigaylov's, and how odious Luzhin is. He should love Dunya as she loves him: "her love for you is boundless; she loves you more than herself. She is an angel" (I, iii, 36). Raskolnikov feels that the only way he can reciprocate their "love" is by having a glorious career. He is convinced that Dunya has agreed to marry Luzhin because in this way "his happiness may be secured, he may be kept at the University, made a partner in the office, his future provided for; perhaps later on he may be rich, respected, honoured, he may even die famous!" (I, iv, 41). There is a great deal of bitterness here.

There is ample evidence that Raskolnikov has understood his sister correctly, that she was prepared to make an "infamous" marriage for the sake of his future glory. After Svidrigaylov tells her that her brother is a murderer and explains his theory of the extraordinary man, he recognizes that Dunya's distress is not entirely on moral grounds and says, "Calm yourself. He may yet be a great man" (VI, iv, 473). In parting from his sister, Raskolnikov also tries to reassure her: "Don't cry for me: I shall try to be honourable and manly all my life, although I am a murderer. Perhaps one day you will hear me spoken of. I shall not disgrace you, you will see; I may yet prove . . ." A "strange expression come[s] into Dunya's eyes at the promise of his last words" (VI, vii, 499).

Pulkheria Alexandrovna is even more obsessed than her daughter with visions of Raskolnikov's greatness. This is most evident near the end of the novel in a series of stunning passages to which I had paid little attention before rereading the novel during my visit with my mother. Despite being distraught by Raskolnikov's state and full of foreboding that "some great misfortune" is in store for him, Pulkheria is tremendously excited by his article and tries to convince herself that he has been so distracted and neglectful because he has been busy with new ideas. Although there is a lot that she does not understand, she has read his article three times and tells him that, "however foolish" she may be, she "can tell that in a very short time you will be one of the first, if not the very first, among our men of learning. And people dared to think you were mad! Ha, ha, ha! You don't know, but they really did think that. Wretched crawling worms, how can they understand what true intellect is?" She had been grieved about his living conditions, but she sees that she "was just being foolish again, because you could get anything you wanted tomorrow, with your brains and talents" (VI, vii, 493).

We are looking here, I think, into Raskolnikov's unconscious, into the attitudes he absorbed from his mother in childhood, that have governed him as an adult, and that he has elaborately rationalized in his theory of the extraordinary man. He will be one of the first, if not the very first, among men, most of whom are wretched crawling worms who are unable to appreciate true intellect. With his brains and talent, he should be able to get anything he wants immediately. This corresponds exactly to Raskolnikov's view of himself at the beginning of the novel and helps to explain much of his behavior.

Although Pulkheria understands "that something terrible [is] happening to her son," she cannot relinquish her concern about his career. She asks if he is going far away:

"A very long way."
"What is there there? Some work, a career for you?"
"What God sends . . . only pray for me . . ."
Raskolnikov went to the door, but she caught at him and looked into his eyes with an expression of despair. Her face was disfigured with fear.
"That's enough, mama," said Raskolnikov, bitterly regretting that he had ever thought of coming. (VI, vii, 496)

Raskolnikov is bitter because he understands that at least part of his mother's despair derives from the collapse of her dream of glory. Unlike Sonya and Dunya, she is not a source of spiritual support. We do not see her praying for him.

Pulkheria is so excited about Raskolnikov's article because it seems to promise the fulfillment of her dream. She tells him that his father had "twice sent something to a magazine—first a poem (I have the manuscript still, I will show it to you some time), and then a whole novel (I copied it out for him, at my own request), and how we both prayed that they would be accepted—but they weren't!" (VI, vii, 493). With her husband's failure to redeem their impoverished existence through a glamorous achievement, Pulkheria turned to her son, investing him with all her hope and trust. Now he, too, has disappointed her, and she soon becomes deranged.

I am not suggesting that her derangement results only from the frustration of her ambition or that she has no other concern for her son, but she remains obsessed with his career. After she falls ill, Dunya and Razumikhin "agreed on the answers they would give to her mother's questions about her brother, and even worked out together a complete story of Raskolnikov's having gone away to a distant place on the Russian frontier on a private mission which would bring him in the end both money and fame." They know what she needs to hear. Pulkheria does not ask questions, however, but produces her own account of Rodya's departure (he is hiding from powerful enemies) and assures Razumikhin that her son will "in time be a great political figure, as was proved by his article and his literary brilliance" (Epilogue, i, 515). She reads his article incessantly, sometimes aloud, all but sleeps with it, and talks about it to strangers. My mother did not read my articles, but when she became manager of a hosiery shop in a mall after retiring from the grocery business, she kept my publications at hand and showed them to teachers from a nearby high school when they came into the store.

Pulkheria falls into long spells "of dismal brooding silence and speechless tears," from which she often rouses herself "almost hysterically" and begins to talk "of her son, of her hopes, of the future . . ." Trying "to give her a moment of pleasure," Razumikhin tells her about a student and his infirm father whom Rodya had helped while he was at the university and about how he "had suffered from burns in saving the lives of two little children a year ago." This brings Pulkheria Alexandrovna's "already disordered mind to a pitch of feverish exaltation," and "in public vehicles or in shops, wherever she could find a hearer, she led the conversation round to her son, his article, his helping of the student, his being injured in a fire, and so on." Finally, she falls ill, becomes delirious, develops a burning fever, and dies. In her delirium she reveals "that she suspected far more of her son's terrible fate than they had supposed" (Epilogue, i, 517). It is the frustration of her hopes, I think, that kills her, more than the suffering of her son. She cannot go on living after her dream of glory has died.

When we appreciate the all-consuming character of Pulkheria's need for her son to become a great man, we can begin to understand her effect upon him and the sources of his ambivalence. He reacts to her letter at the beginning of the novel with "a bitter angry smile" because it puts him in an unbearable position. He is supposed to be their source of protection and glory, but instead they are making terrible sacrifices for him and he is impotent. Their sacrifices make him feel like more of a failure and put him under even greater pressure to fulfill their lofty dreams. He shares his mother's attitude that he *ought* to be able to fulfill these dreams easily by virtue of his superiority to the crawling worms around him. He has dropped out of school in part because completing his education would only have led to a mediocre career, one that would have enabled him neither to protect them nor to satisfy their craving for glory. Instead he has begun to brood about committing a crime that would permit him to achieve these objectives. But he has powerful taboos against committing the crime and hates himself for even considering it. His mother's letter makes him feel that he *must* go ahead, and he is full of rage with her as a consequence. When he remembers her injunction to love Dunya, who loves him more than herself, and her statement that he is their only hope, "resentment well[s] up in him, more and more bitter, and if he had chanced to meet Mr. Luzhin at that moment, he would have felt like murdering him" (I, iv). This is clearly a displacement of his rage toward his mother and sister.

There are many evidences of Raskolnikov's rage toward his family. In order to insure that her precious son will "be rich, respected, honoured," and "may even die famous," Pulkheria Alexandrovna is ready to carry her "conscience . . . to Rag Fair" and sell her daughter into prostitution. Raskolnikov feels that "Sonechka's fate is no whit worse" than Dunya's would be if she married Luzhin; indeed, Dunya's may be "even worse, fouler, more despicable" because with Sonya "it is a question simply of dying of hunger." He envisions his sister's "laments," "curses," and "tears" after such a marriage and his mother's suffering "when everything is clearly revealed." "And what of me?" he asks, "How indeed have they been thinking of me?" (I, iv, 41–42). Under the guise of unselfish love, they subject him to unbearable guilt by proposing to destroy themselves ostensibly for his sake but really to further their own ambitions. "Oh, ignoble natures! Their love is like hate. O how I hate them all!" (III, iii, 223).

It is quite possible that he displaces his rage toward his mother onto Alyona, just as he displaces it onto Luzhin. As a loving son, he usually represses his resentment toward his mother and is mystified when it erupts, but he immediately feels "an irresistible dislike" of the moneylender, who arouses no filial taboos (I, vi, 60). In killing her, he may be symbolically killing Pulkheria. During a spell of near-delirium when he is in the grip of despair and self-hate, he exclaims to himself, "Oh, nothing, nothing will make me forgive that old witch!" He is, in effect, blaming the murder on Alyona. This is followed immediately by thoughts of his mother and sister: "how I loved them! What makes me hate them now? Yes, I hate them, hate them physically; I cannot bear them near me." The connection, I think, is that he blames them for his crime, just as he blames Alyona, whom he hates so much that he thinks he "should kill her again if she came back to life!" (III, vi, 265). He later tells Sonya, "I killed myself, not that old creature! There and then I murdered myself at one blow" (V, iv, 402). He hates his mother and Alyona because both, in somewhat different ways, have led him to murder himself.

In murdering Alyona, he is not only symbolically killing his mother but is showing her what she has done to him and punishing her for it. By murdering Alyona, he kills himself (or at least his "future") and thereby kills Pulkheria Alexandrovna as well. Though only forty-three, she dies not long after. Raskolnikov's crime is an act that he does *for* his mother, *at* his mother, and *to* his mother. He knew in advance that he could not carry it off and what the consequences would be both for himself and Pulkheria. He had almost killed his mother once before, when he became engaged to his landlady's plain, sickly daughter. "Would you not think," Pulkheria complains to Razumikhin, "that my tears, my entreaties, my illness, my possible death from grief . . . would have stopped him? No, he would have trampled coolly over every obstacle. But surely, surely he loves us?" (III, ii, 207–8). He does love her, but he hates her as well and has a need to torment her, as this episode shows. She presents herself as an easy victim, much as Alyona had done, by her readiness to die of grief. It is difficult to say what might have happened if his fiancée had not passed away. Pulkheria Alexandrovna would have been crushed had her son made a marriage so out of keeping with her conception of his worth.

Not only Raskolnikov's murder of Alyona but also the conflicting side of his personality is influenced by his relationship with his mother and the values and example of his family. Pulkheria's letter reinforces his ambition by reminding him that he is their only hope and trust, but it also urges him to pray to God, to "believe in the mercy of our Creator and Redeemer." Afraid that he "may have been affected by the fashionable modern unbelief," his mother reminds him of his religious upbringing: "Remember, my dear, how, when you were a child and your father was still alive, you lisped your prayers at my knee, and remember how happy we all were then!" (I, iii, 37). She wants her son to be a great man but also a good Christian.

Raskolnikov's childhood was steeped in religious feeling. Once or twice a year his pious family visited the cemetery where his grandmother was buried, paying for a requiem in the old stone church: "He loved this church with its ancient icons, most of them without frames, and the old priest with his trembling head." The cemetery also contained the grave of a younger brother who had died in infancy. Raskolnikov could not remember his brother, but "every time they visited the cemetery he devoutly and reverently crossed himself before the little grave and bowed down and kissed it" (I, v, 52). He was a sensitive boy who disliked the village tavern, pressing closer to his father when they passed it, and who felt so sorry for horses when he saw them being beaten that his mother took him away from the window.

Raskolnikov grew up in an atmosphere in which generosity and self-sacrifice were glorified. Indeed, in Dunya and his mother he has examples of women who are heedless of their own well-being and seem only to live for other people. Dunya even tries to save Svidrigaylov, who astutely tells Raskolnikov that "she is the kind of person who hungers and thirsts to be tortured for somebody, and if she does not achieve her martyrdom she is quite capable of jumping out of a window" (VI, iv, 456). Raskolnikov admires Dunya, though he hates being the object of her sacrifice, and he is drawn to martyrs like Sonya, who turn the other cheek and seem to love others more than themselves. He is a very compassionate person who is compulsively generous and is given to taking burdens on himself. He is attracted to his fiancée not only because it torments his mother but also because she is unattractive and ill: "If she had been lame as well, or hump-backed, I might very likely have loved her even more . . ." (III, iii, 221). Like his mother and sister, he glorifies sacrifice and derives a masochistic satisfaction from suffering for others.

Pulkheria is extremely proud of this side of her son, which she has done much to cultivate. In her deranged state, she brags not only about his article, but also about his having helped a fellow student and his father while he himself was in poverty and saved two children from a fire, burning his hands in the process. She wants him to be a great man, to be sure, but also to be a very good one. When he apologizes for having given twenty-five roubles for Marmeladov's funeral, she says, "Don't go on Rodya. I am sure that everything you do is right!" When he says that he "may be no good" but that Dunya ought not to marry Luzhin, she becomes extremely distressed: "And why will you persist in saying you are no good? That I cannot bear" (III, iii, 218, 222). And when he does not come to see her, she rationalizes his neglect: "You may have God knows what plans . . . in your mind, or all sorts of ideas may have sprung up in you; am I to be always jogging your elbow to ask you what you are thinking about?" (VI, vii, 492).

This reminds me of my mother who, as she grew old and ill, told me her troubles every Sunday, but often ended by saying, "Now, don't worry about me, Bernard. You need a clear head for your writing." She wanted me to worry about her, of course, but also to get on with my work. There is a similar conflict in Pulkheria between the need for a loving, dutiful son and one with impressive achievements. Pulkheria tries to balance her needs by telling Raskolnikov that he "mustn't spoil" her, that she'll know he loves her even if he can't visit: "I shall read your writings, I shall hear about you from everybody, and from time to time you will come to see me—what could be better?" (VI, vii, 494). She then bursts into tears.

Raskolnikov knows how important it is for his mother that he be both great and good, and he strives desperately to reconcile these imperatives, which he has internalized. It seems that if he is good he cannot be great and that if he is to be great he cannot be good. No course of action is satisfactory. If he follows his mother's injunction to remember his religious upbringing, not only will he fail to achieve greatness, but he will be unable to lift himself out of poverty in time to save her and his sister from sacrificing themselves. He feels that he must commit the crime in order to do his duty toward his mother and prevent Dunya's immoral marriage. If he commits the crime, however, he will be a sinner in the eyes of his family and will be separated from them by guilt. His mother would be destroyed should she learn of what he had done. He would be violating his own humane and conscientious feelings, moreover, and would loathe himself intensely. He will be damned if he commits the murder and damned if he does not.

Pulkheria is afraid that her son has been corrupted by the fashionable modern unbelief, and Dostoevsky wants us to see that as Raskolnikov's problem. Porfiry diagnoses him as a contemporary intellectual with a one sided-development who has been led astray by abstract reasoning. Believing that he can govern his life by reason alone, he justifies his crime in utilitarian terms, as a matter of simple arithmetic. From a thematic point of view, Raskolnikov illustrates how modern unbelief leads to crime. He gets into trouble because he has left the religious environment of his native village and has come to St. Petersburg, a hotbed of atheistic humanism.

But why is Raskolnikov so receptive to modern ideas, and why do they lead to such an extreme result in him? Dostoevsky does not raise such questions, since they would not serve his ideological purpose, but as a great psychological novelist he provides so much information about Raskolnikov's character, motives, and background that I cannot help asking them. Dostoevsky's psychological realism subverts his thematic intentions, for when we understand Raskolnikov as an imagined human being, he escapes his illustrative role.

Just after his plan has begun to take form in his mind, Raskolnikov overhears a conversation in a public house that has "an extraordinary influence on the subsequent development of the matter." A student is telling an officer that he "could kill that damned old woman and rob her, without a single twinge of conscience." He then presents a utilitarian rationale for such an action: "Kill her, take her money, on condition that you dedicate yourself with its help to the service of humanity and the common good. . . . What is the life of that stupid, spiteful, consumptive old woman weighed against the common good? No more that the life of a louse or a cockroach—less, indeed, because she is actively harmful.

She battens on other people's lives, she is evil." The officer agrees that "she doesn't deserve to live," "but there you are," he says, "that's nature." "But don't you see," replies the student, "nature must be guided and corrected, or else we should all be swamped with prejudices. Otherwise there could never be one great man" (I, vi, 62–63). The conversation ends with the student saying that "of course" he would not kill the old woman himself.

What most impresses Raskolnikov, I think, is the idea that unless we get rid of our prejudices there can "never be one great man." Raskolnikov does not need to be a great man because he has fallen prey to modern unbelief but is attracted to the new ideas in part because they serve his psychological needs. Dostoevsky suggests that these ideas are responsible for the increase in crime and derangement in contemporary society, but in the case of his protagonist he shows them leading to crime when combined with his individual psychology. Atheistic humanism seems to provide Raskolnikov with a way out of his psychological impasse, enabling him to dismiss the conscientious scruples that block his path to greatness and at the same time satisfy his moral needs by seeing himself as a benefactor of mankind. According to the ethical calculus articulated by the student, he will be doing far more good than harm by killing the noxious old moneylender.

The trouble is that murdering the old woman still *feels* wrong. Raskolnikov tries to explain this feeling as a residue of conventional prejudices, traditional ideas that a truly enlightened man should be able to transcend. He divides the world into ordinary people who are governed by such prejudices and extraordinary ones who, realizing that there is no God, become their own law-givers and are able to step over the old arbitrary barriers without experiencing guilt. Murdering the old woman will not only give him the means to launch his career but will signify that he *is* a great man—if he can do it without conscientious qualms, without feeling that it is a crime. It becomes the means of proving to himself that he is the superior being he needs to be if he is to fulfill his mother's expectations, to actualize his idealized image of himself, and to escape self-contempt.

After the murder, Raskolnikov finds himself behaving in just the ways he had predicted for the ordinary man. He feels guilty, goes to pieces, gives himself away, and seeks punishment. He hates himself for what he has done and hates himself for hating himself, since that shows he is not the Napoleonic figure he had aspired to be. He oscillates between impulses to make peace with his conscientious side by confessing and efforts to hold onto his claims to be an extraordinary man by denying that he has committed a crime. He has committed a blunder, perhaps, or a criminal offense, but not a violation of moral law, the existence of which he must deny. Raskolnikov can give up neither his need to be good nor his need to be great, and since there seems to be no way in which he can reconcile these needs, he is driven to the verge of madness.

Raskolnikov's psychological conflicts continue after he goes to prison and eventually make him physically ill. In a dream he has during his illness he finds a way out of the bind into which first his mother's contradictory demands and then his own inner conflicts have put him. In his dream the whole world is condemned to fall victim to the pestilence of unbelief, a pestilence in which people regard themselves as "the sole repository of truth" and are unable to agree on "what was evil and what good." They go mad, kill "one another in senseless rage," and fall into chaos and cannibalism. All are "destined to perish, except a chosen few, a very few," who, founding "a new race of men and a new life" will "renew and cleanse the earth." When Raskolnikov recovers, he cannot shake off "the impressions of his delirious dreaming" and is distressed that "this ridiculous fantasy" lingers in his memory. But he soon finds himself "seized and cast" at Sonya's feet. "Restored to life," he takes out the New Testament from which Sonya had read to him of the raising of Lazarus, and the idea flashes through his mind that her beliefs can now become his (Epilogue, ii, 523–24, 526–27).

Raskolnikov's dream shows him how to reformulate his search for glory in such a way that he can be both great and good. In his article, ordinary men were believers while extraordinary men were those who saw that the traditional morality had no foundation and that each person was a law unto himself. In his dream he envisions the consequences of the spread of his atheistic beliefs. Here ordinary men are unbelievers while the "chosen handful of the pure" are presumably those who have preserved religious truth. Having worked out the solution to his problem unconsciously, he finds himself embracing Sonya and her beliefs, thus becoming one of the chosen few. He no longer has to violate the traditional morality in order to be great, since he can become great by being one of the handful who prepare the way for the renewal and cleansing of the earth by upholding the teachings of Christianity. Had she lived long enough to see Raskolnikov's vision for himself fulfilled, his mother would have been proud.

While my understanding of my relationship with my mother sensitized me to Raskolnikov's problems, it was my analysis of another aspect of my experience that influenced my interpretation of his solution. As I have already indicated, in graduate school I was in some ways a more innocuous version of Raskolnikov. Influenced by my mother, I had a dream of being one of the first, if not the very first, among our men of learning. Like many of my fellow students, I felt that my talents should exempt me from the expectations governing ordinary mortals. Some of them stole books and records on the grounds that these things should be in the hands of those who could properly appreciate them. I did not do that, but I felt that most other people were considerably less important than I was, and I neglected or exploited them accordingly. In my mind, I was doing my parents and my wife a favor by allowing them to finance my education, since that would give meaning to their lives. My dream of glory came crashing when, for reasons I came to understand in therapy, I went blank during my doctoral oral and had to retake two fields. What happened after that has certain parallels with Raskolnikov's "conversion."

I felt under enormous pressure to write a magnificent dissertation in order to restore my pride and vindicate myself. This pressure made the dissertation almost impossible to write, and I frequently despaired of completing it. Confronted with the prospect of a humiliating failure, I became a convert to George Eliot's Religion of Humanity, in which the emphasis was on giving value to our lives by living for others rather than for our own selfish objectives. Like Dorothea in *Middlemarch*, I was looking for something that "would reconcile self-despair with the rapturous consciousness of life beyond self" (Prelude, 3). My importance to others, rather than ambitious triumph, became the meaning of life, and I sought to be a good husband, father, and friend. My dissertation developed a proselytizing tone, as I preached my new gospel. George Eliot had the answer to the value problems of modern man, and I was proclaiming her truth to the world. Even if I did not complete the dissertation, I would exemplify her teachings by my life. I was still trying to work eighty hours a week, I might note, and was largely deluding myself.

I somehow finished the dissertation, which was very well received, and promptly lost my enthusiasm for George Eliot's beliefs. This puzzled me greatly until I read Karen Horney's *Our Inner Conflicts*. In this book, Horney describes three defensive strategies—moving toward, against, and away from people—and the constellation of character traits, behaviors, and beliefs that accompanies each solution. The aggressive solution (moving against) describes me in graduate school and Raskolnikov before his conversion. The compliant solution (moving toward) describes Raskolnikov and me after our conversions. Sonya exemplifies an extreme form of the compliant solution, and George Eliot glorifies compliant attitudes, values, and character traits. Often, both the aggressive and compliant solutions co-exist in the same person, with one being predominant and the other subordinate. Since they are so opposed to each other, the individual is torn by inner conflicts. Raskolnikov's mother and mine wanted contradictory things of us, fostering both sets of trends.

If our predominant strategy fails, we may embrace our subordinate solution. Thus when I could not write my dissertation, I adopted George Eliot's philosophy of living for others. Raskolnikov oscillates between the two solutions all through the novel, but after he goes to prison he realizes at some level that his aggressive solution cannot work, he has a dream that shows him another path to glory, and he embraces the compliant Sonya and her beliefs. The enthusiastic reception of my dissertation made me feel that *my* aggressive solution *could* work, and I resumed my ambitious course. Hence my loss of enthusiasm for Eliot's Religion of Humanity.

When I asked earlier why Raskolnikov was so receptive to modern ideas, I said that although Dostoevsky does not raise this question, he presents Raskolnikov in such psychological detail that I cannot help asking it. I would not ask this question in the absence of psychological detail, since there would be no way of answering it, but the question really comes from my understanding of my own experience, which has predisposed me to assume a psychological basis for beliefs.

Self-analysis can be a valuable critical tool. I do not think that I could have come to my understanding of Raskolnikov's relationship with his mother, of his conversion at the end, and of the connection between his beliefs and his psychology without having analyzed similar phenomena in myself.

There are dangers, of course, in understanding literature through our own experience, since we might engage in naive identification and fail to discriminate between the characters and ourselves. One of the values of literature, after all, is that it gives us a sense of what it is like to be other people confronting a different set of circumstances and living in a different world. Our ability to engage with what is different, however, inevitably depends on finding some point of likeness. The more facets of ourselves we are aware of, the more kinds of other people to which we can respond. The knowledge we derive from self-analysis should discourage naive identification, since it involves distance from raw experience and a critical perspective. We need a point of likeness for entry, but the greater our self-awareness, the more conscious we will also be of difference. Ideally, we want to be close enough to the characters to be able to enter into their experience and to have enough psychic distance to keep them separate from ourselves. Although there are parallels between Pulkheria and Raskolnikov, my mother and me, there are many dissimilarities as well, and I have tried not to conflate the two relationships. Using my understanding of my relationship with my mother as a starting point, I have tried to do justice to the specific ways in which Pulkheria Alexandrovna and Raskolnikov drive each other crazy.

Notes

1. I am using the Jessie Coulson translation of *Crime and Punishment* as published in the first edition of the Norton Critical Edition. To make it easier for readers to find the quoted passages in other translations or in other editions of this translation, I shall include part and chapter as well as page numbers in the text.
2. This essay, "The Two Selves of Rodion Raskolnikov," was published in *Gradiva* 1 (1978): 316–28. There is a serious printing error, corrected in the following issue, that garbles several pages of the text. Drawing on this essay, I discussed *Crime and Punishment* again in "A Horneyan Approach to Literature," *American Journal of Psychoanalysis* 51 (1991): 324–32. These two essays analyze Raskolnikov's character structure and inner conflicts in terms of the psychoanalytic theories of Karen Horney and are complementary to the present discussion. They make some of the same points about Raskolnikov's

relationship with his mother that I shall make here, but this chapter is in many ways a fresh reading of the novel, since I did not grasp the dynamics of the relationship in detail until I was invited to write on the topic of self-analysis in literary criticism.

For other discussions of Raskolnikov's relationship with his mother, see Wasiolek 1974, Kiremidjian 1975, 1976, and Breger 1989. I arrived at my view of the relationship independently, but I find much to agree with in Breger.

3. There is a good discussion of Pulkheria's letter in R. D. Laing, *Self and Others* (Harmondsworth, England: Penguin Books, [1961] 1971), 165–73. Laing reports that "when this letter was read to a group of eight psychiatrists, all testified to feelings of tension in themselves" (166). My analysis of the letter is compatible with Laing's.

Works Cited

Breger, Louis. *Dostoevsky: The Author as Psychoanalyst.* New York: New York University Press, 1989.

Dostoevsky, Fyodor. *Crime and Punishment.* Trans. Jessie Coulson. Norton Critical Edition. Ed. George Gibian. New York: W. W. Norton, 1964.

Eliot, George. *Middlemarch.* Ed. Gordon Haight. Boston: Houghton Mifflin, 1956.

Horney, Karen. *Our Inner Conflicts.* New York: W. W. Norton, 1945.

Kiremidjian, David. "Dostoevsky and the Problem of Matricide." *Journal of Orgonomy* 9 (1975): 69–81.

———. "*Crime and Punishment:* Matricide and the Woman Question." *American Imago* 33 (1976): 403–33.

Rosten, Leo. *The Joys of Yiddish.* New York: McGraw-Hill, 1968.

Wasiolek, Edward. "Raskolnikov's Motives: Love and Murder." *American Imago* 31 (1974): 252–69.

FIVE

Why Natasha Bumps Her Head: The Value of Self-Analysis in the Application of Psychoanalysis to Literature

Daniel Rancour-Laferriere

On the morning of 8 January 1990, I was sitting and peacefully reading an article in a recent issue of the *Psychoanalytic Review*. The article dealt with Freud's famous 1911 case history of the psychotic German judge, Paul Schreber (*SE* XII, 3–82). I was enjoying the article because it was very detailed and was telling me things I had never heard before about Herr Schreber.

Suddenly I came upon the following words about Schreber's father: "Moritz Schreber's successful years ended in 1851 . . . when a ladder fell on his head. Some months thereafter he began to suffer from head symptoms which troubled him for the next ten years until his death" (Lothane 210).

I had to stop reading. There was a burst of anxiety, followed immediately by guilt, again followed immediately by an awful, familiarly depressive feeling.

I tried to resume reading, but to no avail. Only the words "intermittent depression," "black spots," "shadow" floated before my eyes.

Again I tried to pick up the thread of the article, but to no avail. Finally, I put the journal away, got up, and tried to think about other things.

Of the three feelings I had experienced in rapid succession—anxiety, guilt, depression—the second is now the easiest to remember and understand: I felt a twinge of guilt because at the time I owed a colleague a paper for an upcoming conference, and the paper had not yet been written (the paper—now this essay—was going to deal with my feelings about head injuries).

Much more difficult to reconstruct now are the anxiety and the depression of those moments. The anxiety was apparently provoked by the idea that Schreber's father was *struck on the head*. And the subsequent surge of depression evidently went back to a primitive belief I have always held: being struck on the head means that *life is not worth living*.

These are obviously personal matters. Why should the idea of a head injury provoke this depressive anxiety? Other readers of the passage in question are hardly likely to have the kind of reaction that I did.

And what has this whole subjective process of mine got to do with Natasha Rostova, a heroine of Lev Tolstoy's great novel *War and Peace?*

A couple of months before reading about Schreber's father being hit on the head, I had completed a psychoanalytic study of Tolstoy's novel. The study focused on the character Pierre Bezukhov, who marries Natasha at the end of the novel. Natasha, as we will see, bumps her head in the presence of Bezukhov.

Originally I had planned to include a chapter in that book about the role my own fantasies played in the decipherment of Pierre's numerous fantasies. This chapter was not written, however, on the advice of my lawyer, who also happens to be my wife, and who is always looking out for my good interests.

But sooner or later, I felt, the topic had to be dealt with. The upcoming conference, which was entitled "The Fantastic Imagination in New Critical Theories" (held at Texas A&M University in March 1990) seemed to offer the perfect opportunity to deal with self-analysis. It was a forum where one could openly discuss the topic of the literary scholar's own fantasies arising in response to fantasies proffered by the author (narrator, hero, character, etc.). So I wrote the previously suppressed chapter.

The book itself has since been published under the title *Tolstoy's Pierre Bezukhov: A Psychoanalytic Study* (1993). However, while writing the book, that is, at the time of most of the events to be described in this chapter, the title was simply *Pierre on the Couch*. The original title will be retained here for reasons which will become obvious.

The typed manuscript of the book runs to 237 single-spaced pages. In the two and one-half years I was writing *Pierre on the Couch* I was also keeping a diary, much of which was self-analytic in nature. The diary adds up to 189 handwritten leaves (most written on both sides). Many of the diary entries deal with Tolstoy, his novel, and especially with Pierre himself. In addition to the straightforwardly self-analytic prose, there are poems, dreams, daytime fantasies, philosophical musings, doodlings, blank spaces, memory flashes, and so forth—which for me are inseparable from the self-analytic prose passages because they often generated them, or were generated by them.

All of these materials I now consider leftovers, trash almost. Yet they were very useful at the time of writing the book (not to mention their now helping me to write this essay).

The diaristic leftovers do not include the rough drafts of *Pierre on the Couch*. There were those too, of course, but they were cannibalized one after the other by my computer as the book grew in size.

The diary entries, by contrast, were handwritten, and were not destroyed. Nor do I plan to destroy them. Here I differ from Freud, who destroyed his papers on more than one occasion.

What I want to argue is that a diary is a very good device for making initial contact with the subject of psychoanalytic study, for generating crude, preliminary hypotheses, for maintaining and deepening contact with the subject through the production of useful fantasies over extended periods of time, and, most importantly, for minimizing transferential distortion and partiality. A potential ancillary benefit is the continued existence of the diaristic material beyond the lifetime of the analyst: should some psychoanalytic scholar return to the same subject in some future generation, further transferential distortion can be removed, further refinements of the analysis can be made.

I realize that not all scholars are inclined to keep a diary, and that those who do so *gladly* are probably using the diary in some neurotic way that itself has nothing to do with generating hypotheses or clearing the air of potentially false interpretations. In my own case, for example, a diary seems to be a substitute for certain kinds of conversations I used to have with my mother during early childhood. I have the impression that these conversations were about my father. Associations lead from there to some old narcissistic difficulties.

Nevertheless, a diary need not be *only* a scene for neurotic reenactment—any more than is a novel, or a painting—or a creative psychoanalytic study for that matter.

As it turns out, Pierre Bezukhov spends a good deal of his time lying on a couch, which is why my book was originally titled *Pierre on the Couch*. Obviously this title refers to more than just Pierre's horizontal position. In writing the book I thought of myself as a psychoanalyst listening to a patient. Of course the patient did not know he was a patient, and could not have known that he was being listened to in a manner that had not yet been invented at the time of the novel's time frame, which was roughly from 1805 to 1820, or the time of the novel's writing, 1863–69 (on the other hand, the earth was very likely revolving around the sun before Copernicus said it did, and natural selection was undoubtedly taking place long before Darwin was born).

Early on in my research on Pierre I noticed a strong tendency to identify with my subject. On 19 August 1987 I wrote: "There is an 'ierre' in both 'Pierre' and 'Laferriere' " (in fact this is not true, or is only phonologically true; many diary entries deal with the parallel of my French name with Pierre's French name). On 29 October the diary reads: "That silly smile on Pierre Bezukhov's face—it's just the same one I see when I catch myself, unawares, in a mirror." On 10 May 1988: "I keep thinking Pierre has a moustache. But he doesn't. *I* have the moustache."

The identification with Pierre, as can be seen from these examples, had a certain admixture of projection. For Pierre to have a moustache, for instance, is an objectively unwarranted fantasy. But I felt free to project in the diary, I enjoyed it even. It helped me to "loosen up," to "get into the swing" of living with Pierre. The fantasy was not shameful because it was not in the "objective" book I was simultaneously trying to write about Pierre, where of course it would have been out of place and would have distorted *Tolstoy's* image of Pierre.

Sometimes my tendency to project was manifested in more subtle ways, so subtle in fact that sometimes I barely caught the element of projection:

23 [April 1988]
Hunting around for evidence of a connection between the folkloric Petrushka and Tolstoy's Pierre, I came across this description of Petrushka in the Brokhaus-Efron encyclopedia: "Petrushka govorit khriplym i vizglivym golosom [Petrushka speaks in a hoarse and shrill voice] . . ." For a moment I thought that

this did indeed apply to Pierre at the moment he challenged Dolokhov to a duel. But then I checked, and Tolstoy only says "Ne smeite brat'!—*kriknul* on [Don't you dare take it! he shouted"—*SS* V, 29]. Perhaps I confused "khriplyi" with "kriknut'," because of the sound similarity. But then I realized I was thinking of myself, of how my voice goes way up and squeaks sometimes, like a woman's voice.

So I was looking for Pierre, but I found myself.

It is possible that this sort of thing happened on other occasions, but without my catching the error. I hope not. I wouldn't have wanted to give Pierre a high, feminine voice if he didn't "really" have one. On the other hand, Pierre really *does* manifest feminine characteristics on some occasions (especially in the attachment to the Freemason Bazdeev), and it was thus not entirely irrelevant for ideas about my own feminine side to be coming into play.

At times I would *be* Pierre:

7 August [1987]
A portion of a dream: I enter an elevator somewhere in Cambridge [Massachusetts]. As I enter I am Pierre Bezukhov, when I come out on the other side I am Napoleon.

In this fantasy the transformation into Napoleon rather resembles Pierre's own grandiose fantasies about being the biblical "beast" numbered 666 who would overcome Napoleon (*WP*, 736–39).

If in some situations I had difficulty disentangling myself from Pierre, in others I complained about being too *un*like Pierre. Usually this was not a serious problem, as when one day (24 September 1988) I noticed what seemed like something new about Pierre: "How come *Pierre* is not a perfectionist too, like me, like Prince Andrei?" There is no further discussion of this in the diary, and I seem to have accepted Pierre's lack of anal preoccupations (which are what perfectionism sublimates). Besides, I had already written a book on *that* subject (I call it "the kaka book," which is about Nikolai Gogol's highly anal character Akakii Akakievich—see Rancour-Laferriere 1982).

On other occasions, however, Pierre's "objective" dissimilarity to me was a real point of conflict:

[20 May 1988]
Sometimes I don't like Pierre Bezukhov. . . . He is such a rich bastard. Why do I need a rich man's problems? I am from the proletariat. Pierre never worked a day in his life. What does *he* know about digging ditches, hoeing potatoes, or feeding swill to the pigs?

Yes, indeed, what did *he* know? Nothing, of course. He was one of the richest noblemen in early nineteenth-century Russia. I, on the other hand, was a workaholic academic of very humble social origins (French-Canadian working class).

This class difference between myself and Pierre was very important for the writing of the book. On occasion it engendered great psychological tension. But I *knew* it was a problem, and I *reveled* in the difference, enjoying a kind of reverse snobbery, or what in psychoanalytic terms was a reaction formation: I was Pierre's social inferior, and because of that I was superior to him. *I* knew what his poor, exploited serfs were going through, while he, the dummy, could not even manage to free them when it was his intention to free them. He was just a bumbler. He was outwitted by his steward, who embezzled his money and prevented the serfs from being freed, and so on.

These feelings were useful. They were based on my personal internal conflict, but they gave me a certain distance from my subject as well. It was not good to be *always* identifying with Pierre. On the other hand, those moments of overidentification with him did tend to provoke self-analytic breakthroughs (cf. Ticho 314–15, on the potential advantages of overidentification with literary and film characters).

Sometimes I would think I was not identifying with Pierre, when in fact I was. Here, for example, is a pre-sleep fantasy where he became my father:

[12 June 1988]
. . . fat Pierre was sitting down to eat his dinner in some restaurant. I was watching from the other side of the room. Suddenly he got up and started walking toward me. I was afraid.
Associations: Dad eating ham and eggs, which we children weren't allowed to have. Envy. Longing to be fed.

I remember that the fear of my father in this fantasy was considerable, and I knew it had something to do with death. The passage continues:

But ham and eggs have high cholesterol. Dad should be dead? Recently [I] had my own cholesterol checked—it's too high.

So, when Pierre got up and started walking toward me, it was not only my father's death, but my own death approaching as well.

Sometimes, having become very sick of Pierre, I had fantasies of psychoanalyzing somebody else—anybody else, it did not matter. But in fact it did matter, for the somebody else usually bore some systematic relationship to Pierre in my mind. For example, there was Philip Carey from Somerset Maugham's *Of Human Bondage* (I read the novel for the first time in the summer of 1988):

> [19 July 1988]
> Seriously. There is more for me to identify with in Philip Carey than in Pierre Bezukhov. Philip has known poverty, degradation, desperate love. I have known all these. Has Pierre known them? Maybe the trials of his imprisonment make up for the fact that he is basically a spoiled bastard . . .

I forced myself to keep writing the book about this "spoiled bastard," but the disgust was building up, and it had to be handled somehow.

The immediate occasion for a breakthrough was Richard Wollheim's fascinating book *The Thread of Life*. I happened to be reading it over lunch in a cafe on 4 August. Like so many philosophical treatises on the mind, this one struck me as being an incomplete autoanalysis. I was particularly fascinated by a chapter titled "The Examined Life." This chapter got me to thinking about the way Pierre constantly examines his own life, and from there—surprise !—I started thinking about myself again. It seems that Pierre's narcissism was not unrelated to my narcissism:

> It has been said that the unexamined life is not worth living [Plato, *Apology* 38]. This is true in a more profound sense than was perhaps intended.
> It means: if I do not examine my life it is worthless, it is shameful, I am worthless, I am unloved, etc.
> It has finally dawned on me that Pierre's constant self-examination is a symptom [among others I had written about in the book and in the diary] of damaged narcissism. His relentless inwardness compensates for insufficient attention being paid to him in early life. He is always trying to figure out what is right and what is wrong—but primarily in relationship to *himself*. He cannot make up his mind what to do with *himself*—and in the process gives an extraordinary amount of attention to himself, and forces others to pay attention to him too (e.g., his indecision about marrying Hélène, his conversations with Bazdeev).
> At the same time (or perhaps two or three hours later) it dawned on me why I am so interested in psychoanalysis: it gives me an excuse for thinking about myself. Auto-analysis especially (which this diary is full of) is a form of narcissistic gratification. That ought to have been obvious. After all, Joel [a colleague who is a professor of philosophy] had already some months ago pointed out to me how "self-indulgent" my planned chapter on auto-analysis would be. But somehow it didn't hit me then. I was too interested in convincing Joel that

autoanalysis is a useful methodological tool (which it is). But today it hit me as I was thinking about Pierre thinking about himself, that I very often do what Pierre does.[1]

Perhaps I would not have understood what Pierre was up to if I had not been up to it myself. Or perhaps I would not have understood what I have been up to if I had not had extensive contact with this Pierre fellow. I don't understand which direction the process works—it seems to be bi-directional.

This sense of bi-directionality strikes me, in retrospect, as itself a symptom of how deeply entangled I had gotten with Pierre's personality. There was more than just identification and the attendant dangers of projection. In Kohutian terms, Pierre was not merely an object, he was a selfobject (on this not always clear distinction, see Heinz Kohut's book *The Analysis of the Self*). But I think it was even necessary for me to be involved with Pierre as a selfobject because, early in the novel at least, he was himself treating others as selfobjects. He had trouble separating himself from Hélène, for example. At one point he perceived himself as possessing *her* great beauty (*WP*, 228). Similarly, I would sometimes think I saw *him* in the mirror. The important thing is that, seeing him in the mirror helped me to understand that *he* was treating Hélène as a mirror.

In the book I argue that Hélène is one of the substitute mothers in Pierre's life. Pierre is always searching for a substitute mother, because he lost his real mother early in life (Tolstoy's own mother died when the writer was a toddler).

The topic of Pierre's motherlessness fascinated me no end. Originally I was going to write a book about the national character of "Mother Russia," and Pierre was merely going to be one of her foremost "sons." But then I abandoned the larger topic and zeroed in on motherless Pierre. The question of who Pierre's mother was never left me during the two and one-half years of writing. To this day the question is unanswered in my mind, and I believe Tolstoy unconsciously intended that his novel have this puzzling effect on the reader. Pierre, through all his transformations during the fifteen-year time frame of the novel, remains a lost soul, an orphaned child. At one point I had a fantasy of Pierre going around to all the various older ladies in the novel—Anna Mikhailovna Scherer, Countess Apraksine, Anna Pavlovna Drubetskaia, and so forth—and asking: "Excuse me, are you my mother?" (28 August 1989).

138   Daniel Rancour-Laferriere

For a while I was trying to *feel* what it would be like to be motherless. But since I had not lost my mother, this presented a difficulty. The solution I happened upon was to fantasize something just a little different, but not *too* different from losing a mother. At the time I was in the throes of paraphrasing Tolstoy's depictions of Hélène early in the novel:

[26 January 1988]
. . . I began considering the fact that Pierre has no mother, that he must have lost her very early. I did not lose my mother. But I lost someone else. Kakrin [a sister who died at the age of two when I was four].
   Now it hits me. I can understand the way Pierre deals with Hélène if I just think of Kakrin, not Ma. Sister, not mother.
   Or sister-icon. Many of the women I have fallen in love with have been sister-icons . . .

There is some truth to this (I have had intense relationships with sister-icons), but in retrospect it looks defensive in context, too intellectual. I am not sure that I will *ever* understand what it means to lose a mother, unless my mother dies before I do. This belief is reinforced by the experience of a good friend of mine whose mother died recently. He insists that I could not possibly know what it feels like, and that he had not the slightest idea what a blow it would be until it actually happened to him. I accept his judgment.

Some of my thoughts of Pierre seem to have been merely pressed into the service of psychological issues having little to do with the book. For example, when I was visiting my large family in rural Vermont for several days during the summer of 1988 I was not actively working on the book. But events during the visit reminded me of events in *War and Peace*, and in particular my visits with my aging father reminded me of Pierre's relationship with the novel's aged Freemason, Osip Bazdeev. For example:

[3 July 1988]
The thing about dad is that he has gotten so old he almost looks dead—
   There is that passage where Pierre looks at Bazdeev—*pochti mertvoe litso* [almost dead face].

The entry goes on to deal with the intense feelings about my father which I was experiencing during those visits. The focus was on those feelings—not on Pierre.
   At some level of course the entire Pierre book was a means of dealing with personal issues. All books are about their authors. But when the

author is away from his or her book-in-progress and is dealing with personal issues in a direct fashion, then the book becomes rather irrelevant. Instead of pleasant sublimation there is raw affect, which for me can range from exhilaration to depression. In general I much prefer to write books than to deal with my family.

Sometimes, though, writing comes very close to direct confrontation with the family. On a day in August of 1989 I was hammering out a paraphrase of Pierre's first meeting with Natasha after the war with Napoleon was over. The part which I have italicized is what caught my eye:

"Well, that's all—everything," said Natasha.
She got up quickly just as Nicholas entered, almost ran to the door which was hidden by curtains, *struck her head against it,* and tore out of the room with a moan either of pain or sorrow [stuknulas' golovoi o dver', prikrytuiu port'eroi, i s stonom ne to boli, ne to pechali vyrvalas' iz komnaty].
Pierre gazed at the door through which she had disappeared and did not understand why he suddenly felt all alone in the world. (*WP*, 1238; *SS*, V, 248)

This was puzzling. Why did Natasha bump her head? Something seemed not quite right here. I felt disturbed, alarmed even, as if heavy thunder were rolling in the distance. And why did Pierre suddenly feel abandoned at this moment?

The second question was perhaps answerable, because Pierre had just realized he was in love with Natasha, so perhaps he was just missing her because she had temporarily left the room. But the wording seemed inappropriately strong ("on vdrug odin ostalsia vo vsem mire"). He had been in and out of love with her many times, but had never felt *abandoned* by her. And Natasha had done many odd and quirky things in the novel, but to me banging her head just sounded *too* odd.

Here I remembered that the Russian critic Konstantin Leontiev had once been similarly disturbed about the passage: "this is just an accident for accident's sake, this is a *straining* of realism" (93).

The next thought that came to my mind as I continued to ruminate about this problem was: Tolstoy himself must have felt abandoned in that same way when his mother died. Since in *Pierre on the Couch* I had argued that Natasha was a mother-icon for Pierre, and since Pierre himself was so very much like Tolstoy, it was only natural to wonder about Tolstoy's mother in this context. But my idea that Tolstoy had felt abandoned by his mother when she died seemed a bit questionable, because Tolstoy was only slightly less than two years old when that happened, and he always claimed that he could not even remember what she looked like.

But the idea of Tolstoy's mother would still not go away, because at that point I remembered reading something about a *head injury* that Tolstoy's mother suffered shortly before her death, and which may even have been the cause of her death (see Gusev 58).

But then *that* memory quickly led me away from Tolstoy altogether and into my own past:

[15 Aug 1989]
Tolstoy's mother had died [word crossed out] as a result of complications following a *head* injury. *Then* I remembered my *own* aversion to being hit on the head. I remembered the time [D] hit [F] on the head with his crutch, causing blood to flow. I remembered [M] beating [R] so hard that I could hear his screams a quarter of a mile away. And then there was the time when I had a scene with [D] when I refused to let him cut my hair (he used to enjoy our cries when the scissors would get tangled in our hair because they were too dull [word crossed out] for cutting).

And I remembered the time when, as I was putting dishes away in the cupboard, one of the cupboard doors was open and I hit my head against it. Such pain. I wanted to smash the cupboard door to pieces.

As I enter this handwritten document into my computer I can feel the original affect ebb away. But I remember being in a state of excitement and anguish when I wrote the passage into the diary, and I recall the even greater excitement (and dread) I felt when I originally noticed that *Natasha bumped her head.* The oddness of that detail *and* my personal connection to the detail seemed to double the affect, to make me feel the excitement I always feel when I discover something that is true about the world *and* about myself.

I am sure I would have noticed the detail of Natasha bumping her head if it had not been directly relevant to me. But it would not have bothered me much. I would most likely have just gone on with the writing and not attempted to explain the detail (*Pierre on the Couch,* like most scholarly books, leaves many more details unmotivated and unexplained than it attempts to explain). But because the detail was in fact tied to very strong feelings of my own, I was pushed to account for it, to explain it, to intellectualize as all intellectuals do.

I thought, for example, about the connection of *doors* with *death* in

Tolstoy's works (recall the door Prince Andrei dreams of as he is dying). I thought also about how a seemingly minor blow can lead to death in Tolstoy's writing, as in *The Death of Ivan Ilyich* (this idea was not my own, but was suggested to me in conversation with Heinz Insu Fenkl).

I thought also about what my head (my literal, physical head) means to me: most of my eight brothers are strong, muscular, and make a living by manual labor, whereas I am not muscular, but I have a large *head* which I *use* to make a living. Injury to my *head* means *death*—I would not only be unable to make a living, but I would think of myself as worthless with a defective *head* and would be obliged to *die*. This latter idea is a simple consequence of the perception I had, in childhood, of a person I loved who used to strike me on the *head:* this person wanted me to *die*. As an adult I cannot shake the feeling: *To be struck on the head means that life is not worth living.*

All of this was, of course, highly transferential material and had no place in my book on Pierre. It was a good thing I was getting it off my chest in the diary, or reserving it for what eventually became this essay, for otherwise it might have spoiled the objectivity of certain parts of the book.[2]

The transferential material was also quite apart from the fact that Tolstoy himself had to have had a reason for introducing the detail of Natasha bumping her head. In my self-analytic scrambling about I eventually did come up with a theory, although the theory was relevant to Tolstoy, not Pierre, so it is not included in the book. It goes something like this: Tolstoy's beloved Natasha represents his mother, Pierre represents Tolstoy himself, and the sudden and intense feeling of loss that Pierre experiences right after Natasha bumps her head is a reference to the still unextinguished grief Tolstoy felt over the loss of his mother, who had died as the result of a blow to the head. This complex hypothesis would certainly require detailed study of all the relevant biographical source materials, such as Tolstoy's own description of the crying spells he had in old age whenever he tried to think about his mother.

As for motivating the image of Natasha bumping her head *within the narrative sequence of Tolstoy's novel,* I am still at a loss, as was Leontiev. There is no comparable head injury suffered by any of the other women in Pierre's life, for example, with which to compare this particular bump. In context, the bump is truly gratuitous, and modern readers do not seem to mind its being so. As Gary Saul Morson says of the incident: "we are now used to accepting events that reveal character without materially advancing the story" (79).

I could multiply examples. The diary material is truly massive, and even it is very incomplete. It shows every sign of being an "interminable" self-analysis.

Meantime, I think I have offered enough samples to show that, in my case at least, personal concerns have a lot to do with the scholarly analysis of literature. Hopefully it is also apparent that personal concerns, when managed by means of persistent self-analysis, can assist with intellectual creativity.

The fantasies I produced and wrote down in response to Tolstoy's fantasies brought me into a closer contact with Pierre than I might otherwise have achieved. They also encouraged the production of hypotheses about Pierre.

With continued self-analysis, on the other hand, I was forced to discard at least some of the hypotheses as irrelevantly transferential, and was encouraged to produce alternatives.

Given the natural limitations of self-analysis, it has to be pursued vigorously over a considerable period of time. A little self-knowledge is a dangerous thing. One should drink deep, or taste not the self-analytic spring. There has to be a sense that the analysis is "interminable" before it can be safely terminated.

Self-analysis is a useful tool for humanistic scholarship. It is certainly not the only tool, nor is it an obligatory tool. It is also not a tool that is suited to every scholar's temperament (each scholar's neurosis is different). But when it is used—as it must be in most scholarship that is specifically psychoanalytic in orientation—it should not be used sparingly. Otherwise there is a danger of both intellectual shallowness and inappropriate acting out in the supposedly "objective" scholarly text.[3]

Notes

1. Compare Jeffrey Berman who, at the end of his excellent book *Narcissism and the Novel* (245–56), openly discusses his own narcissism.

2. There are perhaps some further implications of the fantasy material that I was not aware of at the time I was thinking about the significance of head injuries. Two readers of the first draft of this essay wrote to me and argued (independently of one another) that my concerns about head injury signified castration anxiety. Alan Elms (7 February 1990) pointed to the "life not worth living" passage, compared it with a remarkably similar passage in Freud's *Psychopathology of Everyday Life* (which I had read many years ago), and noted that Freud often said that fear of death disguises fear of castration. Steven Rosen (8 August 1990) wrote that the physical comparisons with my "muscular" brothers indicated anxiety about my masculinity, and that the concerns about head injury should be understood in terms of "the familiar Freudian association (head = penis)." As for the painful haircutting, Rosen stated: "the blunt shears both symbolize his [D's] phallus and threaten your castration (while actually injuring the head)."

I confess that I had not thought much about this sexual aspect of the problem before hearing from Elms and Rosen. I was thinking in a Kohutian rather than a Freudian mode. But Elms and Rosen could well be right, and my self-analysis may have been incomplete in this area. I have myself written about the death-castration and head-penis equation in previous books (Rancour-Laferriere 1985, 315; 1982, 154–65; there is also considerable discussion in *Pierre on the Couch* of the castration imagery applied to Pierre by Tolstoy). In any case, the self-analysis seems to have been extensive enough to prevent me from making unwarranted, projective conclusions about the head-bumping incident in the novel (very little is said about the incident in *Pierre on the Couch*).

3. I wish to thank Barbara Milman, Alan Elms, Steven Rosen, Brett Cooke, Joel Friedman, and Heinz Insu Fenkl for their constructive comments on this chapter.

Works Cited

Berman, Jeffrey. *Narcissism and the Novel.* New York: New York University Press, 1990.

Freud, Sigmund. *Standard Edition of the Complete Psychological Works of Sigmund Freud.* Trans. under direction of J. Strachey. London: Hogarth Press, 1953–65, 24 vols. (abbreviated as *SE* in the text).

Gusev, N. *Lev Nikolaevich Tolstoi: Materialy k biografii c 1828 po 1855 god.* Moscow: Izdatel'stvo ANSSSR, 1954.

Kohut, Heinz. *The Analysis of the Self.* New York: International Universities Press, 1971.

Leontiev, K. *Analiz, stil' i veianie: O romanakh Gr. L. N. Tolstogo.* 1912. Providence: Brown University Press, 1965.

Lothane, Zvi. "Schreber, Freud, Flechsig, and Weber Revisited: An Inquiry into Methods of Interpretation." *Psychoanalytic Review* 76 (1989): 203–62.

Morson, Gary Saul. *Hidden in Plain View: Narrative and Creative Potentials in "War and Peace"*. Stanford: Stanford University Press, 1987.

Rancour-Laferriere, Daniel. *Out from under Gogol's Overcoat: A Psychoanalytic Study*. Ann Arbor: Ardis, 1982.

———. *Signs of the Flesh: An Essay on the Evolution of Hominid Sexuality*. Berlin: Mouton de Gruyter, 1985.

———. *Tolstoy's Pierre Bezukhov: A Psychoanalytic Study*. London: Bristol Classical Press, 1993.

Ticho, Gertrude R. "On Self-Analysis." *International Journal of Psycho-Analysis* 48 (1967): 308–18.

Tolstoi, Lev. *Sobranie sochinenii v dvadtsati tomakh*. Moscow: Gosudarstvennoe izdatel'stvo khudozhestvennoi literatury, 1960–65, 20 vols. (abbreviated as *SS* in text).

———. *War and Peace*. Ed. G. Gibian. 1869. New York: W. W. Norton, 1966 (abbreviated as *WP* in text).

SIX

Wimp or Faggot? Subjective Considerations in Understanding the Alienation of Dostoevsky's Underground Man

Steven Rosen

Serendipitous Introduction

Many beggars work my Manhattan neighborhood. I recently saw two fighting over turf. One challenged the other: "Swing, then, nigger. Come on, faggot, you just full of hot air!" Before my eyes unfolded an actual version of my literary study: the multiple meanings, some spurious but still significant, that the gestures of males in physical confrontations generate. If the fellow fails to throw a punch, he not only shows himself meek (and thereby unmasculine), but a "faggot"—though we really know nothing about his sexual orientation. Furthermore, he is called a "nigger," by another African American, before a gathering crowd of whites. Not wishing to encourage the brawl, I moved on, noting that we Jewish academics are not the only ones concerned about these issues.

Walking on, I passed an elderly beggar, one I find too aggressively charming, uncomfortably Uncle Tomish, in his ritual well-wishings to all passersby. He begged, and I, preoccupied by the previous confrontation, exercised the sage's prerogative to obliviousness. But as I walked on by, I heard him mutter, "You jerk, you could at least look at a person if you don't give them anything." I first thought, no, you have no more right to coerce a kind look from me than a quarter, not if you station yourself in my path every day. But then I reflected that Dostoevsky would have sided with the beggar. He too put a need for public, physical significations of respect and affection over money.

Then why wouldn't I look at an old black beggar? Because I am an intellectual and like to think without interruption? Because I am a wimp and fear to acknowledge my refusal of money? Because I am a Jew and find it excruciating to look cheap before gentiles? Because I am—as he called me—a jerk?

The Gist of the Essay

Why does Dostoevsky's Underground Man spend years pursuing a strapping officer who once unceremoniously moved him aside? In "Homoerotic Body Language in Dostoevsky" (*Psychoanalytic Review,* Fall 1993), I hypothesized that the intellectual anti-hero not only feels offended when the officer grips his shoulders, but sexually aroused. I claimed that a hypersensitivity to body language, which pervades Dostoevsky's descriptions of men in confrontations, frequently has a homoerotic motive. And I argued that Freud, in his still controversial study "Dostoevsky and Parricide," was right to explain the writer's ideological development (which he deplored) on this basis.

I still think that interpretation plausible. But the psychoanalytic focus of the journal which accepted my Dostoevsky essay obliged me to suppress perspectives perhaps equally important to understanding Dostoevsky's treatment of body language. Even then I felt my analysis was uncomfortably partial, in both senses of the word—incomplete and biased. First, it reduced to a single meaning passages whose fascination lies in the multiplicity of interpretations they provoke. Second, it discredited Dostoevsky's religious and political idealizations by stressing their hypothetically homoerotic motive. Like Freud himself, I thereby indulged an ethnic animus against Dostoevsky, whose anti-Semitic writings have been cited in defense of pogroms and ritual murder accusations (Goldstein 131). Like Freud, as I will argue, my treatment of Dostoevsky was in part motivated to defend Jewish masculinity—though recent, African American (not nineteenth-century Russian) anti-Semitism then preoccupied me. My journal entries concerning former and current personal parallels to the Underground Man's situation also pointed more clearly to our mutual anxieties about masculinity than to any homosexual motives. So this subjective essay supplements, not contradicts, my prior explanation of Dostoevskian body language. Here I attribute his hypersensitivity to the postures men assume in confrontations, not to repressed, conflicted homosexuality, but to ambivalence about male bonding or masculinity proving. And here I consider the force that factors of ethnicity and class, family history, and sexual temperament have had upon my own and some others' psychoanalytic interpretations.

The Homoerotic Hypothesis

Before considering alternative approaches to Dostoevsky, and to myself, it is necessary to summarize my original, Freudian interpretation more fully.

Though the Underground Man does shoulder into the officer to pay back an earlier physical slight, he also fantasizes about the friendly embraces he might enjoy with the "dear fellow" (*Notes from Underground* 68, 72). Likewise, though he claims not to understand the basis of his cohort's attraction to Zverkov, a popular mediocrity, the latter's physical presence fascinates for the same reason that his libertinism offends him. The bitterly jealous narrator loves the handsome fop both more intensely and physically than the men who frankly admire Zverkov's coolness and share his shallow attitudes.

Likewise, Trusotsky, the cuckold in Dostoevsky's *The Eternal Husband,* confronts his deceased wife's lover, not so much to avenge his dignity, but to signal his own, unreciprocated attraction to the handsome roué. Homosexual feeling being unmentionable, he is compelled to signal it silently through mysteriously outsized postures and gestures. These culminate in violent grapplings and bizarre nursing—for example, Trusotsky pressing hot irons against Velchaninov's naked flesh—which, I maintain, are barely symbolized copulations.

The violent conspirators in *The Possessed* all tend to seduce or repel one another through provocative postures and gestures. The libertine nihilist Stavrogin, perhaps himself seduced in childhood by his liberal tutor Stepan Verkhovensky, once preached Slavophilism to a disciple, Shatov, who (like Trusotsky) lent Stavrogin his wife. Later Shatov figuratively "dance[s] naked" before Stavrogin, hoping to get the latter to "raise the banner" (of Slavophilism), and confesses a desire to kiss his footprints (240). Shatov's killer, Peter Verkhovensky, praises Stavrogin's handsomeness, kisses him impulsively, and can hardly keep his hands off him. Verkhovensky, in turn, manipulates his murderous stooge, Erkel, through the latter's hapless homoeroticism, typically signified through Erkel's hypersensitivity to the gestures of salutation. His chief concern after helping kill Shatov was not having committed murder, or endangered himself, but his boss's failure to "have pressed his hand a bit harder" in leavetaking (647).

Likewise, in *The Brothers Karamazov*, Smerdyakov kills old Karamazov for love of his half-brother Ivan. A cowardly, affected dandy who shows "much contempt for the female sex" (114), Smerdyakov cannot speak directly of either the murder or his love, so he fills his conversations with smirks and gestures, torturing Ivan with the coyly erotic intimations of his body language (248–49).

Recurrently, a Dostoevskian character type emerges: the touchy *(Notes from Underground)*, confrontational *(Eternal Husband)*, or conspiratorial type *(The Possessed, The Brothers Karamazov)* whose resentment and violence stem from rejected homosexual attraction. Furthermore, my point was not that Dostoevsky occasionally portrayed a bitter recluse, an ambivalent cuckold, a political conspirator, a suggestible murderer, a paranoid hallucinator *(The Double*'s Golyadkin) or a saint *(The Idiot*'s Myshkin) as motivated by a frustrated, repressed homosexuality, but that such feeling pervaded Dostoevsky's own sensibility.

For Dostoevsky's letters, his prison memoirs, and his journalistic writing do indicate some unusually intense, apparently homoerotic relationships. One, alluded to in *Notes from Underground*, involved a fellow schoolboy, Ivan Berezhetsky, a wealthy fop, with whom Dostoevsky read Schiller and protected younger boys from hazing (Frank 1976, 80). Dostoevsky wrote to his brother of this "companion at my side, the one creature I loved in that way" (Frank 1976, 80) and that he "desire[d] to keep silence about it forever" (*Letters* 12). Another friend and fellow literary enthusiast, the somewhat older, father figure, Ivan Shidlovsky, was "tall and striking in appearance" (Frank 1976, 94); Dostoevsky wrote to his brother Mikhail about "the moral beauty of his face" (Frank 1976, 97). Homoerotic attraction and resentment probably influenced Dostoevsky's long, difficult relationship with Ivan Turgenev. Dostoevsky professed to "loathe" the hypocritical kisses of his handsome literary rival, who had once seemed "in love" with him but who betrayed Dostoevsky by mocking his social ineptitude (*Letters* 33, 121). The fatally charismatic conspirator Nikolai Speshnev (the model for *The Possessed*'s Stavrogin) was also known for his "masculine good looks" (Frank 1976, 258). He embroiled Dostoevsky in far more seditious activity than their imprisoners ever detected; "he and Speshnev had coolly considered mass slaughter as a possible outcome of the peasant revolt they were conspiring to effect when Dostoevsky was arrested" (Frank 1986, 148). When Dostoevsky, awaiting mock-execution, expressed the hope that they would "be with Christ" (and thus together) after death, Speshnev answered with a "twisted smile" (Frank 1982, 58).

Note that these youthful romantic friendships with Westernizing liberals turned sour; in Dostoevsky's later life, homoerotic feelings flowed through Christian-national contexts, which sanctioned them. In his fictionalized prison memoirs, *The House of the Dead*, homoerotic attraction leads the narrator to teach the beautiful young Muslim Aley to read the Bible. In his later years, Dostoevsky complimented the youthful beauty of his friend, the Christian philosopher Vladimir Solovyov, whose head he compared to Christ's in a favorite painting. Indeed, homoerotic feeling appears to have informed Dostoevsky's feeling for Christ himself, since he proclaimed there to be "nothing lovelier . . . and more manly . . . than the Savior," whom he professed to regard with a "jealous love" which "may never be touched on in society and . . . makes the others uncomfortable" (*Letters* 71). What signals homoerotic interest in all these figures is the potency ascribed to their physical presences, especially to such gestures as Christ's kissing the Grand Inquisitor (*Brothers Karamazov* 243) or the Peasant Marey's putting his finger to the lips of little Dostoevsky (*Diary of a Writer* 208). The reason, then, that Dostoevsky's ideological antagonists—Stavrogin and Shatov, Ivan and Alyosha—remain strangely empathetic to one another is that their divergent ideological commitments originate in commonly homoerotic feeling.

My study concluded by defending Freud's "Dostoevsky and Parricide" against the criticisms of Dostoevsky's biographer Joseph Frank. Freud attributed Dostoevsky's intense "male friendships," his "strangely tender attitude towards rivals in love," and his ideological development from conspiratorial rebel to tsarist propagandist to the writer's "latent homosexuality" (Rancour-Laferriere 1989, 47). Granting that Frank found factual errors in Freud's account of Dostoevsky's life, and that

Freud had felt a (fundamentally ethnic) animus against Dostoevsky, I nonetheless agreed with Freud about Dostoevsky's "remarkable understanding of situations which are explicable only by repressed homosexuality, as many examples from his novels show" (47). Since Freud specified none of those novelistic examples, I considered many—all marked by a character's or narrator's hypersensitivity to masculine body language, the postures and gestures men assume in close confrontations.

It is surely legitimate to construe such interpretation as Freudian. Though I did not know it when I wrote about Dostoevsky, Freud, in "Certain Neurotic Mechanisms in Jealousy, Paranoia, and Homosexuality," did attribute the resentful over-interpretation of body language (as slights) to homosexual tendencies. One might recall the Underground Man when Freud remarks that such touchy people

> expect from every stranger something like love; these "others" show them nothing of the kind, however—they laugh to themselves, fiddle with their sticks, even spit on the ground as they go by—and one really does not do these things while anyone in whom one takes a friendly interest is near. One does them only when one is quite indifferent to the passer-by, when one can treat him like air. (163)

In the same essay Freud claims that marital jealousy (like that of *Eternal Husband*'s Trusotsky) is often "experienced bisexually" (160). He cites a pathologically jealous husband's "observation of the smallest possible indications"—his preoccupation with the way his wife touched, turned toward, and smiled at other men—as motivated by his libido's "homosexual component" (163). Likewise, Freud authorized my attribution of Dostoevsky's passionate political involvements, both the early revolutionary conspiracy and the late nationalistic Christianity, to homoerotic affect. In the same essay, Freud wrote that "in the light of psychoanalysis, we are accustomed to regard social feeling as a sublimation of homosexual attitudes towards objects" (170). Indeed, "Certain Neurotic Mechanisms" fits Dostoevsky so well that the essay seems to have been written (as "Dostoevsky and Parricide" was explicitly) to analyze and refute the (here unnamed) novelist. It says that men who overly resent physical slights, who are inordinately jealous (or compliant) husbands, and who have pronounced social concerns, are more or less self-deluded homosexuals. It exasperated Freud that Dostoevsky seemed both to have preceded him in this understanding, and to have retrogressed from it.

Other Critics and Initial Reconsiderations

I must acknowledge the influence of several writers on my understanding of Dostoevsky—those who helped or provoked me to develop this psychoanalytic interpretation and those who forced me to reconsider it, eventually in a personal context.

One who did both is Daniel Rancour-Laferriere. His analyses of homosexual and sado-masochistic components in Gogol's humor and Stalin's tyranny roughly paralleled my approach to Dostoevsky's presentation of body language and his ideological development.[1] And like myself, Rancour-Laferriere had defended Freud's analysis of Dostoevsky against Joseph Frank's objections. I wrote to Rancour-Laferriere, who confirmed my psychoanalytic approach to Dostoevskian body language, made supporting scholarship available, encouraged my willingness to investigate personal parallels to Dostoevskian fictions and, subsequently, invited me to contribute to this volume. Nonetheless, as our dialogue developed, contentious as I am, I found myself propounding alternative explanations of Dostoevsky's preoccupation with the physical aspects of masculine salutations, and even defending Freud's detractors.

One of those is the aforementioned Joseph Frank. As Rancour-Laferriere observed, "Evidently, Frank does not like Freud's theory of the male psyche, and gives the impression that he somehow has a better theory hidden up his sleeve" (9). Frank's theory—more narrowly, his sense of what motivates ideological novels—stresses public rather than private considerations.[2] He explains Dostoevsky's achievement by his passionate and reconciliatory immersion in then current cultural conflicts. Receptive to Dostoevsky's Christianity, Frank stresses his consistent sympathy for the downtrodden and his prescient opposition to totalitarian tendencies in Russian radicalism. Frank endeavors to rehabilitate the character of a remarkably generous, brave, and productive writer, easily confused with his crazier characters. And Frank has done well to correct Dostoevsky's image, "for an average Western reader . . . of a tormented genius existing on the edge of madness" and draw attention to his moral and intellectual seriousness (1990, 153). Indeed, while some readers do prudishly dismiss psychoanalytic approaches to Dostoevsky, others, only too interested in sexual issues, remain complacently ignorant of Dostoevsky's important journalistic and critical writing, some of which remains untranslated.

It is undoubtedly better to learn from Dostoevsky than to snicker at him, and Frank's pointedly respectful treatment, in its cumulative massiveness, made me worry whether my psychoanalytic approach unfairly degraded Dostoevsky. However, Frank's focus on Dostoevsky's participation in the public literary world, and upon his religious, aesthetic, and political commitment does *not* account for the remarkable tensions of tender and menacing affect in Dostoevsky's most characteristic writing. For this reader, these tensions are most consistently concentrated in the frequently bizarre, sometimes dreadful, always microscopically meaningful, physical and largely silent confrontations between men, which saturate *Notes from Underground, The Eternal Husband, The House of the Dead, The Possessed,* and *The Brothers Karamazov.*

Another writer who shook my satisfaction with my Freudian account of Dostoevsky, but ultimately failed to replace it with his own focus, is the psychoanalyst Louis Breger. Breger, like Frank, wants to defend Dostoevsky's moral authority against Freud's animus and also, evidently, to counter Freud's emphasis on the homosexual tendencies he ascribed to Dostoevsky. Whereas Freud stressed Dostoevsky's love, hate, and guilt reactions toward father figures, Breger explains both Dostoevsky's novelistic development and his epilepsy as a pattern of feelings—longing, rage, regret, and reconciliation—directed towards mother figures.

Though Breger's Dostoevsky may be more in line with current psychoanalytic thought, I think Freud's focus closer to what most readers (and certainly I) find compelling in Dostoevsky.

Which is more interesting? Stavrogin's relations with his male cohorts or with Liza Tikhin? The interactions between the Karamazov brothers or Dimitri's with Gruschenka? Neither the attention that Dostoevsky's female characters elicit from their lovers, nor their own behavior, is so charged with microscopic, ambiguous, and volatile meaningfulness as are Dostoevsky's closely observed, often largely silent physical confrontations between men. Breger rarely discusses those scenes; when he does, such as "Myshkin['s] l[ying] so close that his tears run down Rogozhin's cheeks" (250), Breger never ascribes homoerotic feeling to them.

I found Breger's virtual refusal to consider homoerotic motive in Dostoevsky rather outrageous. Yet his study did somewhat shake my confidence in the homoerotic hypothesis. More precisely, it made me wonder why I never wished to discuss women in Dostoevsky—though

I could well identify with the Underground Man's treatment of the prostitute. Indeed, as I will discuss below, what that unproductive intellectual did once, I used to do always: compulsively seduce, dismiss, reseduce, and eventually abandon somewhat disadvantaged women. So Breger's contrasting treatment of Dostoevsky helped me to understand how my selective focus functioned as a personal statement—both through what it said and what it avoided.

There are many teachers. When I imagine meeting Breger, I feel that I should show him a more respectful attitude than our different views and my resentment of his authority had at first led me to develop. Certainly I would want his respect and be glad to learn from him. To consider intellectual conflicts in terms of actual personal dialogue apparently has moderating, constructive effects. This brings me to another view of Dostoevsky I have taken to heart—that of Mikhail Bakhtin.

Like Frank and Breger, the great literary theoretician Bakhtin wished to stress positive ethical values in Dostoevsky's literary power. Accordingly, Bakhtin understood scenes between Myshkin and Rogozhin (242), which a Freudian would regard as homoerotically charged, as open-ended dialogues expressing "the soul's freedom and unfinalizability" through the capacity for empathy (61). Similarly, Bakhtin treats body language in Dostoevsky as expressing a comical, communally realized, vital relativism. His Dostoevsky draws upon the popular, uninhibited, familiar, and abusive gestures which Bakhtin calls "carnivalistic" (122). Of course this does illuminate Dostoevsky. However, Bakhtin tends to minimize the cruelty and violence of such gestures. And he neglects to account for the intensely mysterious, often ambivalent and fearful fascination which other men's postures and gestures generate in Dostoevsky's touchy characters.

I persist in thinking that these pervasive, hypersensitive confrontations have to be dealt with, if not, as Freud did, by the hypothesis of covert and conflicted homoeroticism, then by some other concept which takes account of their predominantly masculine, silent, physical, and ambivalent aspects. What makes an alternative desirable is that a Freudian approach such as mine does tend to degrade Dostoevsky. Not because arguing for Dostoevsky's "intuitive knowledge of homosexual feelings" (Rancour-Laferriere 1989, 9–10) implicitly disparages Dostoevsky, but because questioning attractions that the writer and his heroes voiced in fraternal or religious terms endeavors to unmask Dostoevsky.

Often, Dostoevsky's characteristically hypersensitive confrontations can be conceived less problematically and more precisely in terms of ambivalence about male bonding. I define *male bonding* as *an urge to signify masculinity, through proximate and parallel postures and gestures with men.*[3] Military drilling, religious (and masonic) ritual, hunting, sports, gambling, criminal adventuring, drinking, and dancing have furnished traditional vehicles for this urge, which is often not conscious of itself as such. Like many literary intellectuals, both Dostoevsky and his Underground Man felt ambivalent about male bonding—shrinking from confrontations with more impressive men which disadvantaged them or from common practices which they morally reproved, while longing for respectful recognition from masculine authority figures. Obviously, male bonding may coexist and be complicated by homoerotic tendencies, but its subjects generally feel it to operate apart from sexual motives.

Since I could have understood Dostoevskian hypersensitivity to body language in terms of ambivalence about male bonding (which I define as an urge no less fundamental than libidinal ones) why did I construe it as homoerotic? In defending Freud's interpretation of Dostoevsky, I suspect I was motivated, as I think Freud was himself, to repair a wounded Jewish masculine identity. To explicate this subjective motive (and, hopefully, shed additional light on Dostoevsky), I need to consider one additional, more fundamental, and provocative personal influence, that of the sociologist J. M. Cuddihy. It was in reaction to his work that I first put Freud and Dostoevsky together.

Cuddihy and the Jewish Context of Psychoanalysis: Dostoevsky and Ethnicity

Cuddihy argues that Jewish intellectuals have suffered from inordinate self-consciousness in (mixed) society, and that ideologies developed mainly by Jews, such as psychoanalysis, have responded to that problem. But Cuddihy's analysis can also be applied to Dostoevsky's hypersensitivity to body language and his Slavophilism. Accordingly, I might have applied a Cuddihyan sociological perspective to Dostoevsky. Instead, I recapitulated Freud's original response to Dostoevsky, because locating homoerotic motives in the latter better suited our mutual need to defend Jewish masculinity against such anti-Semitic denigrations as Dostoevsky himself once produced.

Wimp or Faggot   155

In my doctoral dissertation, published in 1976 as *Samuel Beckett and the Pessimistic Tradition*, I first dealt, briefly, with Dostoevsky, discussing the Underground Man on the futility of hyperconsciousness, but not his hypersensitivity to body language. After that protracted labor among abstractions, I cast about for more socially and physically grounded subjects and soon fell under the influence of Cuddihy's controversial study of Jewish intellectuals, *The Ordeal of Civility*. According to Cuddihy, ideologies propounded by Jews, such as psychoanalysis, functioned as "exercises in antidefamation" (4) by universalizing or valorizing the stigmatizing traits of Jews, who were backward in assimilating modern behavioral norms, and consequently embarrassing to their own intelligentsia. Citing the sociologists Berger and Luckmann's dictum that "the most important experience of others takes place in the face to face situation" (3), Cuddihy treats the Jewish experience of modern society as a perpetual ordeal because of their "failure of ritual competence" (3), that is, bad manners. Having cultivated an aggressive intimacy among themselves, Eastern European Jews neither internalized nor appreciated the forms and attitudes which enable strangers to relate with effective neutrality; and as parvenus they were preoccupied with gaffes (26).

Freud, as Cuddihy understands him, bore a grudge against the modern (gentile) West for making Jews experience this ordeal (34), as well as for its actual anti-Semitism. Cuddihy relates Freud's formulation of the Oedipus complex to Freud's memory of his father telling him about a gentile once knocking off his cap in the street because he did not promptly move aside (48–53). Cuddihy argues that Oedipus' murder of his father closely resembles the meeting of the gentile with Freud's father—both originating in an incivility over right of way. Naturally, Freud hated bullying gentiles, but he was more crucially ashamed of his father's cowardice, yet felt guilty about that shame. Hence, Freud universalized his father hatred, with the Oedipus complex, thereby falsely extrapolating from East European Jewish intellectuals who committed a kind of "moral parricide" (53) in feeling shame over their timorous and otherwise socially embarrassing parents (102). Furthermore, Cuddihy argues, it was to repay the lack of respect he and other Jews had experienced that Freud programmatically shocked gentiles, unmasking their love and courtship rituals as so much lust (69–71). But in the undervaluation of ritual civility, Cuddihy thinks, Freud erred in a typically Jewish way, as in the Jewish tendency to confuse privacy with secrecy (34).

However malicious Cuddihy's analysis, I found it plausible. But his typical, late-modernizing Jewish intellectual, Freud, sounds even more like the Russian intellectual, Dostoevsky. The covert cultural nationalism Cuddihy teases out of Freud was overt in Dostoevsky and his circle. Cuddihy said that Jewish intellectuals theorized to valorize their cultural backwardness; that is, psychoanalytic talk sessions make a virtue out of traditional Jewish unrestraint, which modern civility toward strangers precludes. Dostoevsky more directly transvalued Russian backwardness in his messianic Slavophilism: the Russians' cultural belatedness had required their intellectuals (e.g., Pushkin) to develop a talent for universal empathy, which in turn qualified them to lead humanity (*Diary of a Writer* 785). Dostoevsky's discoverer, Belinski, famously deplored the humiliating backwardness of Russian violence—the endemic beatings of serfs, convicts, wives, horses. Accordingly, Dostoevsky's Underground Man denies that violence lessens as civilization progresses. As Cuddihy said of psychoanalysis, this makes a covert ethnic apology. As for Dostoevsky's father, he was not just unhatted, as Freud's father was, but murdered by his class enemies—serfs he had scandalously oppressed—and Dostoevsky kept this shameful family secret.

Russia's position of cultural backwardness led Dostoevsky, like Cuddihy's Jews, to unease among Western Europeans—even to absurdly personalized confrontations with monuments he alternately felt insulted by and wanted to bow down to (*Winter Notes* 82–83). He complained of feeling ignored, shunned, perhaps even loathed among Europeans—not that the Englishmen he found buried in their newspapers actually said so. (To say, "I disregard you" almost constitutes a contradiction in terms.) Rather, Dostoevsky inferred this neglect and hostility from the body language of Western Europeans, who gave him no friendly looks. He found himself defending the relatively wholesome beating and kowtowing of Russian landlords and peasants (55–65). One of Dostoevsky's Russian characters says to another, adrift among Western Europeans, "I bow down humbly like a true Russian" (*Gambler* 102).

Among his fellow Russians, however, at school, at literary salons, and especially in prison, Dostoevsky was noted for his reserve, unsociability, and awkwardness. At school he was aloof; to his credit, he refused to participate in "hazing" and "mass beatings" (Breger 102). As an arriviste in literary circles, he was ridiculed for his odd blend of shyness and boastfulness. One night, after some ridicule by Turgenev among his cohort, Dostoevsky suddenly left their salon, *never to return* (Breger 109–10). In prison, he shrank from both haughty Western (Polish) and brutal Russian (serf) convicts (Breger 145).

Clearly, Cuddihy's analysis of Jews as late-modernizing intellectuals does apply to Dostoevsky, who is *more* resentful of the modern West, more anxiously uncomfortable during personal encounters, more ashamed of his disgraced father, than Cuddihy's Jewish subjects. Hence, one might explain the unease which pervades Dostoevsky's presentation and experience of face-to-face confrontations by the ethnic, caste, and similar social considerations Cuddihy analyzes. Instead, I recapitulated the Jewish reaction Cuddihy analyzed in Freud, by reapplying Freud to Dostoevsky. Why? Because anti-Semitic attitudes I discerned in Cuddihy and discovered in Dostoevsky stung me.[4] And explaining Dostoevsky on the hypothesis of his repressed homosexuality best served my purpose of protecting, even championing an insulted Jewish masculinity.

Dostoevsky and Freud on Jews and Masculinity

Let me explain the specifically masculine aspect of the Jewish resentment at work in my psychoanalytic interpretation of Dostoevsky.

No doubt, Jews have male bonded all too adequately among themselves, through the proximate and parallel postures and gestures of religious ritual, the ready availability of biblical patriarchs as paradigms, their performance as breadwinners, and so forth. However, in Dostoevsky's Russia, in Freud's Austria, and in my America, Jews have had difficulty proving themselves manly before gentiles. And that has rankled.

How did Jewish men look to Dostoevsky? How did he describe their body language? The most consistent feature of his few Jewish characters is their violation of male-bonding etiquette. The incongruous Jewish fireman who vainly attempts to dissuade Svidrigailov from suicide in *Crime and Punishment* displays a charmlessness which Dostoevsky ascribed to Jews in general: "His face wore the look of eternal, peevish dolor that is so sourly imprinted on all the faces of the Jewish tribe without exception" (cited in Goldstein 51–52).

Dostoevsky's most developed Jewish character, the convict Isai Fomich Bumstein in *The House of the Dead,* recites his prayers in a clownish and exhibitionistic manner:

in a singsong voice, wailing, sputtering, pirouetting, gesticulating wildly and absurdly. . . . what was absurd was the way in which Isai Fomich seemed to pose before us and make a display of his ritual. (Cited in Goldstein 19, 25)

Bumstein also sobs, howls, and laughs while he prays, suggesting, as opposed to his "posing," a hysterical loss of bodily and emotional control; in both respects, if not feminized, he is demasculinized.

As David Goldstein observes, the moneylender Lyamshin, an ambivalent conspirator in *The Possessed,* encapsulates the stereotypical traits of Jews in nineteenth-century Russian literature: "an exaggerated preoccupation with his health, cowardice, skepticism, cunning, feigned indigence, subterfuge, sham indignation, double-dealing" (80). My point is that most, if not all, of these traits signify *unmanliness.* Hence, when the conspirators murder Shatov, Lyamshin protests, not morally but out of "intense fear . . . wailing, without let up, his eyes popping out of his head, his mouth wide open, his legs tapping the ground as if beating a drum" (cited in Goldstein 82). When he promptly informs to the police, he does so, again hysterically: "he crawled on his knees, whimpered and wailed, kissed the floor," and so forth (cited in Goldstein 84).

Now I do not suggest that their imputed lack of manliness constituted Dostoevsky's chief complaint against Jews.[5] But the few Jewish characters he directly described do lack masculinity or the willingness to male bond with gentiles—for example, in graciously exchanging salutations, or in praying and eating together.

As I am not the first to suggest, Freud's value system can be seen as a response to similar attitudes about Jewish males current in his milieu and background. Sander Gilman has observed that Jewish men were commonly regarded as either womanly or hypomasculine in Freud's Vienna. "The clitoris was known in Viennese slang of the *fin de siècle* simply as the 'Jew' " because it suggested "the Jew with his circumcised, shortened organ" (168). It was commonly assumed that Jews of both genders had "the body type of the female" and that Jewish men more often than gentiles had high-pitched voices (173).[6]

Freud's contemporary Otto Weininger, the notorious Jewish antifeminist, killed himself because (to oversimplify) he felt personally unable to transcend the extreme version of this association between Jews and women he had formulated in *Sex and Character* (Klein 59–70). Freud himself, as Gilman sees it, associated Jews with women, for example, in "parallel" statements on their respective "unknowability" (168). As Cuddihy observes, Freud thought Moses's killing of an Egyptian overseer the act of an Egyptian, not a Jew (55; cf Freud, *Moses and Monotheism* 37, 47). Such physical combativeness contrasted with the "ignominious Diaspora passivity" of Freud's father (Cuddihy 55). Freud did attribute his own moral courage—"the readiness to accept a situation of solitary opposition"—to his Jewish origin (Gilman 66). And I think Freud's ability to "stand being criticized, being isolated, working alone" may well, as he thought, have been facilitated by his "Jewish background" (Freud in Gilman 163). However, *standing alone* is not the same thing as *physically signifying masculinity in concert or through combat with gentiles*. There Jews were commonly thought to be wanting.

So Freud's father had let a gentile knock his hat off in the street, and Freud wanted revenge. No doubt that is reductive, but I think it does elucidate one recurrent motive in Freud and in other Jewish, psychoanalytically influenced thinkers: the desire to defend the Jewish against the Christian male, who had long been pushing him off the streets of Eastern Europe (and would continue to do so). Therefore, Freud formulated a Jewish masculine protest, by selecting and valorizing attitudes relatively prominent in Jewish culture, whether religious or secular, which made Jewish men look more manly than their Christian counterparts and which thereby compensated for the felt inferiority of Jewish men, resulting from their actual physical domination by Christians.[7]

The core attitudes which Freud urged, covertly, on behalf of defending Jewish-secular masculinity, included *science,* as a kind of *toughminded willingness to confront unsettling realities,* which in turn entailed utterly direct *candor about sex* and *sexual naturalism.* Cuddihy has pointed out that "the goyim had a corner on romance," and claimed that Freud resented it, since "courtship," "sexual foreplay," and "all the Christian deferences to women" were undervalued in Jewish culture (69–71). I say Freud found a virtue in the relative lack of woman-flattering ritual and discourse in Jewish tradition: it made European Jewish men look tougher, less woman-dominated than their Christian counterparts.[8]

In America, their toughness, their coolness, their mastery of masculine style, have often seemed in question for Jews. Such insecurity need not derive from physical oppression. Brawling, drilling, drinking, hunting, horse-riding, wood-working, coal-mining, fast-driving, and the paraphernalia that accompany these risk-taking, masculinity-proving rituals and occupations have been *relatively* foreign to Jews. Such alienation helps explain why the Jewish critic Leslie Fiedler, in his epochal essay, "Come Back to the Raft Again, Huck Honey!" construed male bonding as homoerotic motifs in Twain and other classic American writers. This, perhaps, is why the biographer Albert Goldman (1981) hypothesized about homoeroticism in the gentile male icon Elvis Presley (but minimized the far more overt bisexuality of the Jewish culture hero Lenny Bruce); and why the hero of Roth's novel, *Portnoy's Complaint*, who yearns for a sense of "manhood" (40) his anxious middle-class Jewish background denies him, describes Jesus Christ in a kitschy portrait as "The Pansy of Palestine" (189). These Jewish interpretations may well be correct, but they also are hostile. They discern unconscious homoerotic motives in gentile culture heroes or their representations to compensate for an insecure or insulted Jewish masculinity.[9]

My own interpretation of homoerotic hypersensitivity to body language in Dostoevsky can certainly be understood as such a case of Jewish masculinity proving. And that realization suggests an alternative understanding of Dostoevskian body language, one closer to the surface meaning of his writing: Dostoevsky's characters are frustrated and ambivalent male bonders. They yearn to exchange physical significations of respectful, mutual masculinity, but they find themselves shrinking from and disadvantaged in such performances. At times this unease can be explained by factors of national culture, at times by class considerations, at times by the temperamental reserve, moodiness, and vanity common to literary intellectuals. Although I called the Underground Man a repressed homosexual to indicate that I was not one, I did identify with him on this other basis. Embarrassment about our insecure masculine styles drove each of us "underground"; additionally, in a generically (though not exclusively) Jewish reaction, it led me to formulate a psychoanalytic interpretation of Dostoevsky.

I now move to consider some personal experience which apparently paralleled the Underground Man's or conditioned my understanding of Dostoevsky. Ironically, such analysis shows that other approaches to Dostoevsky which I criticized above—Breger's focus on rage toward the mother, Frank's on ideological engagements, Bakhtin's on carnivalistic fraternity—do apply to my own experience, conditioning the development of my own preoccupations with masculinity.

Me and the Underground Man

While working on my analysis of Dostoevskian hypersensitivity to body language I suffered a few humiliations at a community center where I frequently play jazz piano. Those current experiences reminded me of another, adolescent disgrace, culminating, thirty years before, in my lifetime withdrawal from the circle of my former schoolmates. In many ways my teenaged fiasco resembled the Underground Man's follies at the party for his classmate Zverkov, where he lost his self control in a self-righteous outburst, and his fellows went off to a brothel without him. Both situations involved disrespectful miscommunication about a social engagement; a failure to share transportation; rivalry in relationship to a group of desired though somewhat stigmatized women; ridicule before a group of men (playing on anxieties about class, as signified by clothes); and a final revelation of unacceptably low rank on a masculine pecking order. Shy, awkward intellectuals, whatever their vanity, expect to feel alienated from and rejected by groups of popular, "cool" people, whom they may think intellectually and morally inferior but whose acceptance they nonetheless crave. But the sudden, public, and unmistakable manifestation of our lowly status provoked both me and the Underground Man to lose control and, by those failures of masculine dignity, to finalize our isolations.

These parallels clearly pointed to the wounded masculine pride at the bottom of both our confrontations with and flights from our fellows, but not necessarily to the unreciprocated homoeroticism which I assigned to Dostoevsky's anti-hero. I argued that the latter bitterly withdrew from his cohort because the handsome Zverkov (like the manly, anonymous officer) hardly noticed him and thereby failed to reciprocate his homoerotic feeling—not because, as the text more plainly indicates (and like me in diverse but recurrent situations) he refused to accept his lower place on the male hierarchy.

To explain my unusual touchiness in this regard, and its relevant ethnic contexts, will require a brief sketch of my early childhood, refracted, no doubt, through the lens of self-pity. Compared to the abusive and impoverished childhoods of so many, I really had nothing to complain of my gentle and responsible parents. Nonetheless, I was an unhappy youngster, basically, because both my mother and the boys around me apparently thought me unmanly.

I was a would-be momma's boy; she did not reciprocate my feeling. Though I loved my kindly, manly father almost unambivalently, I rarely thought about him. I could not imagine attaining his relaxed, assured masculinity, his ease in his huge, hairy body. I identified with her completely—a nervous, unhappy talker. At school, I would pretend that she was with me, conducting imaginary conversations with her. At home, I talked to her constantly. This invariably irked her, so I would resolve by each night not to speak to her the next day, then break my vow the following morning, and thus begin anew the cycle of resented, unreciprocated love and self-loathing.

It seemed that my incompetence in (and indifference to) proper physical presentations was what most provoked her. My tendencies to lose gloves, leave my shoes untied, wear my underwear backwards drew forth daily, heartfelt derogations. I felt that my mother, whom I cannot recall embracing me, rejected me physically; I was not manly enough for her. Likewise, my poor younger sister was not womanly enough. It stung me to hear some relatives once say that she, who was outgoing and rambunctious, should have been the boy, and I . . .

I knew that my mother saw me as a sissy because she was angrily unsympathetic when I came home crying from neighborhood tussles. In retrospect, I understand her concern about my alienation from the local male-bonding culture. I lived until ten in a gentile, working-class neighborhood. The other boys aspired to be tough, and I did not. Hence, they scorned me when they did not abuse me. I now believe that their bullying only rarely took an explicitly anti-Semitic turn, but then I cultivated a myth of my ethnic persecution. My propensity to verbal, rather than physical, expression and general lack of manliness seemed connected to my Jewishness. And, gallingly, I felt that my own Jewish mother preferred my antagonists—the taut-bodied, tousle-headed, relatively fearless gentile boys on our block. She almost said as much—that I ought to be like them.

Indeed, as icons of masculinity, I preferred them myself. I used to spend weekends beneath the window of one relatively kindly, tough Irish kid, yelling "Mike" for hours until his mother would tell me to go away. I liked to play ball as well as anyone, and I had no girlish interests. But I was talkative and timorous, they laconic and daring. I feared to swim, to dive; I remember an intense humiliation before the local group when I could not start a bicycle without help, for fear of falling, and lost a race for my relay team. I was often in an impotent rage. Bullies would settle disputes, for example, make athletic calls, by sheer intimidation—and everyone else would admire them. The others' seeming lack of ethics and respect for facts perpetually appalled me. I spent my early childhood feeling like a modern-minded, middle-class, miserably lonely little adult, exiled among bold, male-bonding barbarians.

I suppose I was an odd young boy. I had an early visceral horror of the military—the lack of privacy, the regimentation, the silent standing at attention, the haircutting, the repression of individual expression. (Fortunately, student deferments later kept me out of the Vietnam War.) I had a great fear of being seen naked by women. Once, when my sister entered a room while I, aged around seven, was dressing, I freaked out in a hysterical rage, and fell upon her, pummeling and shrieking. My father, undoubtedly embarrassed, gently pulled me off her.

He told me that he had no fear of being seen naked. And occasionally he would articulate wise and wonderful words about respecting less fortunate people. Nonetheless, we moved uptown because Negroes, in the terminology of the times, were expected to settle in our neighborhood. I was inclined to like them, sight unseen, since my antagonists, the gentile boys, voiced fear and hatred of them.

In any case, the Jewish neighborhood to which we moved, when I was ten, proved wonderfully congenial. At once, the pressure to be tough was off; fights were few. I got along. Such conflicts as I had were with my mother, but I generally obeyed her. As my friends entered adolescence, gambling became the rage. She forbade it, so I spitefully stayed away from my friends altogether for a few weeks, amazed at their apparent indifference to my absence. After my father died, when I was fifteen, I had one protracted conflict with my mother about taking a gentile girl, whom I hardly knew but who looked appropriate, to the prom. I rather liked being a martyr to my mother's bigotry, but she relented. She clearly despaired, however, of my ever becoming a *mensch*.

The world at large, on the other hand, proved unexpectedly welcoming. My high school, with a well-deserved reputation for anti-Semitic thuggery, had been suddenly "integrated" by a mass of us Jews from our newly built-up, near-suburban neighborhood. But we were almost never hassled by gentile students. We wound up dominating, not only academics, but the student clubs and government, and even had good representation on the sports teams. Then, as graduation approached and passed, a series of drunken parties made clear to me and my friends that the Christian girls, far from finding us unmanly or unattractive, couldn't wait to get their hands on us. (Philip Roth, Joseph Heller, and other Jewish novelists of their generation have described that amazing discovery, a joy that only those who have dreaded a pariah's sexual status can appreciate.)

I myself had a very fortunate high school experience. I won many school-wide elections, and got an anti-Semitic teacher disciplined. I starred in a musical I wrote for our Jewish social club to perform at the high school. I did not play on any teams, disdaining hard training for probable bench-warming. And I was socially immature: By graduation I had not yet gotten laid. And I had failed my driver's license test several times. When I was finally able to drive, my mother refused to co-sign for my insurance. Carless, I depended on the good will of richer, more independent friends with wheels to get to those incredibly sweet, Dionysian parties the summer after graduation.

And here I clashed with a nemesis, a young man named Michael Field. Field was not in the honors classes. He was not a team athlete. He was neither handsome, nor (to judge from his parent's apartment) rich. However, he dressed well, had a perfect haircut, and was one of the first people I knew to assimilate the preppy look. He had an implausibly wonderful girlfriend, who studied ballet and performed with grace, the elegant daughter of a wealthy local bandleader. And through a ready wit that could turn cruel, he ingratiated himself with the "coolest" guys in our circle—generally those with money, hence cars and golf clubs, who had established a sufficiently secure style of masculinity. Once, early in our high school days, Field had successfully twitted and nettled me, as I carried my lunch tray in happy oblivion down an aisle of the school cafeteria, about the unfashionable cut of my pants bottoms. I remembered that. He seemed disposed to scapegoat me—to insure his own solidarity with the dominant clique at my expense.

At least, he disliked me enough to tell me the truth. He was on to my ridiculous vanity. As graduation neared, and class elections approached, I dreaded to be automatically designated "Most Likely to Succeed," the title always accorded to the glib Jewish nerd like me who had presided over the student council. Of course, no one campaigned for such honorary designations, but, hoping to avoid the go-getting label, I began telling people I deserved to be selected "Most Versatile" (the trait Dostoevsky proposed to distinguish his Russians). That had an agreeable openness. Actually, I wanted to be elected "Most Handsome," and in a foolish moment, proposed that outcome to Michael Field. Field told me in a tone of flattened scorn, "Rosen, you're not the most handsome." It rankled me that I had made my vanity so vulnerable to him.

One early evening, shortly after graduation, twenty or so of our Jewish cohort were to gather at Field's house, get into a few cars and drive off to a party of drunken shiksas amazingly disposed to adore us. But I would need to be picked up separately, or at least know when the cars from Field's had left without me, so as to plan my own route to the party. I called Field, and he started joking around with me on the phone, contradicting himself, evading my questions, and, I began to suspect, making fun of me for the benefit of a small crowd standing around him. I hung up in an uncharacteristic rage. Unexpectedly, a friend with a car then did show up, and we drove to Field's. I bounded up the steps to his apartment three at a time, and as he opened the door with a shit-eating grin, smashed my fist into his face, then fell upon him, pummeling wildly and screaming (in a none-too-masculine vocal register). I had simply freaked out—freaked and shrieked. I couldn't stand the thought of him ridiculing me to a group, behind my back. Two or three big athletes gently lifted me off Field, shaking their heads in shame at my craziness. I left, and I never saw any of those people—that is, my high school crowd—again in my life.

A couple of months later, one of those who pulled me off Field happened to see my mother on the street. Herbie Cohen, a big, tall, already prematurely balding athlete, was a nice, utterly unpretentious guy with a working class father (a house painter). It was him, on the strength of his baseball and basketball talents, that my class had (absurdly) elected "Most Versatile." Cohen was also known for regularly having sex with his family's black cleaning woman, which he described not boastfully but gratefully. I remember his astonishment at the various postures they could employ.

This Cohen told my mother that "What [I] did was wrong." He did not elaborate his remark and I did not contemplate it until recently. Of course, he was right, and I was wrong: (1) Probably wrong to suppose, paranoically, that I was the butt of the whole group's amusement; (2) certainly wrong to sucker-punch Field, confirming my lack of masculine style while defending my masculine ego; (3) wrong to take pride (as I have) in that shameful loss of self-control, (thinking that the violent and unrepentant outburst, like those of *The Eternal Husband*'s Trusotsky, at least asserted my unpredictability); and (4) most consequentially wrong to be too proud to apologize to Field and the group, to acknowledge that I had gone haywire and acted badly. (Now, when business takes me in middle age to my old hometown, I have no old friends to visit.)

It recently occurred to me that Herbie Cohen functioned as a father figure in this actual but also mythical occurrence. He was big, hairy, physically competent, sexually active, unpretentious, gentle, wise, remote.

And that implies that Michael Field, despite his gender, functioned like my mother. What Michael Field and my mother had in common was a tendency to denigrate my (l) obliviousness and (2) unmanliness, as signified in things like driving and clothes; they both blocked my path to shiksas. As Cohen pulled me off Field, my father gently pulled me off my symbolical mother, as he once pulled me off my actual sister, both of whom I wanted to vent a raging fury upon, in defense of my insulted masculinity.

Field's representing my mother might help explain what seems most odd about my behavior—not attacking my tormentor, but feeling so ashamed of my outburst that I avoided all witnesses for the rest of my life. Attacking the mother is the ultimate taboo. That is about as psychoanalytic as I can get here. I cannot affirm, as a Freudian might, that attacking Field was like sexually mounting my mother, or inviting the sexual punishment of my father. It does not feel that Freudian.[10]

But it sure was Dostoevskian.

Like the Underground Man, I found myself unwanted and ridiculed among former classmates. One unaccountably popular, though fashionable mediocrity, prone to mock my unclassy clothes and deride my vanity, kept me uninformed about a party's arrangements. Offended, I lost self-control in a self-righteous outburst. I actually forced the scandalous and clownish brawl which the Underground Man planned to have with Zverkov and his retinue (96–97). Our friends went off to see women without us, and we both went underground.

When the Underground Man runs after his friends to fight them at a whorehouse and finds them gone, he takes up instead with a wretched prostitute (Liza). With her, he finds himself caught in an oscillating pattern, compelled to seduce and dismiss and reseduce and be free of her. In my "Homoerotic Body Language" paper, except to remark that the anti-hero's failure to sustain this relationship might also betray his homosexual orientation, I scanted this heterosexual narrative development. Here too, though, I had much to identify with.

Once again, I found college at the University of Chicago very congenial. Among a collection of nerdy maladjusts, unconcerned to flaunt their masculinity, for once I cut a sufficiently confident figure. But since I still had trouble approaching women, I found myself becoming sexually involved with a few aggressive and flattering black women in the neighborhood. These relations led to some gratifying brawls with white racists. And, becoming a habitué of blues clubs, I braved the dangers of the ghetto. I proclaimed myself a Negrophile. In my twenties, I had sex with black women exclusively; in my thirties, predominantly. I supposed that the danger associated with such relationships, perhaps even a certain masculinization in these tougher, bolder black women, enhanced my masculine identity. Meanwhile, it enabled me to keep from competing for women with the Jewish, middle-class men of my native cohort.

I had some long romantic relationships, but like the Underground Man, usually found myself wishing to be free of women once I had secured their affections, then, when free, needing once again to persuade them of my love and virtue. The pattern was compulsive, but it was also exploitative.

It also kept my scandalized mother at bay. She would not meet any of my black girlfriends, and I too readily acquiesced in her racism because I did not want her to meet them. I wanted to protect myself from her denigration in front of them. I wanted to enjoy a grandiose sense of myself I could only have in my mother's absence. To bring my mother and girlfriends together was a horror to contemplate. In "A Special Type of Object Choice Made by Men," Freud opined that those whose erotic attractions are limited (that is, to "whores," which my girlfriends were not, but they were of a stigmatized group) suffer from protracted, relatively unresolved Oedipal attractions to their mothers, with whom they paradoxically associate their "degraded" object choices. That sounds right enough to me.

The exclusiveness of my attraction to black women became increasingly inconvenient as middle age approached. The racial climate had changed. Interracial sexual relationships, which looked bold and idealistic in the sixties, began to look predatory and pathetic in the eighties. I was never misused by black women or embarrassed by my involvements with them. But I no longer felt my masculinity enhanced around the flamboyant, assertive black women I kept winding up with. Shifting political contexts and personal aging left me feeling liable to restricted opportunity, categorical rejection, humiliation, and guilt if I remained a Negrophile. What had begun as a sexually enabling liberation (they made a man of me) and a badge (as I thought) of hipness became an increasingly disenabling addiction.

Additionally, over the years, I got robbed a couple of times by black men and lost my sense of invulnerability around them. And eventually, I could no longer deny that anti-Semitism was rampant among black intellectuals. All this motivated me to pass out of Negrophilia as I entered my forties—an ordeal perhaps comparable to a former generation of Jews leaving the Communist Party, in that my public and private identity was so bound up in my connections with blacks.[11]

Meanwhile, I had learned to play jazz piano. And for the last twenty years, in an odd recreation of Jewish male bonding, I've ritually played once a week at jazz jam sessions run at African American Community Centers, first in Los Angeles and then in New York. At jam sessions, which are open to all players, amateurs like myself often get to play alongside distinguished professionals. There is sometimes a competitive element and consequently opportunities for humiliation. But jam sessions are male-bonding rituals, par excellence: They facilitate the making of proximate and parallel postures and gestures, while brandishing masculinity confirming paraphernalia (musical instruments). Some people come to the sessions just to carry their horn cases in public. There is a lot of ritual handshaking and other exchanges of civilities. There are also episodes, as Bakhtin would put it, of carnivalesque uncrownings.

An intellectual in these circles can feel like Dostoevsky's narrator in his prison memoirs, *The House of the Dead*—both shrinking from but highly sensitive to the nuances of physical salutations. Despite my tendency to sit apart grading student papers when not playing, and despite my refraining from male bonding by helping to set up and put away house instruments, and despite my considerable musical limitations, the black musicians and coordinators of these sessions have generally made me feel quite welcome there.

However, at the time I was writing my Dostoevsky piece, I suffered a few weeks of scorn at the jam session I normally attend, particularly from one hypermasculine black saxophonist, who plays with tremendous rhythmic force and authority. Though a fairly well-known recording artist, for years he played on the streets. Bitterly independent, and angry, he is understandably prone to put down lesser players, who lower the level of the music, regardless of personal, racial, or other non-musical factors. I greatly admired and rather dreaded him. Sure enough, one night he mocked me when I responded to his question by calling out too many chord changes. (Too much talking spoils male bonding; it seems white, middle-class, and intellectual.) The following week, he told me loudly and repeatedly before fifty other people not to accompany him, then not to accompany others. He insisted that I solo, led the crowd in applauding me, but he forbade me to male bond—that is, to play in unison with others. Alas, my loud, thick, overemphatic playing, in its misconstrued hypermasculinity, can often be insensitive, and I did not have the heart to defend it.

I just stormed out, both indignant and humiliated, then walked around and decided to go back to the session, feeling that I shouldn't let him run me out of there. But once I started to walk up the stairs I reconsidered that my Dostoevsky article was coming due and went home to work on it.

I hit the computer and found myself writing about my own humiliation. How dare he insult me so publicly? Did they all think me a wimp? In the street sense, a faggot? How awful. I might be a wimp, but I wasn't a faggot. I thought how sweet it would be *never* to go back there again, to show a kind of spiteful power, to avoid the whole crowd, the witnesses of my disgrace. I'd rather be alone than be the low man on the totem pole. My adolescent debacle with my Jewish cohort was recurring among blacks in this mini-mid-life crisis.

Fortunately, by middle age, I had acquired a little more sense. Humility? Masculinity? Sociability? I went back the following week and found the fellow unaccountably friendly. (Better yet, he left town the following day.) I reimmersed myself in the jam session scene. I need it.

I must admit, however, that I wrote my piece on homoerotic body language in Dostoevsky when these subjective resentments were strongly influencing me. I was endeavoring to repair a wounded Jewish masculinity. I had hardly been wounded by the anti-Semitism of dead white men—Dostoevsky and his fellow Russians (who happened to be the sometime ethnic antagonists, among other Eastern Slavs, of my ancestors)—but rather by African Americans. And there, the injuries were rarely personal, but came from the pronouncements of public figures I did not know. And I had struggled to free myself from an inconveniently exclusive attraction to black women, dreading eventual rejections as a dirty old Negrophile, but not because black women had mistreated me. On the contrary. I was liable to criticism as a jazz musician, but knew I had received, especially from blacks, really more encouragement than my playing deserved.

I was mainly mad at blacks for the kind of political and ideological reasons which, according to Joseph Frank, best explain the enduring interest in Dostoevsky. Anti-Semitic discourse, from some of my favorite black writers, as well as fanatics, had increasingly characterized African American public rhetoric.[12] (It worried me, just as irreligious Russian radicalism worried Dostoevsky.) It rendered increasingly untenable the meaning of my life, the defining project of my adulthood. I had bonded with blacks in compensation for an insecure Jewish masculinity—insulted first by my mother's irritable sense of my deficiencies, later in childhood by tougher, gentile white boys, and in adolescence by my Jewish circle, who knew my ridiculous vanity all too well and were getting snotty about cars and other signs of class distinction. Additionally, I had recently been stung by some personal dissing among black musicians.

These ethnic and male-role concerns, which had covertly motivated my piece on Dostoevsky, were directly addressed in my subsequent study, "African-American Anti-Semitism in Himes' *Lonely Crusade.*" There I argued that the African American (and very Dostoevskian) novelist Chester Himes, a personal favorite, had prefigured the mood of the next generation's black writers by constructing (in the forties) an African American anti-Semitism in specific response to (supposed) insults which Jewish businessmen, leftists, and entertainers had offered to black *masculinity*. And here too (as in attributing homosexual motives to Dostoevsky) I found it convenient to cite Himes' little known homosexual experiences.

In this chapter, I have been explaining such interpretations as the products of touchy Jewish male intellectuals—e.g., Freud himself, Leslie Fiedler, Albert Goldman, and Philip Roth—who, whether in response to actual anti-Semitism or resentful of masculinist codes which disadvantage Jewish men, degrade gentile male-bonding activity by interpreting it as covertly homoerotic.

One inference from such a perspective is that these interpretations may be *mistaken:* that male-bonding activity may be *misconstrued* as homoerotic. Since I conceive male bonding as *mutual physical demonstration of masculinity,* chiefly through posture and gesture, I might well have interpreted Dostoevsky's hypersensitivity to masculine body language in such terms.

Wimp or Faggot? Dostoevskian Figures as Ambivalent Male Bonders

The Underground Man frequently cites his feelings of masculine insufficiency and unimpressiveness to explain his usual avoidance patterns and occasional ridiculous blustering around other men. His conflicts come with hypermasculine figures: one officer who clanks his sword (*Notes from Underground* 26–28), the other who moves him aside in the tavern and before whom he "beat a respectful retreat" (66), and Zverkov, who "swaggers" (77). He compares himself, alternatively, to a "hunchback or dwarf" (30) or "fly" (68). He denigrates "men of action" (32), with capacity to take revenge, as "stupid"; then suggests that, since those who charge forward against opponents like "bulls" do retreat before "stone walls" (34), they are really less heroic than tortured intellectuals, who remain preoccupied with unalterable humiliations. His problems with his schoolmates derive from his inability to assimilate masculine etiquette: he both takes and gives too much offense (86). His vanity and intellectuality call for individual attention where camaraderie is wanted. Therefore, his former schoolfellows take to "cutting him in the street" (78), seem to be "warding off something" (86) when compelled to shake his hand, "turn carelessly from him" (87), and laugh off his challenges to duel (92). These failures to male bond—to affirm common masculinity through proximate and parallel postures and gestures—provoke his desperate fantasies of clownish brawling (96–97), since exchanging blows will affirm his masculinity however much they hurt.

The narrator of *The House of the Dead* finds himself shunned by tough convicts in work parties, and like the Underground Man, regularly avoids confrontations. Nonetheless, as mentioned above, he accords great significance to whether his fellow prisoners either shake or shrink from his hand in departure. It would be far-fetched to apply a homoerotic motive to those handshakes, which *powerfully signify shared masculinity since they cross class (and ethnic) lines.*

Similarly, the conspiratorial criminal violence in Dostoevsky's major novels, which I analyzed as motivated by homoerotic love (e.g., in Erkel and Smerdyakov) more or less consciously manipulated by others, can also be seen as a passionate masculinity proving—a motive which suffices to explain most of humanity's destructive behavior: war, hooliganism, fast driving, drinking, drug-taking, sexual harassment. Dostoevsky's own revolutionary activity (with the iconic male adventurer, Speshnev) might well have been similarly motivated.[13]

Altogether, crucial, recurrent aspects in the Dostoevskian character type—hypersensitivity to masculine body language, self-consciousness of masculine weakness or unimpressiveness, and violent outbursts of masculinity-proving criminal adventurism—are readily explained in terms of an intellectual's intense ambivalence about male bonding. And such an approach might suffice to explain a good deal of material which I, like Freud, attributed to Dostoevsky's homoeroticism. Why? As a timorous Jewish intellectual who felt charmless in his own mother's eyes and had problems relating to male groups, I had temporarily solved my masculinity problems by bonding with blacks. But aging and the changing political climate made that less tenable. Focusing on Dostoevsky's hypothetical homosexuality, where I *dis*identified with him, enabled me to engage in some compensatory swaggering—a function which, I believe, often motivates such interpretations.

Nonetheless, when we Jewish and other intellectuals, in resentment of being regarded as wimps, explain male-bonding behavior as homoerotic, we choose plausible cases to do so. Dostoevsky is one of them. He attracted Freud's and Freudians' attentions because his ambivalence about male bonding was complicated by homosexual attractions. In Dostoevsky, hypersensitivity to masculine postures and gestures was overdetermined by various factors, including homoeroticism. See my article on the subject.

Some Values of Subjective Criticism

Considering personal parallels to my critical subject has helped me to see just how subjective my criticism has been. Naturally, my defense is to generalize: One tends to select texts and develop interpretations which work out personal conflicts, usually by flattering or at least defending one's type and group—does one not? Accordingly, one ought to question those interpretations. Paradoxically, self-analysis—that is, more probing and careful considerations of limited parallels between oneself and literary characters—can provide an opportunity to restore a plurality of meanings to texts which personal agendas have kept one from considering.

Perhaps, as in the training analyses of psychoanalysis, professional interpreters of literature ought to be encouraged (if not required) to perform some such criticism. One effect of that training might be more responsible efforts to broaden one's sympathies. (If it were not for feminist pressures, I might still be teaching my personal canon of pessimistic/libertine literature exclusively.) Another effect might be to recruit more expressive (if narcissistic) types to our profession. Obviously, subjective criticism affords gratifying opportunities for self-knowledge and for more direct expression of one's personal and political concerns—though also for exhibitionism, for masochism, and for the venting of absurdly petty personal resentments. Given readers' limited interest in critics, as opposed to their subjects, subjective criticism risks seeming impertinently egocentric. Nonetheless, I like to think that self-analysis has helped me, ultimately, to deal more thoroughly and justly with Dostoevsky.

Notes

I dedicate this chapter to my wife, Victoria Sullivan.

1. Cf. Rancour-Laferriere's *The Mind of Stalin* and *Out from under Gogol's Overcoat*.
2. Frank wrote, in *Through the Russian Prism:* "If Dostoevsky's books are the greatest dramatizations in modern literature of the clash of competing moral-social ideologies, it was not because he brooded over his Oedipus complex.

... It was because he was passionately plunged into the merciless ideological warfare of Russia in the 1860s and 1870s, and was able to project its issues both in terms of his own inner conflicts and with a brilliant grasp of their larger significance" (95).
3. Unlike its best-known theoreticians, Lionel Tiger and Robert Bly, who conceive male bonding as woman excluding, my conception allows women to male bond, i.e. through proximate and parallel postures, gestures, and brandishings—e.g., raising beer mugs alongside men at sports bars, toasting touchdowns.
4. When I interviewed Cuddihy at his home in 1980 he very civilly denied feeling any anti-Semitic animus.
5. The charge of ritual murder ventilated in *The Brothers Karamazov* suggests a polar resentment of Jewish patriarchy (i.e., of Jews as castrating father figures). The prior claim of Jews to be a "God-bearing" people conflicted with Dostoevsky's Messianic Russian nationalism. In his journalism (notably, "The Jewish Question" in *Diary of a Writer*, 637–53) Dostoevsky complained (sometimes eloquently, sometimes crazily) about Jewish exploitiveness and ethnocentricity. It should be noted that he was even more intensely anti-Catholic.
6. "According to a contemporary guidebook," Gilman observes, "in Vienna the first question one asks about any one seen on the street is 'Is he a Jew'?" (175). Gilman's observations imply that men were sometimes suspected of being Jews because of their hypo-masculine or androgynous traits.
7. For instance, as a secular Jew, Freud regarded all religion as an "anodyne" (*Moses and Monotheism* 67), whose eschewal accordingly signified his toughness. However, he also thought Judaism manlier than Christianity. The later religion "did not keep to the lofty heights of spirituality to which the Jewish religion had soared," since, among other lapses from patriarchal monotheism, it "re-established the great mother goddess" in Mary (*Moses and Monotheism* 112).
8. It was also as part of Freud's (unstated) project to stress the relative masculinity of Jewish men that he analyzed anti-Semitism as a consequence of repressed homosexuality. According to Gilman, "Freud's later work on the psychology of mass movements"—which explain crowd psychology in terms of libidinal attraction to father figures—"are his unstated analyses of anti-Semitism" (156). More specifically, in *Moses and Monotheism*, Freud "venture[d] to assert that the jealousy which the Jews evoked in others peoples by maintaining that they were the first born, favourite child of God the Father has not yet been overcome by those others" (116). Similarly, Freud's imputation of homoerotic motives to Dostoevsky served to denigrate the masculinity of a Christian sage, who was incidentally anti-Semitic.
9. Similarly, it may be true that hypermasculine thugs and fascists resist unconscious feminine identifications, and that Theodor Adorno rightly discerned

"pseudo-masculinity" in "authoritarian men" (cited in Pleck 32). But it seems even more likely that such interpretations defend the masculine egos of their makers.

10. I realize that the internal logic of Freud's system, political correctness, common sense, and fair play require me to consider my own behavior in light of a homoerotic hypothesis; nonetheless, I have not *felt* it as such. So I am not inclined to regard the Michael Field incident as I did the Underground Man's; that is, I don't regard the source of my bizarre behavior as wounded homoeroticism. Unlike the Underground Man, I never followed strapping men around or invited myself to their parties.

11. Incredibly, I coordinated the Afro-American Studies Department of my college for two years—a happy experience among others, including reconciliation with my mother and marriage in my forties, which are omitted from this paper, since it focuses on personal humiliations paralleling the Underground Man's.

12. See my Himes article, cited above, for derogatory references to Jews by Chester Himes, Ishmael Reed, James Baldwin, Jesse Jackson, and Spike Lee, among other highly reputable African Americans. Whether such criticisms constitute "anti-Semitism" (as I think some have) is debatable. Since this chapter criticizes a tendency in Jewish intellectuals, I can hardly deny other people the right to do so.

13. Some of Dostoevsky's personal traits, previously psychoanalytically interpreted, can also be understood in terms of male-bonding ambivalence. Freud explained Dostoevsky's compulsive gambling (in reference to a story by another writer) as masturbatory by its gestures, hence a kind of circle jerk. Compulsive gambling is more obviously motivated by masculinity proving, through publicly taking risks. The gambler also demonstrates sophistication in the (masculinist) language and ritual gestures of gambling. As Frank points out, Dostoevsky thought he could become a successful gambler if "he could impose an iron self-control on his feelings" (1986, 262); Frank does not see, however, that this "iron self-control" implies a *public demonstration of masculinity*.

Even Dostoevsky's religious sentiment, with its insistence upon the "manly" quality of Christ, can be seen in terms of masculinist (rather than homoerotic) preoccupations. (He naturally needed to assert the manliness of someone known for turning the other cheek.)

Works Cited

Bakhtin, Mikhail. *Problems of Dostoevsky's Poetics.* Ed. and trans. C. Emerson. Minneapolis: University of Minnesota Press, 1984.

Bly, Robert. *Iron John: A Book about Men.* New York: Vintage, 1992.

Breger, Louis. *Dostoevsky: The Author as Psychoanalyst.* New York: New York University Press, 1989.
Cuddihy, John Murray. *The Ordeal of Civility: Freud, Marx, Levi-Strauss, and the Jewish Struggle with Modernity.* New York: Basic Books, 1974.
Dostoevsky, Fyodor. *The Brothers Karamazov.* Trans. C. Garnett. Rev. and ed. R. E. Matlaw. New York: W. W. Norton, 1976.
———. *The Diary of a Writer.* New York: Braziller, 1954.
———. *The Eternal Husband: Three Short Novels by Dostoevsky.* New York: Doubleday, 1960.
———. *The Gambler/Bobok/A Nasty Story.* New York: Penguin, 1966.
———. *The House of the Dead.* New York: Dell, 1959.
———. *Letters of Fyodor Michailovich Dostoevsky to His Family and Friends.* New York: Horizon, 1961.
———. *Notes from Underground/Poor People/The Friend of the Family.* New York: Dell, 1960.
———. *The Possessed.* Trans. Andrew MacAndrew. New York: New American Library, 1962.
———. *Winter Notes on Summer Impressions.* New York: McGraw-Hill, 1965.
Fiedler, Leslie. "Come Back to the Raft Again, Huck Honey!" In *A Fiedler Reader.* New York: Stein and Day, 1977.
Frank, Joseph. *Dostoevsky: The Seeds of Revolt, 1821–1849.* Princeton: Princeton University Press, 1976.
———. *Dostoevsky: The Years of Ordeal, 1850–59.* Princeton: Princeton University Press, 1982.
———. *Dostoevsky: The Stir of Liberation, 1860–1865.* Princeton: Princeton University Press, 1986.
———. *Through the Russian Prism: Essays on Literature and Culture.* Princeton: Princeton University Press, 1990.
Freud, Sigmund. "Certain Neurotic Mechanisms in Jealousy, Paranoia, and Homosexuality." In *Sexuality and the Psychology of Love.* New York: Collier, 1963.
———. "Dostoevsky and Parricide." In *Russian Literature and Psychoanalysis,* ed. D. Rancour-Laferriere. Amsterdam and Philadelphia: Benjamins, 1989.
———. *Moses and Monotheism.* Trans. Katherine Jones. New York: Vintage, 1955.
———. "A Special Type of Object Choice Made by Men." In *Sexuality and the Psychology of Love.* New York: Collier, 1963.
Gilman, Sander L. "Freud, Race, and Gender." *American Imago* 49, no. 2(1992): 155–83.
Goldman, Albert. *Ladies and Gentlemen—Lenny Bruce.* New York: Penguin, 1964.
———. *Elvis.* New York: McGraw-Hill, 1981.
Goldstein, David I. *Dostoyevsky and the Jews.* Austin: University of Texas Press, 1981.

Klein, Viola. *The Feminine Character: History of an Ideology.* Second ed. Urbana: University of Illinois Press, 1971.

Pleck, Joseph H. "The Theory of Male Sex-Role Identity: Its Rise and Fall, 1936 to the Present." In *The Making of Masculinities: The New Men's Studies.* Ed. Harry Brod. New York: Routledge, 1992.

Rancour-Laferriere, Daniel. *Out from under Gogol's Overcoat: A Psychoanalytic Study.* Ann Arbor: Ardis, 1982.

———. *The Mind of Stalin: A Psychoanalytic Study.* Ann Arbor: Ardis, 1988.

———, ed. *Russian Literature and Psychoanalysis.* Amsterdam and Philadelphia: Benjamins, 1989.

Rosen, Steven J. *Samuel Beckett and the Pessimistic Tradition.* New Brunswick: Rutgers University Press, 1976.

———. "Homoerotic Body Language in Dostoevsky." *Psychoanalytic Review* (Fall 1993): 405–32.

———. "African-American Anti-Semitism in Chester Himes' *Lonely Crusade.*" *Melus* (Summer 1994).

Roth, Philip. *Portnoy's Complaint.* New York: Bantam, 1969.

Tiger, Lionel. *Men in Groups.* New York: Moyars, 1984.

SEVEN

Attunement and Interpretation: Reading Virginia Woolf

Barbara Ann Schapiro

During the fall of our senior year in the University of Michigan's Honors English Program, my girlfriend Deborah and I amused ourselves by trying to guess which authors our various classmates would choose to write on for their senior theses. We had been with the same group for two years so we had a fair sense of individual personalities. Marisa would go for Jane Austen, we bet, and Fred would undoubtedly pick a poet, a Romantic, probably Coleridge. Although we guessed correctly in only a few cases, when we heard the actual selections of the others, our feeling invariably was, "But of course! We should have known!"

We felt similarly about our professors and their fields. Alexander Allison, with his string tie and biting quips, muttering over his ubiquitous coffee cup, seemed the perfect guide through the eighteenth century. Then there was Herbert Barrows, who would read a Keats ode in his quiet, pensive, almost whispering voice and make us understand it as we never had before. Had we asked them, our classmates or professors might have explained their literary choices on the basis of an author's complex ideas, formal elegance, or intriguing use of language. What we were responding to, however, was less an intellectual than an emotional alliance—a resonance rooted in feeling.

"Literary criticism can be no more than a reasoned account of the feeling produced upon the critic by the book he is criticizing," wrote D. H. Lawrence, remarkably anticipating reader-response criticism.

"The touchstone is emotion, not reason." Consequently, he argues, the good critic must be "of good faith. He must have the courage to admit what he feels, as well as the flexibility to *know* what he feels" (539). The statement is a cogent declaration of the importance of self-analysis to literary study. Though I would not go so far as Lawrence to proclaim all critical writing about style and form as mere "twiddle-twaddle," I share his conviction about the emotional foundation of literary response. With psychoanalytic criticism, which deals explicitly with the unconscious and affective dimensions of a text, the courage to admit and the flexibility to know one's own feelings are perhaps more crucial than with other critical approaches.

If the emotional resonance between a critic and the literary text is real, then the reasoned account of the critic's feelings can tell us much about the work—its affective patterns or feeling structures—as well. Thanks to current psychoanalytic theory, affect no longer belongs to some fuzzy realm outside of critical discourse. Affect is indeed now understood as one of the most profound structuring forces of the psyche. Deborah and I were responding to an intuited complex of emotions we associated with both our classmates and their chosen writers, a complex related to general sensibility or personal style.

Norman Holland might argue that Deborah and I had a murky awareness of "identity themes" which we were trying to match. I wouldn't disagree, although I prefer Christopher Bollas's term "personal idiom" because it implies structure and style as well as thematic content. According to Bollas, "each of us at birth is equipped with a unique idiom of psychic organization that constitutes the core of our self, and then in the subsequent first years of our life we become our parents' child, instructed by the implicate logic of their unconscious relational intelligence in the family's way of being" (*Being a Character* 51). Our idiom, in other words, is a personal "aesthetic of being" that is to some degree both inherited and acquired. We seek out objects, Bollas says, that "stimulate our idiom," that enhance its articulation and "release it into lived expression" (53). From Bollas's perspective, the literary critic's preferred texts would be those that most articulate and release the critic's idiom.

Jonathan Culler has argued that the dialectic of reader and text in reader-response theory inevitably breaks down into either one pole or the other dominating interpretation: either the reader structures the text or the text provokes certain responses and controls the reader (70). If we can incorporate the idea of resonance or attunement into our understanding of literary response, however, then the dialectic can remain intact. At least in regard to one's favorite works, the reader is not so much "re-creating" the text in terms of his or her own identity themes, as Holland has argued, as "re-cognizing" an idiom that resonates with the reader's own and triggers its expression.

Affective attunement is a focal concept of psychoanalytic intersubjective theory, and it can offer a useful lens through which to view literary and aesthetic response. The work of Daniel Stern, based on laboratory studies of infant behavior, suggests that "infants at about nine months notice the congruence between their own affective state and the affect expression seen on someone's face," and "that the infant somehow makes a match between the feeling state as experienced within and as seen 'on' or 'in' another, a match that we can call *interaffectivity*" (132). Such interaffectivity, Stern claims, "may be the first, most pervasive, and most immediately important form of sharing subjective experiences" (132).

Interaffectivity expands into a category of behavior Stern calls "affect attunement." Attunement behavior is not simply imitation; it expresses "the quality of feeling of a shared affect state without imitating the exact behavioral expression" (142). Attunement is a matter of transposing or recasting feeling states, and the process is crucial to the formation of the sense of a subjective self. According to Stern, attunement is also a precursor to language and symbol use and to the experience of art.

Bollas talks about aesthetic experience in terms similar to attunement when he stresses the "fit" and "uncanny rapport" that we experience with a work of art: "As the aesthetic moment constitutes a deep rapport between subject and object, it provides the person with a generative illusion of fitting with an object" (*Shadow of the Object* 32). Feminist psychoanalyst Jessica Benjamin also emphasizes the concept of attunement in her theorizing, though she includes in it the dimension of "mutual recognition." For the infant, emotional attunement is a deeply pleasurable, reciprocal state that involves recognition of an other along with the experience of being recognized by an other. Benjamin sees intersubjective development as a spectrum in which recognition of the other as both like and different becomes increasingly conscious. As full intersubjectivity emerges, the awareness of a separate other only enhances the feeling of connection: "this *other* mind can share *my* feeling" (30).

These psychoanalytic concepts of attunement and intersubjectivity can be applied to the experience of reading literature. The pleasure we feel while involved in a text may be mirroring our earliest, most intense mode of being and relating, in which we feel deeply attuned to another subjectivity. In our favorite texts, we recognize and feel recognized by an other. Our critical interpretations are perhaps elaborations of that sense of intersubjective recognition. When I write critically, I feel as if I am seeing or recognizing something in the text that I want others to see or recognize too. Self-analysis can help us to articulate this recognition process more fully and consciously. The more cognizant I am of my own subjective patterns or idiom, the more able I am to re-cognize patterns in texts to which I am emotionally attuned and in unconscious, as well as conscious, rapport.

Recently a few literary critics have been stressing similar notions of attunement or rapport. Michael Steig explains the premise of his reader-response study, *Stories of Reading,* as follows: "Because of personality and experience, some readers are capable of more original and deeper understanding of emotionally puzzling aspects of particular literary works than others; and such understanding can be conceptualized by such a reader through a reflection upon the emotions experienced and upon personal associations with those emotions" (xiv). In a similar vein, John Clayton, in a critical study of the modern novel, explicitly connects a particular emotional constellation in his own family with that of the families of the novelists he's analyzing. As a result, he says, he is especially sensitive and "attuned" to these writers and the type of anxiety their novels present. He admits, however, that his attunement is not total; it is limited "only to *particular aspects* of their work" (17).

If my classmates at Michigan had been playing my same game, I wonder if they would have guessed that I would choose Virginia Woolf as the subject of my thesis. Looking back, it seems obvious to me now. My undergraduate years were an emotionally intense period for me, and intensity apparently was one of my hallmarks. I recall a male classmate confessing to me over coffee one afternoon that he and several other guys in the class had all agreed that they wouldn't want to date me because I was "too intense." Another signal I seemed to have been giving off at the time was sadness, though it was a sadness with which I was curiously out of touch. Repeatedly during those years, as I walked down the street or through the corridors of Angell Hall, a stranger passing me by would chirp, "Cheer up!" or "Don't look so sad!" I was always startled; I had no consciousness of feeling sad at all. Still, I remember a dream from that period. I was sitting in a circle of people and a photograph was being passed around which everyone was murmuring over. When it got to me I was shocked: it was me—a close-up of my face with the most sorrowful expression I'd ever seen in my life. "I look so sad! I look so sad!" I exclaimed, and woke up.

The emotional issues with which I was struggling at the time—the depression, the anxiety that fueled my intensity, problems with boundaries and identity—found expression in and an affinity with the fiction of Virginia Woolf. I studied her work with the intensity for which I was known, reading everything she ever wrote. I think I was unconsciously reenacting the theme of merging and union that runs throughout her work in my very act of reading and studying her, in my extreme identification with and absorption in her writing. Such identification, in fact, got me into trouble stylistically in the writing of my thesis. I incorporated (again unconsciously) the extraordinary fluidity of her style,[1] but while she could get away with endlessly subordinated sentences, I couldn't. "Miss Schapiro," one reader scrawled at the back of my essay, "You are absolutely diabolical with the semi-colon!"

The title of my thesis was " 'The Perfect Dwelling-Place': Art as Life Principle in the Fiction of Virginia Woolf." The phrase "the perfect dwelling-place" was drawn from Rhoda's meditation on music in *The Waves:*

> There is a square; there is an oblong. The players take the square and place it upon the oblong. They place it very accurately; they make a perfect dwelling-place. Very little is left outside. The structure is now visible; what is inchoate is here stated; we are not so various or so mean; we have made oblongs and stood them upon squares. This is our triumph; this is our consolation. (139)

Art as a metaphor for the battle against formlessness and disintegration in general was the ruling argument of my essay. Mrs. Dalloway and Mrs. Ramsay were artists, working not with paints or words, but with the domestic medium of human relationships. All of the characters in *The Waves*, I maintained, were also metaphorical artists, each attempting to construct a perfect dwelling-place in a different mode or medium. I tied this theme to some formal, stylistic analyses and brought in a little late nineteenth-century aestheticism as well. The essay wasn't bad for an undergraduate effort; I still consider some of the specific insights valuable today. What interests me most in retrospect, however, is how closely my analysis reflected my particular emotional state and psychological struggles of the time.

I wrote that thesis at a moment when my own psychic stability felt exceedingly fragile. The fight against disintegration, the focus of my argument, was a battle I was waging myself, though I was not aware of it in those terms at the time. Lyrical lines from *The Waves*—"The door opens; the tiger leaps," or "Death is woven in with the violets. Death and again death"—reverberated with my dreams. The longing for the perfect dwelling-place, the perfect protective environment in which everything coheres and "very little is left outside," springs from the experience of a dangerously disconnected, unreliable environment in which nothing seems to hold. In one of my recurring dreams from that period, I would be looking at the moon and it would suddenly drop out of the sky.

I was routinely writing down my dreams in those years, mainly because they were so vivid and disturbing, but I did not truly begin to self-analyze until graduate school and my introduction to psychoanalytic theory. I do not understand critics like Jane Tompkins who, while arguing vigorously for the importance of recognizing personal feeling in literary criticism, can then seem so mistrustful of psychoanalysis. Because it "systemizes" emotions, Tompkins believes, psychoanalysis has often been used defensively by reader-response critics; they take refuge in the system rather than dealing with their own emotions.

Certainly psychoanalysis can be used defensively, as any theoretical framework can, but it can also serve as the very path to the conscious acknowledgment of emotion by providing a vocabulary, by naming and mapping that nebulous realm of human feeling. Tompkins herself eloquently states that readers need to acknowledge their feelings because "feeling, the most powerful determiner of human action, is itself determined; and its ancestry in the self can never be traced, its causes in the text never adequately explored, until the feeling has a name" (178). This is precisely what psychoanalysis made possible for me: it allowed me first to name and then to trace the ancestry of my own feelings.

One of those feelings, oddly, was non-feeling. Another line from

Woolf that had a peculiar resonance for me was Mrs. Dalloway's "There was an emptiness about the heart of life; an attic room." An LSD trip years ago dumped me smack in the middle of that room. Besides an intensity of sensation—everything looked magnified, with an electric edge—I experienced what I can only describe as a complete draining of affect, an emptiness or nothingness, a state of utter despair. Although the man who was to become my husband helped me out of that state, I didn't really begin to understand it until I started reading certain psychoanalytic theorists: Heinz Kohut, Harry Guntrip, and Donald Winnicott. They helped me to name and map that emptiness, to trace it back to early empathic disturbances. In addition, the more I followed back the intricate routes of my own feelings, the more avenues opened up in the literature I was analyzing.

As an undergraduate, I had taken Woolf's vision, because it confirmed my own, as an objective, universal, or existential given. As I began to understand the specific relational context of my own feelings, however, I was able to see the specific personal and historical context for Woolf's vision as well. This in no way diminished my appreciation of her work. On the contrary, the more I saw the limits and specificity of her vision, the richer and more nuanced her work became for me.

In my senior thesis, for instance, I had completely idealized her maternal characters. My idealization was in part a reflection of the idealizing aspects of the characterizations themselves. Mrs. Dalloway and Mrs. Ramsay are powerful, magical figures. Their mere presence, stated in the barest declarative terms—"For there she was," the line that concludes *Mrs. Dalloway*, or "There she sat," referring to Mrs. Ramsay—holds the key to all meaning, depth, and coherence in life for the other characters. "And directly she went a sort of disintegration set in" (168), Lily observes about Mrs. Ramsay. Yet this is only one dimension of the characterizations: Mrs. Dalloway and Mrs. Ramsay are themselves supremely fragile, and while they may be defending others against chaos and emptiness, they are equally defending themselves against an emptiness within.[2] Peter Walsh refers to Clarissa's "coldness, this woodenness, something very profound in her . . . an impenetrability" (91). For Lily, Mrs. Ramsay is "sealed" and achingly inaccessible; Mr. Ramsay thinks her "heartless," though "It was only because she never could say what she felt" (185), Mrs. Ramsay believes.

Awareness of the full ambivalence and emotional complexity of

Woolf's maternal characters was not available to me until I became aware of the ambivalence and complexity of my own emotional life. Twenty years ago it was too threatening for me to see these characters as anything other than strong and heroic. New dimensions opened up after I was able to analyze my narcissistic anxieties and to understand and empathize with my own mother's fragility. When I came to write on Woolf again in a recent study, I actually incorporated my original undergraduate thesis. I embedded it, however, within a very specific psychological context: Woolf's characters, I wrote, "ceaselessly strive to make connections, to assemble, to unify, and to create a sense of order and permanence. In a sense, they approach their lives as works of art, and thus their fragile selves are bolstered through the creation of a cohesive artistic whole" (Schapiro 82–83).

The psychological context made my argument at once more particular and more encompassing. Though the battle against chaos now became representative of a specific psychological condition as opposed to a universal, existential condition, the psychological condition itself is contextual and opens up not only to the familial, but also to the social and cultural dynamics of Woolf's time as well. The anxiety, fragmentation, and sense of hollowness and futility expressed in so much modernist literature and art reflect, as Kohut, Guntrip, and others have suggested, a cultural pathology distinctive of the age.

The particular psychological context also allowed me to encompass more textual elements in my critical analysis. The need to impose order—the struggle against disintegration—could be tied to the ambivalent maternal characterizations and also to the underlying theme of emptiness or nothingness. In rereading Bernard's experience of the world without a self at the end of *The Waves*, I recognized that place I had tripped to on a tab of windowpane:

> I waited. I listened. Nothing came. I cried then with a sudden conviction of complete desertion. Now there is nothing. . . . No echo comes when I speak, no varied words. This is more truly death than the death of friends, than the death of youth. . . . A man without a self, I said. . . . A dead man. With dispassionate despair, with entire disillusionment, I surveyed the dust dance. (284–5)

I no longer consider Bernard's vision as reflecting an existential truth underlying the false identities of our everyday lives, as I had originally thought. My self-analysis and reading in psychoanalytic theory allowed for a more singular, focused perspective. I now see his world without a self as informed by a specific relational dynamic that the language of the above passage enforces. The lack of "echo," of any answering response, suggests, I more recently wrote, a "lack of recognition at the heart of the self's relational experience, a lack or loss that Virginia Woolf's art itself persistently seeks to repair" (82).

I have always felt attuned to Woolf's writing, and as I became more conscious of my own affective patterns and development, the better I was able to recognize the specific components of that attunement and to articulate its structure. Like Clayton, however, I would never claim that attunement to be total or all-encompassing. Attunement, furthermore, is not the equivalent of sameness or identical oneness. As Benjamin repeatedly stresses, intersubjective attunement involves a dynamic tension between sameness and difference. In analyzing a text we discover ourselves, but we also discover the text. In fully attuned interpretations, likeness and otherness co-exist.

Attunement is also related to empathy. According to Stern, empathy begins with emotional resonance but also "involves the mediation of cognitive processes" as we abstract and integrate knowledge gained from that resonance, leading to a transient form of identification (145). Reading is thus empathic as it includes emotional resonance and the accompanying cognitive processes.[3] Paradoxically, a strong empathic connection with a text sharpens our awareness of distinctions, of the text's unique and separate contours. "The paradox of empathy," as Judith Jordan explains, is that "in the joining process one develops a more articulated and differentiated image of the other and hence responds in a more accurate and specific way" (73).

Self-analysis can enhance empathic reading because it, first of all, encourages empathy with oneself. To a significant degree, self-analysis involves the ability to tolerate one's own negative and painful affects, to own and acknowledge frightening and shameful feelings. The more we are open to and able to identify with our own feelings, the more open we will be to the range of feelings given expression in a literary text. Our resonance with a text will inevitably involve not only certain feelings, but also certain defenses against feeling, as my idealizing interpretations of Woolf's characters matched idealizing strains in her novels. If our psychoanalytic interpretations aim, among other things, to analyze a text's defensive strategies, then some awareness of our own characteristic defensive patterns is critical. Above all, self-analysis promotes, to use Lawrence's term, flexibility—flexibility in both feeling and consciousness—and thus it makes us more empathic readers.

One's self-analysis, however, is never complete, nor is one's empathy with a text ever perfect. Our interpretations are always subjectively limited, but that makes them no less capable of genuine insight. Peter Gay has discussed the subjective limitations of historical analysis, how a historian's style "is a repository of biases" and his perceptions inevitably compromised. Still, Gay maintains, "style can also be a privileged passage to historical knowledge and . . . the historian's particular vision of what made the past world move, however distorted that vision may be by his neuroses, professional deformations, or class prejudices, may yet assist him in securing insights into his material that he could not have gained without them" (viii-ix). Relating Gay's view above to clinical psychoanalytic interpretation, Jay Greenberg remarks, "The narrow instrument is also sharp; it penetrates beneath the surface" (128). The same holds true for literary interpretation.

We are all drawn to some texts over others, and in that very attraction lies much of our potential strength as critics. Our particular subjectivity resonates with certain others and can provide an edge in the analysis and understanding of those other subjective worlds. Obviously a literary text can never be wholly or objectively known, just as I can never truly know the psychic reality of another human being. I can, however, approximate the text's psychic domain from the particular vantage of my own subjective position, and sometimes that position affords an especially good view.

I've always been unusually drawn to Romantic and modern literature. These works, I now see, display a predominance of the kinds of emotional and psychological issues I've come to recognize in myself: narcissistic loss and rage, issues regarding boundaries, merging, and separateness. These matters are equally prominent in the specific psychoanalytic theories with which I've chosen to work: relational theories that stress pre-oedipal dynamics.

We can't escape our own subjectivity. Nevertheless, we can, I believe, make genuine contact with other subjectivities and engage in intersubjective play. This is possible particularly in our intimate relations with others and in our aesthetic relationships, in which we interact with the vivid representations of subjective experience that art and literature provide. A key task in literary interpretation, it seems to me, is to maintain the sort of tension Benjamin describes—to hold an awareness of simultaneous commonality and difference. And it is the differences, finally, every bit as much as the commonalities, that assure us that we are not alone, that the world we inhabit is not all self but is, thankfully, a world of both self *and* other.

Notes

1. Cary Nelson has written about the general phenomenon of literary critics imitating stylistic patterns of the texts they are analyzing, noting how a critic "incorporates the vocabulary and style of his texts into his own writing" (809).
2. Jeffrey Berman, J. Brooks Bouson, and Ernest and Ina Wolf all discuss the extreme narcissistic vulnerability and corresponding defenses of Woolf's central female characters.
3. See Bouson for a discussion of empathic reading from a strictly Kohutian point of view.

Works Cited

Benjamin, Jessica. *The Bonds of Love: Psychoanalysis, Feminism, and the Problem of Domination.* New York: Pantheon, 1988.

Berman, Jeffrey. *Narcissism and the Novel.* New York: New York University Press, 1990.

Bollas, Christopher. *Being a Character: Psychoanalysis and Self Experience.* New York: Hill & Wang, 1992.

———. *The Shadow of the Object: Psychoanalysis of the Unthought Known.* New York: Columbia University Press, 1987.

Bouson, J. Brooks. *The Empathic Reader: A Study of the Narcissistic Character and the Drama of the Self.* Amherst: University of Massachusetts Press, 1989.

Clayton, John J. *Gestures of Healing: Anxiety and the Modern Novel.* Amherst: University of Massachusetts Press, 1991.

Culler, Jonathan. *On Deconstruction: Theory and Criticism after Structuralism.* Ithaca: Cornell University Press, 1982.

Gay, Peter. *Freud for Historians.* New York: Oxford University Press, 1985.

Greenberg, Jay. *Oedipus and Beyond: A Clinical Theory.* Cambridge: Harvard University Press, 1991.

Guntrip, Harry. *Schizoid Phenomena, Object Relations, and the Self.* New York: International Universities Press, 1969.

Holland, Norman. *The I.* New Haven: Yale University Press, 1985.
Jordan, Judith V. "Empathy and Self Boundaries." In *Women's Growth in Connection: Writings from the Stone Center.* Ed. Judith V. Jordan, Alexandra G. Kaplan, Jean Baker Miller, Irene P. Stiver, and Janet L. Surrey. New York: Guilford, 1991. 67–80.
Lawrence, D. H. "John Galsworthy." In *Phoenix: The Posthumous Papers of D. H. Lawrence (1936).* Ed. Edward McDonald. New York: Viking, 1972. 539–50.
Nelson, Cary. "Reading Criticism." *PMLA* 91 (1976): 801–15.
Schapiro, Barbara A. *Literature and the Relational Self.* New York: New York University Press, 1994.
Steig, Michael. *Stories of Reading: Subjectivity and Literary Understanding.* Baltimore: Johns Hopkins University Press, 1989.
Stern, Daniel. *The Interpersonal World of the Infant.* New York: Basic, 1985.
Tompkins, Jane. "Criticism and Feeling." *College English* 39 (1977): 169–78.
Wolf, Ernest, and Ina Wolf. " 'We Perished, Each Alone': A Psychoanalytic Commentary on Virginia Woolf's To the Lighthouse." In *Narcissism and the Text: Studies in Literature and the Psychology of the Self.* Ed. Lynne Layton and Barbara Schapiro. New York: New York University Press, 1986. 255–72.
Woolf, Virginia. *Mrs. Dalloway* (1925). New York: Harcourt, Brace & World, 1953.
———. *To the Lighthouse* (1927). New York: Harcourt Brace & World, 1955.
———. *The Waves* (1931). New York: Harcourt, Brace & World, 1959.

EIGHT

Unearthing Buried Affects and Associations in Reading: The Case of the Justified Sinner

Michael Steig

I have for the past sixteen years used my own version of associative reader-response in teaching literature classes and in writing literary criticism. In teaching I require all students to write response-papers and distribute copies to the entire class, and I participate in all assignments. Personal associations and self-analysis are encouraged, and I have frequently used students' papers, as well as my own, as the basis for my published criticism. Because this approach has been rewarding for both myself and my students, I am willing to risk being called an exhibitionist, narcissist, or solipsist—or an amateur therapist, for that matter. And during that decade and a half I have, through the self-analytical aspect of this approach, begun to understand who I am and what factors have helped to make me that person.

Interested in myself? Yes—who is not?[1] But I am also interested in other people, and have learned a great deal which otherwise might have been closed to me, in reading and discussing students' response papers and having them read and comment on mine: first of all, about the wide range of ways of reading literary works, but also about families, about the experiences of women, and about sameness and difference across genders, ethnic groups, nationalities, and social classes. To me, teaching through the analysis of one's own reading and its personal bases, especially in a process of interaction with others, is both a fruitful and a never-ending process. And I have found that students can do self-analysis if given the opportunity (though they cannot be *required* to do so), and it is sometimes a very important event in their lives. One advantage of literary works as a basis for self-analysis is that though they are verbal, they can give a virtually physical solidity to feelings and memories that have been either intellectualized or repressed. One middle-aged woman, in reading of Maggie's and Tom's death in *The Mill on the Floss*, recalled the family story of the drowning of her brother before she was born, and subsequently Eliot's account of Maggie Tulliver's family brought back repressed memories of the bleakness and unhappiness of this student's childhood home. (Her daughter, who had also been a student of mine, told me that her mother said that taking my course had changed her life.) The concretization of intellectualized or repressed memories can, however, be risky, as with the student who spoke of being sexually and physically abused in childhood and adolescence, and who considered committing suicide after reading Virginia Woolf's *The Waves*. She had been so struck by Woolf's vivid representations of childhood unhappiness as well as continued adult suffering, especially in the case of the character of Rhoda—both the person "with no face" and the suicide—that reading the novel gave new flesh to past experiences which had become rather abstract memories to this student. Yet she was grateful for the course, in which the level of participation and self-analysis was remarkable. I should say, as well, that even had I not asked for response papers and written my own, that particular student would almost certainly have had the same reaction to *The Waves*—though she might not have told me about it.[2]

The present essay, although it was made possible by my teaching, centers on my own self-analysis. It is in part a demonstration of just how incomplete such analysis can be at any one stage, and how difficult for the reader to progress from one stage to another. In this particular instance, the ongoing process of self-analysis has led me to a better understanding of how I tend to read and why I have read a particular novel as I did for years (and to some extent still do). I shall not claim that it throws any light on the objective meanings of the text; any sense that one understands meanings better would depend on the extent to which another reader shares some part of one's response. I have doubts, in other words, that one can, ultimately, get beyond readers in talking about meanings.[3] This essay is based on one of the few articles I have failed to get published; and whatever those evaluating the original paper found lacking, I now know that what *was* lacking was sufficient self-analysis, a lack that derived from an inability to face the actual factors that have kept me fascinated with James Hogg's *The Private Memoirs and Confessions of a Justified Sinner* (1824). That article was rejected by five or six journals, and as I see things now justifiably so, because I have become aware of repressions and evasions of which I had no idea at the time I wrote what I believed to be my complete response to Hogg's novel. It became evident that I had not made an adequately convincing case for my central point: that this novel is a special instance in which the author through his narrative style intentionally confuses the reader. My argument was that this confusion prevents the reader from coming to what Wolfgang Iser calls a "configurative meaning" (*Implied Reader* 287), thus making it imperative to conceptualize the author. But in the context of my long search for the overall tendencies of my own reading and interpretation, I had not really convinced even myself that this was the sole or central reason for that novel's power over me.

When I submitted a version of that article as the original chapter 7 of *Stories of Reading,* the publisher's reader remarked that it seemed as if it belonged in a different book. I understood this to mean that it read like a piece of the kind of objective and distanced literary criticism to which I was in the rest of the book offering as an alternative my own form of subjective and intersubjective criticism. For in that chapter I abandoned my insistence on personal response and association and made use of theories of Wolfgang Iser's which I had elsewhere rejected, specifically the principle that "the reader" (a term I otherwise avoided) is manipulated by a novel's "places of indeterminacy" to construct the author's intended meanings. I believed that there were no personal associations in my response to Hogg's novel, and that my fascination was wholly determined by the author's clever handling of narrators in such a way as to make the reader (me) repeatedly attempt, and fail, to construct meanings in the interstices and gaps in the story.

Just how much I was in the dark about myself and my own attraction to the novel only became evident when, many years after first teaching Hogg's novel and five years after writing my paper on it, I taught the book again in an undergraduate course, intending it as a sort of prelude to *Wuthering Heights*, with which it has a number of things in common. (Emily Brontë's biographer sees it as a probable influence: for one thing, it is a "cuckoo's tale," as Nelly Dean tells Lockwood when she begins Heathcliff's story; for as Heathcliff pushes Hindley out of the nest as heir to Wuthering Heights, so the presumed bastard Robert, the justified sinner, replaces George, the true heir to the Dalcastle properties [Gérin 217]). I also wanted to see what kinds of reaction Hogg's novel would draw in a class in which I used my "stories of reading" approach; for my first experience of teaching *A Justified Sinner*, when I had not yet fully defined that approach, was not a rewarding one, as the only thing resembling a response I got was from a young man who could do no more than assert and reassert that he had felt "mind-fucked" in reading Hogg's novel. Some years later I learned that he had subsequently been hospitalized for schizophrenia, which, although it may or may not have been a correct diagnosis, seemed appropriate; but given some of the things I am going to say below about my own repressed feelings toward the author, I should not be too haughty about this student's seemingly paranoid sense of being dominated or invaded by the novel or novelist. In the more recent course, the requirement that I distribute a response paper of my own forced me to reconsider just why I was so attracted to this mysterious and frustrating novel—and so I was finally pushed by my own pedagogy into examining what, besides the ambiguities created by Hogg's narrative complexities, appealed to me, although only in the present essay have I come to explore the basis of my responses with anything approaching fullness.

It seems appropriate to insert at this point the paper I wrote as my contribution to the class discussion of *The Private Memoirs and Confessions of a Justified Sinner*. I titled it "Another Crack at Responding to *A Justified Sinner*," and what should become evident is that there are two aspects of my response that I had originally failed to deal with adequately: my attitude to the author and narrator(s), and the attraction I felt to the antinomian concept of the "justified sinner."

1. This has not been an easy paper to write, and it is even less easy to think of allowing an entire group of students to read it; so please bear with me. I have tried now for four or five years to get a paper on James Hogg's novel published—first in scholarly journals, then as a chapter in my book, then again in journals—with no success. Obviously there was something unconvincing about the angle I

took, and to tell the truth, there *is* something both labored and bloodless about that essay. A couple of paragraphs from the paper should give some sense of my approach, and why I call it bloodless:

"There is at least one nineteenth-century British novel in which the author seems deliberately to elude being conceptualized, to be continually in hiding behind the multiple narrators who by their own uncertainties make the satisfactory delineation of a consistent viewpoint, of meaning itself, difficult or impossible. Such characteristics make James Hogg's *The Private Memoirs and Confessions of a Justified Sinner* (1824) for me the most frustrating but also one of the most fascinating among pre-modern novels in English. This work has special relevance for the question of the relations among author, narrator, text, and reader because of the way it seems to convey an author's conscious intention to elude the reader's attempts to understand his meanings, or to know what he knows. Unlike Emily Brontë, Hogg seems deliberately to be *hiding* meanings. Robert Kiely suggests that unlike Brontë, Hogg had an 'abstract' fascination with 'narrative techniques' (236), and I would add that while in *Wuthering Heights* Brontë also may seem to hide behind her multiple narrators in a way that deflects any easy construing of meaning, none of her narrators are as drastically unreliable as Hogg's.

The narrative's ambiguities have motivated in me repeated efforts to discover which parts of [the story] are supposed to be 'real,' efforts that repeatedly end in a frustration which leads to a disturbing set of doubts about both the reliability and the referentiality of texts. The obvious parallel in modern literature is Kafka, many of whose works are so uncertain in meaning, and indeed even in action, that they beckon the reader (or me, at least) to attempt over and over to stabilize both fictional 'facts' and their meaning. But there is the difference that I get no sense of Kafka's playing games with or intentionally mystifying the reader: he and his protagonists seem as mystified as is the reader. Because of Hogg's breaking of eighteenth- and nineteenth-century narrative expectations, *The Private Memoirs and Confessions of a Justified Sinner* may by some standards even be considered a dishonest book written by a willfully elusive author, and some readers may be impelled to reject the novel on that ground; but it also can be seen as a notable example of how a reader may be forced by a text to attempt to conceptualize its author. In my experience of reading and reflecting on it, I find Hogg's novel a stunning instance of the potential power of a determinately indeterminate narrative to hold one's attention and to motivate repeated readings, however frustrating they may be. This power would seem to be at least one explanation of the amount of critical attention that has been paid to it in recent years."

2. The first of these paragraphs is from the introduction to my paper, while the second is its conclusion; and my problem with the whole paper is that as an example of a reader's response it is almost totally literary, taking no account of the strong emotions expressed throughout the novel and how they affect this particular reader. Undoubtedly, one thing that set me off on my attempt to write about *A Justified Sinner* was a student's pointing out to me, years ago, that the

passage on page 18, "A brother he certainly was, in the eye of the law, and it is more than probable that he was his brother in reality. But the laird thought otherwise," has an implicit double meaning (of which the narrator, as distinct from the author, is unlikely to be aware): First of all the obvious, that it is uncertain that Robert *is* the illegitimate son of Pastor Wringhim; but second, that if we accept what seems to be made manifest throughout the novel, that Robert is indeed Wringhim's son, then being George's "brother in reality" would have to mean that the parson is the father of *both*.

3. As no critic seemed to have picked up on this, I felt I had attained special knowledge of a hidden meaning, and in my paper attempted to present reasons why it might be thematically appropriate. But in doing so I got completely away from the matter of how I respond, affectively and on the basis of associations, to what is actually going on in the novel, apart from what I saw as the author's tricks on me. And I tried very hard to demonstrate that the identification of Gil-Martin with Satan is uncertain, especially because he is also repeatedly described as a double of Robert's, and also, strangely enough, as frequently taking on the appearance of his brother, George, whom Gil-Martin has led him to murder. Yet the hints that Gil-Martin *is* Satan—whether his actual embodiment or a projection of the evil within Robert, or somehow both—are too numerous to be ignored.[4] I suspect that I wanted to read Hogg's novel as a psychologically realistic one, rather than as one in which the tenets of either Judaism or Christianity—the existence of God and Satan—have to be taken as true.

4. Reflecting upon my most recent reading (this week), I find that although Hogg's use of what Wolfgang Iser calls "indeterminacy" still fascinates me, it is likely that I have ignored my feelings about the novel's content: most specifically about the idea of the "justified sinner," a part of the antinomian offshoot of the Calvinist belief in predestination and the uselessness of good works to guarantee that one is saved from damnation. The act of denial that I have any emotional response to this seems to have stemmed from the danger of acknowledging the nature of that response.

5. What I am getting at is that there is a tremendous attraction—even or perhaps especially for a non-believer such as I—in the idea that one need not worry, need not feel guilt, about any of one's acts or thoughts, that somehow one is free of the moral strictures that are part of the conscience of most other human beings. And it is a damned difficult thing for me to admit, as I have always considered myself to be sensitive to and considerate of the needs of others, unselfish, generous, and a truly moral person; and some people, at least, actually see me that way. Maybe that *is* my basic nature, but having to think again about Hogg's novel has led me to realize that my character has other, less pleasant, elements.

6. The reason I am now able to acknowledge the terrible fact that I am attracted to the idea of being free of guilt no matter what I do, is that this year [1990] I have become aware of numerous ways in which my actions toward others have produced heavy but largely repressed feelings of guilt in me. I cannot reveal them all in this paper; it will have to suffice for me to say that this has

been a year of catastrophes and crises in my life which have made me aware of long-standing inadequacies as son and husband, and then give just a few examples. My mother's multiple tiny strokes have made her much more helpless (at 86) than she has been, and I am all of a sudden vividly aware of how our relationship has deteriorated since my father's death seventeen years ago, and just how much that deterioration has resulted from my continuing over the years to dispute the many dubious things that she has come more and more to say; to resent her need to be the center of attention at all times—and show that resentment—and altogether to expect too much from her, as if she were still young and I a child. I can say that I understand how Robert might be motivated to murder his own mother! I also dealt badly both with my mother-in-law's presence in our home for three years and her subsequent six years in a retirement home, during which she required a great deal of attention, which she received almost entirely from my wife; I simply did not give enough support, but rather selfishly withdrew, and upon my mother-in-law's death I was not supportive enough to my wife in her grieving.

7. And I have become aware of other ways in which, during the past decade and earlier, I have not been the supportive partner to my wife that I could have been. Given the magnitude of guilt feelings that have arisen in my consciousness, it is now understandable why I have had a kind of sinister attraction to the egocentric doctrines of antinomianism, which psychologically resemble the "I'm all right" tenets of yuppie pseudo-psychology. And my failure for many years to acknowledge that burden of guilt feelings explains why I could not deal with, nor even acknowledge, a substantial part of what attracted me to Hogg's novel. But of course I could not consciously admit the degree of affinity I felt with the odious character of Robert Wringhim Colwan, could not see him as having any similarity to me; and hence, I think, my attempt to write a publishable paper based wholly on my fascination with Hogg's evasive and confusing narrative techniques. The latter attraction I still do feel, but it now seems to me very secondary, except to the extent that I may have been both identifying with and fearing the author's power and duplicity.

8. I know that it is not healthful, and may be a form of egocentricity (even a kind of boasting), to wallow in one's feelings of guilt. But I could never have written a genuine response paper on Hogg's novel for this course without acknowledging the repressed, and possibly the strongest, part of my actual involvement with and attraction to that text.[5]

What I called bloodlessness in this classroom paper might also be described as deep affect hiding behind a mask of purely intellectual enthusiasm. My fascination with Hogg's novel was genuine, but I simply did not explain, nor even search for, its deeper emotional sources. Despite my disclaimers, however, I still think there are many ways in which Hogg does seem to be attempting to confuse his readers. Among other things, he makes the first part of the novel, "The Editor's Narrative," something based on tradition, rather than known history, and gives his Editor any number of qualifying adjectives and phrases with which to throw doubt on the reliability of his story. He even goes so far as to imply the unreliability of one James Hogg, who in the narrative attempts to mislead the Editor as to the location of the burial place of the justified sinner, Robert Wringhim Colwan—in whose grave the Editor, purportedly the author of the first part of the book—found the manuscript of the Memoirs and Confessions and published it as his second part. In 1823, Hogg actually published in *Blackwood's Magazine* a letter describing the opening of a suicide's grave, and, as happens in the novel, finding the corpse remarkably preserved; it is not clear whether this is fact or fiction, but it was first published as if it were fact. Part of this letter then makes its way into the novel, as a detail to lend a sense of authenticity when the Editor's Narrative resumes after the Memoirs and Confessions, and we discover that the corpse is that of the justified sinner.

One may doubt that an author can really want the reader to believe he is a liar, but a question of the Editor's leads to a reply which makes this matter at least ambiguous. When he first decides to look for the suicide's grave, the Editor asks a friend, "Mr. L———t" (presumably J. G. Lockhart, editor of *Blackwood's*), whether he thinks Hogg's letter to the magazine is true. The reported reply is, " 'I suppose so. For my part I never doubted the thing, having been told that there has been a deal of talking about it up in the Forest for some time past. But, God knows! Hogg has imposed as ingenious lies on the public ere now' " (246). Whatever Hogg's conscious reason for thus upsetting expectations of his own reliability near the novel's conclusion, it has already become clear on the first page that we will remain uncertain as to what is really meant to have happened in the novel's action, as we not only get different views of some of the same events, but are addressed by two narrators who are themselves uncertain about the facts.

I originally went on to develop the idea that the phrase "more than likely his brother in reality" is at least ambiguous, and possibly means that *neither* brother is actually the son of the laird, though the laird certainly believes the elder son, George, is his, while his wife's younger son was begotten by her spiritual adviser, Robert Wringhim. And I still think there may be something in this which has a significance for certain aspects of the novel's meaning: that if both sons are Wringhim's, then, according to nineteenth-century practices of writing (and reading) similarities into children of the same parents, high-living George and stern Robert, though they seem to be polarized in the text, are in fact more similar to one another than either believes.

But why should I have grasped at this questionable point, when there are other ways to explain the Editor's language—perhaps as just careless, or, as one critic has suggested, that the Editor's idea that Robert was George's brother "in reality," is "no more than a pious hope" (Oakleaf 60)? Here is where self-analysis provides me with an understanding of the emphasis of my interpretation. Although I cannot say whether I had doubts in childhood, now repressed, as to whether my father, Henry Steig, was my "real" one, I remember entertaining the fantasy—as described by Freud in "Family Romances"—that *both* parents were not mine; and I can say that I have in my writings made frequent claim that it is important for me to believe that I have uncovered "hidden meanings." One possible explanation for this wish is that when I first learned (perhaps at the age of three or four) about mothers carrying babies in their wombs, I was given no sense of how they got there, and it was not until I was nearly seven that I finally asked my father, who did give me most of the facts, but was clearly embarrassed, as he began his lesson with, "Love is a wonderful thing" ("What does that have to do with it?" I thought!). And I remember my mother's explaining the word "virgin" to me evasively as "a woman who is not married."

My parents were by the standards of their generation anything but puritanical—indeed, I met children of my own age when I was about ten who still thought babies came out of their mothers' anuses or stomachs (through the navel); and I doubt they had much idea of how the fetuses got *into* those awkward places. Yet having a correct verbal, or even diagrammatic, knowledge of how reproduction takes place through sexual love between men and women is not the same thing as really knowing, through experience, what sex *is*. If there was any understanding that remained incomplete for me and provoked considerable curiosity it was that one. So I am suggesting that my being drawn to the supposed mysteries of Hogg's novel (and not only that of parentage) has been in part an unconscious reenactment of the wish for and fantasies about sexual knowledge in my childhood and early adolescence, and perhaps as well of my rather compulsive pursuit of sexual experience (with very intermittent success) between fifteen and twenty.

But there is another, related aspect to my fascination with what I consider Hogg's duplicities. If my father and "author" is the one who ultimately held the knowledge for which I, as son, wished, this knowledge was not just sexual. My father had many abilities, and has been described by a family friend as a "renaissance man." He was a professional musician in late adolescence and early manhood, a first-rate easel-painter, photographer, woodcarver, and carpenter, and a professional cartoonist, writer, and machinist. Ultimately he was a successful self-employed artist in metal: for in his last twenty-three years he designed and made hand-wrought jewelry (he died in 1973). Except for the musicianship, in which he and I were both about equally proficient and equally second-rate, I do not have any of these abilities, nor have I tried to develop them, and the fact of having a famous artist (William Steig) as an uncle unquestionably added to my feelings of inadequacy—as it added to my sense of specialness as a Steig (see below). Rather, as a literary critic dealing with both fiction and its illustration, and occasionally with caricature or comic-grotesque art not attached to a verbal text, I have imitated two of my father's talents (and one of my uncle's) at one remove. This lifelong awareness of my inability to equal my father's accomplishments endows my reaction to the author of *The Private Memoirs and Confessions of a Justified Sinner* with Oedipal implications, for a child's view of the father's possessing power, knowledge and abilities which the child does not and cannot have is an aspect of, or analogous to, Oedipal jealousy.[6] I comment in the conclusion to *Stories of Reading* that perhaps my "identity theme" is proven by that book to be "I can do it too." That this involves the sexual as well as the professional, and therefore a jealousy of my mother's love for my father, now seems evident, a meaning of which I was not conscious when I wrote that passage. Yet my father was rarely a man toward whom I could feel rebellious contempt, and the few real arguments we had, much later in life, had mostly to do with trivial factual or linguistic matters, in which I was almost always right and he wrong. In such small victories I found a certain amount of satisfaction: I knew something my father did not, and this whole aspect of our relationship, I now think, to a degree accounts in part not only for my reaction to Hogg, the elusive novelist, but for my general tendency to treat the author as the focal point of my criticism, and of striving to acquire knowledge of an author's meanings that he or she either does not have or is hiding.[7] What happened as I read Hogg was that I felt him besting me by cleverly concealing what was "real" and what false, and my only ways of dealing with this, emotionally, were to claim that I had found him out, and that his duplicity was what I felt most attractive in his novel—which is rather like finding the enemy out and going over to him simultaneously!

Part of the strong emotional connection between my sense of my father as author-of-myself and my reaction to actual authors stems from the fact that my father was, from about 1935 to 1945, a successful writer of fiction and nonfiction, publishing a novel as well as scores of short stories and articles in periodicals. It may occur to my reader that I have set up a metaphor implying that *I* am in some sense a "fiction," that is, not really the son of my father. I think, however, that the phrase "author-of-myself" has as much to do with my father as the main *authority* in my early life, and my tendency to cast writers in the role of authorities, which developed in the face of the new critical (and subsequent poststructuralist) dismissal of the author. *Stories of Reading* began as a study of authorial intention, gradually evolving into a study of response in which I insist that what we know or imagine about an author affects how we respond to and interpret his or her writing.

Although much in one's adult personality may stem from the Oedipal phase, my attitude to my parents was also colored by things that happened at later times. Perhaps my most distinctly Oedipal memory is the one I have already detailed in chapter 5 of *Stories of Reading* (a chapter which I titled—significantly for the present essay—"Response and Evasion in Reading *The Wind in the Willows*"): in the winter of 1939–40, when I would have been four or nearly so, being picked up at nursery school by my father instead of my mother because of snowy conditions, and then not being listened to by my father when I saw my mother waving at us across Central Park West and said I wanted to go to her. Initially in relating this memory I denied having been angry at my father, and required to have the inevitability of such feelings pointed out to me by the late Branwen Pratt, a friend and a psychoanalytic critic. This was an actual incident (occasionally mentioned subsequently by my parents), but, given how I narrate it, the event probably *also* stands in for earlier and more directly Oedipal jealousy—the feeling that my desire for my mother was being blocked by my father.[8]

When I wrote in the classroom response paper quoted above that I understood how a man might be motivated to kill his mother, I was thinking both of the fact that Robert Wringhim Colwan eventually kills his mother because she interferes too much in his life, and of the difficulties in my then current relationship to my mother. A substantial part of the problems derived from the fact that my mother idealized my father, and not long after his death seemed to wish that I would take his place—specifically in the sense of never disagreeing with anything she said (though I doubt that my father, whom I much resemble in a tendency to impatience, was nearly as perfect in this respect as my mother believed after his death). My attachment as late as seven or eight years old to a flannel upper sheet, which I needed at my mouth in order to go to sleep—an obvious substitute for nursing or thumbsucking—suggests some much earlier difficulties in my relationship to my mother; and only after having virtually described myself as having matricidal impulses did I recall what I considered to have been my mother's betrayal of me when I was perhaps seven, in her revealing to friends of hers that I still "kittied" my blanket—an act which made me furious at her. A minor matter from an outsider's perspective, but something that I had considered a shameful secret that would be guarded by my parents. It occurs to me, too, that my mother was actually in a veiled and perhaps unconscious way expressing her own anxiety about this habit, though she never at any time conveyed her concern directly. Were there earlier difficulties in our relationship? I'm not certain, but the fact of her having gone back to work and sent me to nursery school when I was less than three may have had a negative effect on my relationship to her.[9]

Just as significant for my response to what I considered the secretiveness of the novelist in *A Justified Sinner* is an episode from adolescence. When I was about sixteen my father began frequently not to come home for dinner. When I finally asked, "Is it something serious?" he replied, "No, I'm just seeing some new friends." It was obvious to me that he was having an affair, but only my mother's telling me, against his wishes, that he wanted a separation, and asking which of them I would choose to live with (I said I would live with her) comprised a definite revelation of the truth. That this blew over and my parents' marriage became stronger did not lessen my feeling that my father could have been more straight with me, and not left it for my mother to drop a strong hint, nor that my mother had used her own unhappiness to manipulate me into saying I would live with her, when I had had no time to think about it and was not at all sure it was the right choice. I should here stress that my childhood was basically a happy one, especially in contrast to things I hear from my students. My parents were basically loving, kind, and fair; and perhaps it was the very contrast of those acts of betrayal, secretiveness, and manipulation to what I considered my normal relationship to them that causes the acts to stand out more prominently in my memory than they would if I had experienced my nuclear family as a consistent web of secrecy, deception and betrayal. It is as if I had wished my parents, nearly perfect as I saw them, to be *totally* perfect. These incidents must stand in as symbolic of a greater and more complex set of difficulties between my parents and me in my childhood and adolescence, for they (including the snowy day episodes) are the only ones I can recall at present. As a father of two adult sons, I have long since realized just how impossible parental perfection is, but that does not still the anguish I continue to feel when I think about those episodes.

The connection here with my reading of Hogg's novel is that my reaction to the author's use of narrators was, emotionally, one of a betrayed, uninformed, or manipulated child to the parent who commits such an act, and this observation leads me to think that in my reading in general I tend to place narrators and/or authors in the position of my parents. If this is the case, then the term "conceptualizing," which I have used to refer to how we (I) think about the author when we read, should perhaps be "fantasizing." As this self-analysis took place during a year when I was on sabbatical leave, I have not yet had the opportunity to apply these new insights in my teaching; but I should think that the awareness that one's earliest experiences can affect the way one reacts to a narrator or to sexually troubled or ambiguous incidents in fiction will be useful to the understanding of how we do respond, and why there is such a wide range of responses. It may also assist our understanding of how authors place themselves as characters or narrators—whether as children, as in *Sons and Lovers* and the first-person narrative of *Bleak House*, or as wise parents, as in the omniscient narrative of *Bleak House*, and that in Meredith's *The Egoist*.

I had also, until recent years, suppressed the memory that twice within twelve months (when I was nineteen and twenty) I had briefly been "the other man" in two established relationships. I mention these affairs at this point because I want to return to the question of guilt and the avoidance of guilt feelings by styling oneself a "justified sinner" or by otherwise considering oneself somehow free of the normal strictures of honesty and sensitivity to others' feelings—for I had felt no conscious guilt toward either of the men I had cuckolded, even the one who was something of a friend.[10] When I first wrote on Hogg's novel, I quoted in some detail an early dialogue between the laird's wife and Mr. Wringhim, whose theological conversations are described in such a way as to suggest sexual passion.[11] The Lady Rabina claims to be "scandalised at such intimacies" as that of her husband and his mistress "going on under my nose. The sufferance of it is a great and crying evil" (Hogg 12), to which Wringhim replies:

"Evil, madam, may be either operative, or passive. To them it is an evil, but to us none. . . . To the wicked, all things are wicked; but to the just, all things are just and right."

"Ah, that is a sweet and comfortable saying, Mr. Wringhim! How delightful to think that a justified person can do no wrong! Who would not envy the liberty wherewith we are made free?" (12–13)

This is the creed under which the Lady's younger son will live, having been told, first by Wringhim, his adoptive father (or, as I and most other critics think, his biological one), that he is of the elect and can do no wrong, and later by the ambiguous Satan-like figure, Gil-Martin, who actually encourages him to commit what would be sins for those of the non-elect, thus actually sealing his damnation.

In my original paper I expressed little attraction to the idea of the justified sinner, but rather a degree of contempt, and that almost as an afterthought to my conclusion that the novel appealed to me primarily because of its author's stylistic ingenuity, his ability to keep "the reader" (me) both enthralled and confused. Since that time, I have had to recognize that at times in my life I have lived according to a secular version of the same creed. Certainly I had done so during that year when I was the other man in two different relationships; and at the time I wrote the paper on Hogg for class discussion I had recently broken off a close friendship with a woman, a friendship which repeatedly presented the danger of turning into something more, and was causing me great internal conflict and my wife considerable pain. During the course in which I taught Hogg's novel, perhaps three of my four distributed papers bore some marks of my struggle with that situation, but always disguised—although one, a response to George Osborne's planned adultery with Becky in *Vanity Fair*, told much of the actual story, attributing it to an anonymous friend. And one of the peculiarities of my feelings was, that with all the conflict within me, the regret at my necessary loss, and my empathy for my wife, I had been for a time unable to feel guilt toward either woman, though I paid for this subsequently with an access of strong guilt feelings toward both, a change that came about through a regained closeness to my wife, and the ability to take a more objective view of how I had treated (and still was, to an extent, treating) my former woman friend. What is important for understanding my response to Hogg's novel is that I had for a while behaved, and more important, *felt*, like the sublime egocentric I had always believed I was not. Why I have had periods like this throughout my life is likely to have something to do with being an only child and the first male one of my generation among a number of cousins, strongly praised—sometimes excessively so—by my parents and other adults, giving me the feeling that somehow I was governed by different rules from others. The fact that my father had a degree of public recognition, first as a cartoonist (under the pseudonym of "Henry Anton") and then as a writer, and my uncle, William Steig, a good deal more, undoubtedly contributed to this sense, as did the tendency of those relatives to whom I was closest to talk and act as if "we," the Steigs, were always right.[12]

Students in my "stories of reading" class responded a good deal more strongly than those to whom I had previously taught Hogg's novel, including three who reacted passionately to Gil-Martin as a vivid representation of Satan. The most intelligent of these three was, though a devout Christian, the least trapped by religious dogma, and defined Satan as the force of absolute evil in the world. As this young woman subsequently in another course expressed dislike for *Alice's Adventures in Wonderland* because it was *too real*, too much like her own childhood in the irrationality and oppressiveness of its "adults," it seems probable that it was not only her Christian beliefs which operated in her response to Gil-Martin, but also memories of her childhood and adolescence. Only one student reported a response anything like my own, in the matter of wishing to be free of guilt: a woman in the process of leaving her husband of twenty years. Although her reasons for leaving him made sense to me, she was drenched in guilt at what she was doing. So the possibility of being free of guilt feelings was attractive to her, and I believe I was also of some help by letting her know of my own near-transgression and my suffering as a result of it.

Does doing self-analysis make one a better critic? That depends on what is meant by "better." Since I see the individual's background and personality as inseparable from his or her reading and critical work, when self-analysis brings out aspects of reading that have previously remained repressed, it definitely means to me that one's criticism has improved. Among other things I have learned in going through the process of reassessing my responses to Hogg's *The Memoirs and Confessions of a Justified Sinner* is that my earlier insistence (in *Stories of Reading* and elsewhere) that many readers "naturally" conceptualize the author may have been self-serving, for my own conceptualizing, or what I now think might be called fantasizing, authors, is very much tied to my lifelong problem of worrying about whether I can live up to the example of my "renaissance man" father, and my resentment at having to try to do so. In a novel such as Hogg's, where I perceive the author as tricky, deceptive, even dishonest, but awfully clever, a substantial portion of my response seems to have had its roots in the failure of my two "authors" (parents) always to live up to my high expectations of them. And I now know more about the complexities and difficulties of reading and attempting to describe one's responses: that one may resist unpleasant or personally threatening responses and associations for many years before making a breakthrough. The self-understanding I at times obtain during this process, and that achieved by some students, I have come to accept as not merely an incidental but a fundamental result, perhaps even a goal, of reading seriously, personally, and incrementally.[13]

Notes

1. William Steig's *Strutters and Fretters: or, The Inescapable Self* (1992), includes a relevant drawing captioned, "The Self Is One's Chief Interest," showing a man on a pedestal, wound up like a ball, his arms embracing his own head.
2. The course is described, in part, in my 1991 article, "Stories of Reading Pedagogy: Problems and Possibilities."
3. David Bleich first made it clear to me that interaction with the responses and associations of others to literature is more valuable in pedagogy than mere self-analysis. See his *Subjective Criticism* (1978) and *The Double Perspective* (1988). In my own work, at least through *Stories of Reading*, I have been more concerned with the contribution of mutually analyzed affect and asso-

ciation to *textual* understanding, but I have come in recent years to consider self-understanding—Bleich's central concern—to be not just a by-product of the analysis of response, but one of its primary aims, and the possibility of new objective understanding of a text based on one's own or others' responses to be at least doubtful. In discussing my unearthing of repressed response I am not able here to present a full discussion of the values of the mutual self-analysis which at times occurs in my teaching, and is described in some of my other writing.

4. L. L. Lee has argued for the intentional ambiguity of Gil-Martin, as *both* a double or "exteriorization" of impulses in Robert, as well as Satan himself.
5. This was written in the autumn of 1990. My mother died in a nursing home early in 1992.
6. William Steig's drawing "Father and Son," in *Strutters and Fretters,* humorously portrays this archetypal situation: while the father and son have identical noses, the father is tall and decked out in the attire of a king, while the son, much shorter, wears the costume of a jester or fool.
7. My one accomplishment in this latter area has been to have confirmed by Maurice Sendak that I was correct about a major source for his book *Outside Over There,* a source which he had totally blocked out when he wrote and illustrated that book. See *Stories of Reading,* 209, where I quote Sendak's letter on the matter.
8. As for any doubt that I can remember incidents from age four or earlier, all I can say is that there are wide variations in how far back individuals' memories go. I actually remember a few incidents from my first half-year of nursery school, when I had just turned three: I have a very vivid image of the "Group 1" classroom and the outdoor play area on the roof of Walden School, and of a few of the other children.
9. I want to stress "may," as I cannot remember any resentment of this situation. However, in a conference paper on Maurice Sendak's *Dear Mili,* I did remark that I associated one of Sendak's illustrations with my earliest memory—of being lost in the woods with my mother in the late summer of 1939—and speculated that I had subsequently felt "lost" or abandoned when sent to nursery school for full days that September.
10. I have never before thought of those men as "cuckolded" by me, perhaps because the treachery was in both cases so brief. I have also generally thought of myself as sexually quite "pure," quantitatively at least, compared to some men and women of my generation, having been faithfully married since 1956.
11. David Eggenschwiler treats the question of Robert's parentage with a witticism: "Her disputations with the Rev. Mr. Wringhim, with their 'fiery burning zeal,' are parodies of sexual infidelity, especially since they generate a symbolic, if not literal, bastard in Lady Dalcastle's second son" (27). Few other critics have any doubts that the second Robert is a "literal" bastard.
12. A quotation from *People* magazine on the dustjacket of my uncle's *Strutters and Fretters* caused me a doubletake: "A Steig is a Steig and not to be

mistaken for any other artist." When I first read this I missed the word "artist," so much did the preceding words sound like the accustomed affirmation by the Steigs I knew of their specialness.

13. More than one critic has, I think, failed really to write self-analytically while claiming that he or she is taking a radically personal stance. A recent example is Mary Ann Caws' *Women of Bloomsbury,* which, though its author claims to be writing personally, and does express feelings about the lives of Virginia Woolf, Vanessa Bell, and Dora Carrington, conveys no sense of the basis of those feelings, and the author as an individual remains as opaque—to me at least—as any objective and "impersonal" critic, and perhaps gives less ground for accepting her opinions than more traditional critics do.

Another example—and I do greatly enjoy her books—is Jane Gallop's *Thinking through the Body,* which, though its cover shows the birth of her child (in close-up detail, but with no indication of who the mother is), and the text mentions numerous affairs in graduate school both with fellow-students and faculty, provides very little self-analysis, and actually seems rather impersonal to me. This is a pity, because there are responses mentioned, such as weeping and also becoming sexually excited when reading de Sade; but no analysis of these responses is given. (Mary Ann Caws is quoted on the back cover as saying that Gallop's book is "[a]utobiographical criticism at its most recent best.")

Works Cited

Bleich, David. *The Double Perspective: Language, Literacy, and Social Relations.* New York: Oxford University Press, 1988.

———. *Subjective Criticism.* Baltimore: Johns Hopkins University Press, 1978.

Caws, Mary Ann. *Women of Bloomsbury: Virginia, Vanessa, and Carrington.* New York: Routledge, 1990.

Eggenschwiler, David. "James Hogg's *Confessions* and the Fall Into Division." *Studies in Scottish Literature* 9 (1971): 26–39.

Freud, Sigmund. "Family Romances" (1909). Trans. James Strachey. *The Standard Edition of the Complete Psychological Works of Sigmund Freud,* vol. 9. Gen. ed. James Strachey. London: Hogarth, 1959. 137–41.

Gallop, Jane. *Thinking Through the Body.* New York: Columbia University Press, 1988.

Gérin, Winifred. *Emily Brontë: A Biography.* Oxford: Clarendon, 1971.

Hogg, James. *The Private Memoirs and Confessions of a Justified Sinner.* 1824. Ed. John Carey. London: Oxford University Press, 1969.

Iser, Wolfgang. *The Implied Reader.* Baltimore: Johns Hopkins University Press, 1974.

Kiely, Robert. *The Romantic Novel in England.* Cambridge: Harvard University Press, 1972.

Lee, L. L. "The Devil's Figure: James Hogg's Justified Sinner." *Studies in Scottish Literature* 3 (1966): 230–39.

Oakleaf, David. " 'Not the Truth': The Doubleness of Hogg's *Confessions* and the Eighteenth-century Tradition." *Studies in Scottish Literature* 18 (1983): 59–74.

Sendak, Maurice, illustrator. *Dear Mili*. By William Grimm. Trans. Ralph Manheim. New York: Farrar, Straus & Giroux, 1988.

———, author and illustrator. *Outside Over There*. New York: Harper and Row, 1981.

Steig, Michael. "Stories of Reading Pedagogy: Problems and Possibilities." *Reader* 26 (Fall 1991): 27–37.

———. *Stories of Reading: Subjectivity and Literary Understanding*. Baltimore: Johns Hopkins University Press, 1989.

Steig, Michael, and Ann Campbell. "Sendak's *Dear Mili:* Intention, Cultural Rewriting, and Stories of Reading." Conference presentation. Congress of the International Research Society for Children's Literature. Paris, September 16, 1991.

Steig, William. *Strutters and Fretters: or, The Inescapable Self*. New York: Harper Collins, 1992.

Index

Aberbach, D., 45, 52
Adorno, T., 174
aggression, viii, 11–16, 21, 119–25
Alighieri, D., 56
Allison, A., 178
Alvarez, A., 47, 52
ambivalence, 119–20, 147, 148, 154, 162, 171–73, 175, 184–85
anality, 13, 134
anniversary reaction, 52
anti-Semitism, 146, 155, 168, 170, 174, 175
anxiety of influence, 2
Anzieu, D., 2, 30, 31
applied psychoanalysis, 3, 12, 17, 21–23, 27–30
Aristotle, 30
attunement, 178–88
Austen, J., 178
autobiography, 17, 24–27, 207
automatic writing, 7–8

Bakhtin, M., 153, 161, 168, 175
Baldwin, J., 175
Barnet, S., 53
Baron, S., 2, 31
Barrows, H., 178
Bauer, F., 61
Beck, E., 62, 65, 66, 68, 82
Beckett, S., 155, 177
befriending skills, 49
Beiser, H., 2, 3, 31
Belinski, V., 156
Bell, V., 207
Benjamin, J., 180, 188
Berezhetsky, I., 148

Berman, J., xiii, 28, 29, 31, 53, 142, 143, 188
biography, 14–16, 22, 24–27
Bleich, D., xiii, 1, 29, 31, 205, 206, 207
Bloom, H., 2
Bly, R., 174, 175
body language, 146, 151, 153, 161, 171–72, 174
Bollas, C., 3, 17, 19, 20, 31, 179, 180, 188
Bonaparte, N., 134
Boulton, J., 53
Bouson, J., 188
Brandell, J., 19, 31
Breger, L., 129, 152, 153, 156, 157, 160, 176
Brenner, C., 12, 21, 31
Brod, H., 177
Brontë, E., 193, 194
Brown, H., 53
Bruce, L., 176
Buie, D., 49, 53
Burke, W., 19, 33
Bush, D., 110

Calder, K., 2, 3, 4, 31
Camus, A., 37, 53
Capote, T., 13
Carey, J., 207
Carrington, D., 207
castration, 92, 143
Caws, M., 24, 31, 207
Charney, M., 13–14, 31
Chessick, R., 2, 3, 31
Christ, J., 149, 160, 175
Cimbolic, P., 54

209

Clayton, J., 48, 53, 181, 186, 188
clinical psychoanalysis, 3, 5, 12, 17–21, 30, 112–13
Cohen, H., 165, 166
Cohen, R., 60, 81
Coleridge, S., 178
confidentiality of diaries, 46, 49
Conrad, J., 40–42, 43–44, 48, 53
Cooke, B., 31, 143
Copernicus, N., 133
Coulson, J., 128, 129
countertransference. *See* transference
Crime and Punishment, 111–29
Cuddihy, J., 154, 155, 156, 157, 159, 174, 176
Culler, J., 179, 188
cybering, 84–110

Daly, B., 24, 31
Darwin, C., 133
Daston, P., 4, 31
da Vinci, L., ix, 30
daydreams, viii
death instinct, xi, 43
deconstruction, 22, 100
depression, 16, 36, 42, 51–52, 130–31
Devereux, G., 2, 3, 31
Diamant, D., 56, 78, 79
diaries, 5–13, 16, 23, 45–46, 48, 50–52, 71–76, 132–42
Dostoevsky, F., viii, 9, 13, 30, 48, 123, 124, 127, 129, 145–75
Dostoevsky, M., 148
dreams, viii, x, 2, 6, 17, 18, 71, 74
Dubrovner, H., 77
Dunne, E., 40, 53
Dunne-Maxim, K., 40, 53

Edel, L., 2, 31, 57, 62
Eggenschwiler, D., 206, 207
Ehrenreich, B., 19, 31
Eliot, G., 112, 126, 127, 129, 191
Elms, A., 30, 31, 143
Emerson, C., 175
empathy, 186–87
envy, 21
epistemophilia, 11–12, 14

ethnic identity, 29, 57–82, 150, 154–73, 190
exhibitionism, 1, 17, 23, 28–29, 158, 190

Feiner, A., 19, 31
feminism, 16, 24–27, 173
Fenichel, O., 19, 32
Fenkl, H., 141, 143
Ferenczi, S., 4
Fiedler, L., 160, 171, 176
Field, J., 33
Field, M., 164, 165, 166, 175
Flechsig, E., 144
Fleming, J., 2, 32
Fliess, W., vii, 4
Flinn, C., 110
Flynn, E., 110
Flynn-Schweickart effect, 98, 110
Frank, J., 148, 149, 151, 152, 153, 161, 173, 175, 176
free association, 7–8, 16, 21, 195
Freedman, D., 24, 31, 34, 55, 82, 83
Freud, S., vii–xi, 2–5, 7, 12, 17, 19, 20, 30, 32, 35, 43, 52, 53, 81, 110, 132, 143, 144, 146, 149, 150, 151, 152, 154–59, 167, 171, 172, 174, 175, 176, 188, 207
Frey, O., 24, 31, 34, 83
Friedman, J., 143
Friedman, P., 39, 53
Frippon, L., 82
Frye, N., 61

Gallop, J., 24, 26, 32, 207
Garnett, C., 176
Gay, P., 187, 188
Gerin, W., 193, 207
Gestwicki, R., 6, 32
Gibian, G., 129, 144
Gide, A., 5
Gill, M., 32
Gilman, S., 158, 159, 174, 176
Giovacchini, P., 12, 32
Glatzer, N., 81, 83
Goethe, J., viii, xi, 50
Gogol, N., 11–12, 13, 33, 151, 173, 177
Goldman, A., 160, 171, 176
Goldstein, D., 146, 157, 158, 176
Gordin, Y., 65, 68, 69, 75

Index   211

Gordon, A., 110
Gorkin, M., 17, 19, 32
Greenberg, J., 48, 187, 188
Grimm, W., 208
Grosskurth, P., 4, 32
Groves, J., 33
Grundregel, 7
guided imagery, 8
guilt, 41, 131, 195, 202–4
Guntrip, H., 184, 185, 188
Gusev, N., 140, 143

Haight, G., 129
Hartman, G., 2, 32
Heine, H., 13
Heller, J., 164
Hemingway, E., 44, 45, 53
Himes, C., 170, 171, 175, 177
Hoffman, I., 19, 32
Hogg, J., 29, 192–207
Holland, N., xiii, 1, 29, 32, 179, 180, 189
homosexuality, 4–5, 29, 30, 146–54, 170–73
Horney, K., xi, 3, 32, 127, 128, 129
Hughes, O., 14–15
Hughes, T., 14–15

Ibsen, H., 48
idealization, xi, 114
identification, 13–17, 28, 128, 133–36
identity themes, 179–80
interaffectivity, 180
Iser, W., 192, 207

Jackson, J., 175
Jacobs, D., 53
Jaeger, K., 31
Jakobson, R., 27
Jensen, J., x
Jewish identity, 57–82, 113, 146, 154–75
Jobes, D., 54
Johnson, M., 110
Jones, E., 30, 32
Jones, K., 176
Jordan, J., 189
Joyce, J., ix, 58
Jung, C., xi, 5, 17–18, 32

Kafka, F., ix, 6, 16, 29, 32, 45, 48, 53, 55–83, 194
Kafka, H., 63, 64
Kaplan, G., 189
Keats, J., 178
Kiely, R., 194, 207
Kiremidjian, D., 129
Klein, M., 11, 14, 32
Klein, V., 159, 177
Kline, P., 4, 32
Kohut, H., 14, 32, 137, 143, 184, 185
Kramer, M., 2, 3, 32
Kresh, J., 83
Kubie, L., 52, 53

Lacan, J., xi
Lacanian analysis, 26, 29, 86, 92, 95–98, 100
Laing, R. D., 129
Lakoff, G., 110
Larsen, S., 1, 33
Lateiner, D., 73, 75
Lawrence, D., ix, 44, 45, 53, 178, 179, 187, 189
Lawton, H., 2, 32
Layblikh, S., 77
Layton, L., 189
Lee, L., 206, 208
Lee, S., 175
Leontiev, K., 139, 143
Levi, Y., 62, 64, 67, 79
Levi-Strauss, C., 176
Lockhart, J., 197
Lothane, Z., 130, 144
Lowenberg, P., 2, 32

MacAndrew, A., 176
Mailer, N., 76
Malcolm, J., 14, 15, 16, 32
male-bonding, 147, 154, 157, 160, 168, 171–74
Mallard, H., 3, 33
Maltsberger, J., 49, 53
Manheim, R., 208
Maroda, K., 19, 20, 21, 33
Mars, M., 82
Marshall, R., 19, 22, 33
Marshall, S., 19, 22, 33

Marx, K., 176
masculinity, 157–75
masochism, 12, 16, 28–29, 122, 173
maternal imagery, 10–11, 111–29, 137–38, 140–41, 162, 184–85, 198–201
Matlaw, R., 176
Maugham, S., 136
McDonald, E., 189
McIntosh, J., 40, 53
McLean, H., 11–12, 33
Menninger, K., 52, 53
Meredith, G., 202
Messner, E., 19, 33
Miller, A., 76
Miller, J., 189
Miller, N., 25–27, 33, 48
Milman, B., 31, 143
Milner, M., 7–8, 30, 33
Milton, J., 84–110
mindsurfing, 84–110
Mishima, Y., 48
Monroe, M., 75, 76
Moraitis, G., 31
Morson, G., 142, 144
Moser, T., 53
Moses, 159, 174, 176

Nabokov, V., ix
narcissism, ix, 12, 14, 16, 28–30, 49, 132, 136–37, 142, 185, 188, 190
Nelson, C., 188, 189
neurosis, viii, 77, 132, 142, 150
Nietzsche, F., vii

Oakleaf, D., 198, 208
Oates, J., 24
object relations, x, 14
O'Brien, J., 53
Oedipus complex, vii, 2, 155, 167, 173, 199–200
other-analysis (vs. self-analysis), 1–31

Pace, D., 46, 53
Paradise Lost, 84–110
paranoia, 4, 148, 150
Paris, B., xiii, 29
Par-Los, 84–110
Pawel, E., 58, 59, 62, 64, 65, 81, 82, 83
personification, 30

phallic imagery, ix, 25–27, 92, 99, 105
Plath, S., 14–15, 16, 33, 44, 45, 48, 53
Plato, 136
Pleck, J., 175, 177
Pletsch, C., 2, 31
Poland, S., 49, 53
Politzer, H., 59, 60, 61, 83
Pollock, G., 31
Pratt, B., 200
pre-Oedipal period, 11
Presley, E., 160, 176
Progoff, I., 5–6, 32, 33
Pushkin, A., 156
Putnam, H., 107, 110

Raben, J., 110
Rainer, T., 6, 7, 8, 33
Rancour-Laferriere, D., xiii, 2, 31, 33, 134, 143, 144, 149, 151, 153, 173, 176, 177
reaction formation, 12, 135
reader-response criticism, 1, 178, 181, 190, 192
Reed, I., 175
Reik, T., 110
repetition-compulsion, 43
resistance, 3, 18, 19, 28, 50
Rose, J., 14–16, 33
Rosen, S., xiii, 29, 143, 177
Rosten, L., 129
Roth, P., 164, 171, 177
Rousseau, J., 24
Runyan, W., 34

Sade, M., 24
sadomasochism, 10–16, 151
Salinger, J. D., 48
Schapiro, B., xiii, 29, 185, 189
Schepeler, E., 2, 22, 33
Schiller, F., 148
schizophrenia, 4
Schopenhauer, A., vii
Schreber, M., 130, 131
Schreber, P., 4–5, 30, 130, 144
Schwaber, E., 19, 33
Schwartz, J., 33
Schwartz, M., 1, 33
Schweickart, P., 110
Sedgwick, E., 24, 33

Seidemann, M., 77
Seilman, U., 1, 33
selfobject, 14, 137
self psychology, x
Sendak, M., 206, 208
sexism, 59, 81, 84, 92–93, 98–99
Sexton, A., 48
sexuality, viii, 2, 11, 20, 46, 63, 69–78, 92, 98–99, 159, 167
Shakespeare, W., viii, 16, 53, 60
Shidlovsky, I., 148
Shneidman, E., 38, 47, 53
Slakter, E., 19, 31, 33
Slatoff, W., 40
Solovyov, V., 149
Sophocles, vii-viii
Speshnev, N., 149, 172
Stalin, J., 151, 173, 177
Stamler, V., 46, 53
Steig, M., xiii, 29, 181, 189, 208
Steig, W., 199, 204, 205, 206, 207, 208
Stekel, W., 39
Stern, D., 180, 186, 189
Stiver, I., 189
Strachey, J., 32, 53, 143, 207
Styron, W., 44, 51–52, 53
sublimation, 12–13, 96, 139
suicide, 15, 16, 29, 35–52, 61, 191, 197
Surrey, J., 189
Sussman, M., 12, 19, 21, 33
Swartzlander, S., 46, 53

Tansey, M., 19, 34
Tarcher, J., 33
teaching, ix, 28, 35–37, 43–52, 190–96, 202

Thomas, D. M., xi
Ticho, G., 2, 3, 34, 135, 144
Tiger, L., 174, 177
Tolstoy, L., 5, 14, 16, 27, 30, 131–43
Tomkins, J., 24–25, 34, 55, 83, 183, 189
transference, xi, 12, 17, 19–23, 28, 49, 132, 141–42
Tschissik, M., 75, 76, 82
Tse, L., 30
Tucker, R., 2, 34
Turgenev, I., 148, 157
Twain, M., 42

Waldron, S., 19, 20, 34
Walsh, P., 184
Wasiolek, E., 129
Weininger, O., 158
Wilson, E., 36
Winnicott, D., 184
Winston, C., 53
Winston, R., 53
Wolf, E., 188, 189
Wolf, I., 188, 189
Wollheim, R., 136
Woolf, V., 16, 29, 48, 178–88, 191, 207
Wordsworth, W., ix
writing as rescue, 43–45

Yiddish language, 57, 64, 67–81
Yiddish theater, 56, 62, 67–81

Zauhar, F., 24, 31, 34, 83
Zinner, E., 47, 54
Zytaruk, G., 53